THOMAS A. TWEED

CROSSING AND DWELLING

A Theory of Religion

Harvard University Press

CAMBRIDGE, MASSACHUSETTS, AND LONDON, ENGLAND · 2006

Copyright © 2006 by the President and Fellows of Harvard College
All rights reserved
Printed in the United States of America

Library of Congress Cataloging-in-Publication Data

Tweed, Thomas A.
    Crossing and dwelling: a theory of religion / Thomas A. Tweed.
        p. cm.
    Includes bibliographical references and index.
    ISBN 0-674-01944-X
    1. Religion—Philosophy.   I. Title.

BL51.T79 2006
200—dc22   2005051263

To Van A. Harvey

CONTENTS

ILLUSTRATIONS

The Greek term *theorein:* a practice of travel and observation, a man sent by the polis to another city to witness a religious ceremony. "Theory" is a product of displacement, comprising a certain distance. To theorize, one leaves home.

James Clifford, "Notes on Travel and Theory"

This "theory of religion" outlines what a finished work would be: I have tried to express a mobile thought, without seeking its definitive state.

Georges Bataille, *Theory of Religion*

ITINERARIES

⇥

Locating Theory and Theorists

Books don't spring into existence, but, although I didn't realize it at the time, I now can mark the moment that I began the reflections that led to this book. It was a warm September night in Miami, Florida. There was nothing unusual about the weather or the place. Almost all September nights are warm in that subtropical city, where I lived and worked for five years. Yet that night in 1993 was significant because it was September 8, the feast day of Our Lady of Charity, the national patroness of Cuba. She was a shared symbol for hundreds of thousands of Cuban Catholic exiles who had transformed the cultural landscape of Miami in the years after Fidel Castro's rise to power in 1959. It was the third feast-day celebration I had attended in Miami, and I had been doing fieldwork among Cubans at the Virgin's shrine in Miami for two years. So much was familiar that night in Dinner Key Auditorium, where the annual rite was held after Hurricane Andrew displaced devotees from their usual site on Key Biscayne. I recognized the melody and lyrics of the hymn that links Our Lady of Charity with those who fought for Cuban independence in the nineteenth century, "La Virgen Mambisa," which the crowd sang as the diminutive statue of the Virgin entered the auditorium (Figure 1). I knew the bishop on stage presiding over the mass, and I had interviewed the priest who coordinated the liturgy. I had been doing archival research about the history of Cuban and Cuban American religion. I had observed masses, rosaries, *romerías* (annual provincial pilgrimages that involve eating as well as praying), and other rituals at the shrine, and I had talked with pilgrims and listened to their sad stories about exile. I remembered that many Cuban Catholics told me that the annual festival was the most important of their rituals. A fifty-seven-year-old woman who had arrived in 1966 explained, "For me it is a way of celebrating the Virgin's day united with all to ask for the liberty of Cuba." Yet I still didn't have a theory of religion that made much sense of all that I observed as the Cuban Virgin processed into the arena for the collective ritual—or when I wrote about the event later in my ethnography of devotion at the Miami shrine:

> At 8:30 on a Wednesday night in 1993 several Cuban-born men from the confraternity, dressed in traditional white *guayabera* shirts, carried the statue of Our Lady of Charity into an auditorium in Miami for her annual feastday mass. Recently arrived by boat from her short journey from the shrine, the Virgin was welcomed by thousands of devotees. She made her way through a sea of fluttering white, red, and blue as followers waved white handkerchiefs and Cuban flags. Fathers lifted children onto their shoulders for a better view. Flashbulbs ignited. Some in the crowd pushed toward her. From my vantage point a few rows from the altar, I noticed that some elderly women and men nearby were weeping. One woman sobbed aloud, "May she save Cuba. We need her to save Cuba." Many others smiled widely as they waved to their national patroness. As the Virgin weaved her way down the aisles of folding chairs

toward the temporary altar, a local Cuban priest led the crowd in a series of chants. *"¡Viva la Virgen de Caridad!"* he boomed in a microphone to be heard above the shouting and singing. *"Salva a Cuba"* (Save Cuba), the crowd responded again and again. The men from the confraternity lifted her onto the left side of the stage, where she stood in front of a twelve-foot triangular background. Arched across the top a prediction was inscribed in yellow flowers: *"Libre '94,"* signaling the people's hopes that the homeland would be "liberated" from communism during the coming year. Finally, Our Lady of Charity rested triumphantly on the altar, where she would preside over the rest of the ceremony, as the clergy positioned themselves on the altar to begin the mass and the crowd boisterously sang the Cuban national anthem.[1]

What sort of theory, I wondered, would make sense of this Cuban Catholic ritual? Trained in religious studies in graduate school, I had researched the history of Western thinking about the term *religion,* and I had taught an undergraduate course on the topic. I had read many accounts of the nature and function of religion, and almost all of them illumined something of what I observed that night. From the altar and the folding chairs, Cuban participants expressed "belief in spiritual beings," in E. B. Tylor's classic definition, and it is possible to interpret the rosary and mass as an "experience of the Holy," as Rudolf Otto's theory might suggest. Paul Tillich's notion of religion as one's "ultimate concern" offered useful language to talk about Cuban nationalism, and not just Roman Catholicism, as religious. Melford E. Spiro's definition of religion as "an institution consisting of culturally patterned interaction with culturally postulated superhuman beings" accounted for the formalized ritual actions and the venerated "superhuman being" (Mary) and also called attention to the role of "institutions" such as the Archdiocese of Miami and the Confraternity of Our Lady of Charity. Clifford Geertz's popular definition of religion as a "system of symbols" pointed to the image of the Virgin, and maybe the Cuban flag, and—like Friedrich Schleiermacher's and William James's highlighting of "feel-

1. Devotees wave Cuban flags and white handkerchiefs as Our Lady of Charity enters the feast-day celebration in 2001. American Airlines Arena, Miami, Florida.

ings"—provided an idiom for talking about the Cuban devotees' "sobbing" and "smiling" as it acknowledged religion's role in establishing "moods and motivations."[2]

I will return to these and other definitions in Chapter 2—and offer my own in Chapter 3—but here I want to note only that my account of religion originated with my observations in Miami and my dissatisfaction with available theories. Other theories illumined some of what I encountered, but I had a sense—at first, poorly articulated—that there seemed to be more to say than other theoretical lexicons allowed me to say. It was not only that few theories were inclusive enough to consider beliefs, values, rituals, institutions, *and* feelings or that almost all seemed to overlook or minimize some religious expressions—for example, artifacts like the *guayabera* shirts and handkerchiefs or sounds like the shouting and singing. As I tried to name and ease my disquiet I came to the conclusion that I was looking for a theory of religion that made sense of the religious life of transnational migrants and addressed three themes—*movement, relation,* and *position.*

First, the entrance of the Virgin, and a great deal of the religious life of Cuban Catholics at the Miami shrine, is about movement, although most theories offer little help in talking about religion's dynamics. There were movements—waving handkerchiefs and lifting children—and there was movement. The men from the confraternity, who carried the Virgin through the crowd, were on the move. So was Our Lady of Charity, whom (devotees believe) three men found floating in the sea off the Cuban coast in 1611. She also traveled across the water that September night, when she came to the ritual by boat, and she returned to the shrine in the back of a Ford pickup truck. The statue that the confraternity members carried through the crowd had been smuggled out of Cuba in 1961 and driven to a baseball stadium in Miami, where 25,000 exiles greeted her with tears, applause, and singing at the second festival mass in South Florida. So Our Lady of Charity was an exile who had been forced from her homeland—like almost all of the thousands of devotees in the audience and on the altar that evening in 1993. The Reverend Pedro Luís Pérez, who led the rosary and the chants of "Salva a Cuba," had been exiled from the island in the early 1960s, and most of the laity who responded so vigorously to his shouts from the altar were transnational migrants too. The ritual moved participants back and forth between the homeland and the new land as they sang the Cuban national anthem and prayed to the Virgin of Charity, whom the pope had declared the patroness of their island nation in 1916. And the ritual moved them across time. Their religion was retrospective and prospective. It was about the Cuba of memory and desire. The elderly women near me wept as they recalled the homeland, and the people they left behind. The chants from the crowd of "Salva a Cuba" and the floral message "Libre '94" looked toward the future and expressed a hope—that the national patroness would bring democracy and capitalism to Cuba.

Second, my observations in Miami led me to seek a theory that was not only dynamic but relational. Standing amid the fluttering of Cuban flags and white handkerchiefs that greeted the Virgin that night, I found myself wanting to make sense of all sorts of relations: the interdependence of religion and politics; the pathways between here and there, Havana and Miami; the links between the nineteenth-century wars for independence and the contemporary struggles for the "liberation" of Castro's Cuba; the bonds and tensions among the generations; and the contacts and exchanges among religious traditions, especially as those found expression in the continuities and discontinuities between the domestic piety that combined Afro-Cuban and Roman Catholic practices and the public religion that negotiated meaning and power in relation to diocesan clergy who condemned that "syncretism."

Consider two examples from the feast-day ritual in Miami that point to interreligious and intergenerational relations. Some of those waving white handkerchiefs at the Virgin as she arrived that night greeted her as *Ọsun,* the West African *òrìsà* of the river, and not only as Mary, the Catholic saint. Most theories of religions are silent about all this, and they fail to provide language that highlights the historical relations among complex and changing religious traditions—in this case Afro-Cuban and Roman Catholic traditions in Cuba. Yet Cuban American Catholicism as practiced that warm Miami night—though not as prescribed by the clergy—was hybrid, a product of long processes of contact and exchange. The ritual also foregrounds other relations among diverse peoples at the celebration—not only between clergy and laity, black and white, women and men, but also young and old. And familial relations are very important in this rite: "fathers lifted children" to get a better view and children gazed up at parents and grandparents who wept at the singing of "La Virgen Mambisa." The children didn't know much about the Cuban wars for independence alluded to in that hymn. Most didn't remember the homeland their older relatives mourned, and their immersion in U.S. popular culture and public education increased the intergenerational tensions. But any account of this ritual that obscured family relations in Miami and the links with relatives still on the island, devotees told me, would miss a great deal.[3]

To make sense of these myriad relations and movements, in Chapter 3 I argue that religions involve two spatial practices—dwelling and crossing—but as I reflected on religion as I encountered it at the 1993 festival and found it interpreted in the most influential theories, I also felt a need to acknowledge my own shifting position as interpreter: "*From my vantage point* a few rows from the altar . . ."—and from my vantage point as a white, male, middle-class professor of religious studies. Theorists often have obscured their own position, and pretended that they enjoy a view from everywhere-at-once or nowhere-in-particular. I felt a need to consider the position of the theory and the theorist. I deal with the two other themes—movement and relation—in the rest of the book, but in this chapter I consider *positionality*. I try to locate my theory. This entails, first, saying more about what theory is and what theory is not.[4]

THEORIES AS ITINERARIES

Scholars in the humanities and social sciences have understood theory in a variety of ways, and one helpful overview lists five primary notions of what theory is and how it functions: (1) the *deductive-nomological view*, which understands theories as systems of universal laws deduced from axioms and corresponding to mind-independent external reality; (2) the *law-oriented view*, which trumpets the same ideal but suggests we cannot identify universal laws but only "law-like regularities"; (3) the *idealizing notion of theory*, which further refines the deductive-nomological view by suggesting that the regularities—not laws—

should be understood as "ideal types," or the scholar's idealizations of human motives; (4) the *constructivist view of theory*, which goes further still in rejecting the ideal of attaining universal laws as it challenges correspondence theories of truth and proposes that theory offers only "contextual understanding of interacting motives"; and (5) *critical theory*, which agrees with constructivists in their criticism of the deductive-nomological approach but emphasizes power relations and ethical issues.[5]

I will leave it to philosophers of science, and natural scientists working in the laboratory or the field, to decide whether the deductive-nomological view (with its concern for laws, hypotheses, explanations, control, and predication) makes sense of interpretations of the natural world, but this approach presents an unrealizable goal for those who try to understand cultural processes, including religion. Religion's interpreters might offer more or less useful accounts from within culturally and professionally constructed categorical schemes that highlight patterns that are not wholly bound to a time or place, but they cannot discover, or construct, cross-cultural and timeless spiritual "laws." My own view of theorizing takes seriously critical theory's highlighting of power relations while it also resonates with some moderate versions of the constructivist view. As I will explain more fully later, my perspective might be understood as pragmatic or nonrepresentational realism or, to use the philosopher Hilary Putnam's phrase, "realism with a small r"—as opposed to "metaphysical Realism," which champions a "view from nowhere" and aspires to link concepts with mind-independent realities.[6]

But my understanding of theory departs from all five types, since I reject a presupposition they all share, even the constructivists' theory building and the critical theorists' power analysis—that the theorist and the theorized are static. To highlight the shifting position of the theorist, while also acknowledging the movements and relations I found among transnational migrants in Miami, I endorse James Clifford's suggestion that we turn to the metaphor of travel. More precisely, I reimagine theories as itineraries. Drawing on the three primary meanings of the term *itinerary* in the *Oxford English Dictionary,* I suggest that theories are embodied travels ("a line or course of travel; a route"), positioned representations ("a record or journal of travel, an account of a journey"), and proposed routes ("a sketch of a proposed route; a plan or scheme of travel"). Theories are simultaneously proposals for a journey, representations of a journey, and the journey itself. I focus here on the last two meanings of the term.[7]

⤞ Embodied Travels

Theories, in the first sense of the word, are travels. Just as theorists walk the library stacks, shift from idea to idea at their desks, or leap from citation to citation in online card catalogs, theories move too. They are journeys propelled by concepts and tropes that follow lines of argument and narration. But there is not much linear progression. In the imagining and writing—and even in the reader's tracing of the argument on the printed page—there is crisscrossing, stepping down, and circling back.[8]

By imagining theory as movements across space (and time), I employ spatial metaphors, which have been so prominent in recent cultural theory. Yet we should interpret images about movement in ways that retain the dynamism of the process. This means critically and cautiously appropriating the recent "spatial turn" in cultural theory. Michel Foucault noted, "The great obsession of the nineteenth century was . . . history," and that theoretical legacy continued into the late twentieth century. Foucault went on to suggest in that 1986 interview, however, that "the present epoch will perhaps be above all the epoch of space." Taking off from Foucault's comment and extending the insights of others (including Henri Lefebvre, Fredric Jameson, Anthony Giddens, and David Harvey), geographer Edward W. Soja argued in his book *Postmodern Geographies* that we should "reassert" space in contemporary social theory. And a number of theorists have employed spatial images—often toward very different ends—as Bruno Bosteels's survey of the shift "from text to territory" documents. "Anyone even remotely familiar with recent titles, if nothing else, in the humanities must in this regard have been struck by the astonishing appeal of topological and specifically cartographic images." Although I use spatial images throughout this book, we should be careful that our metaphors, especially *map* and *territory*, do not carry implications we might want to avoid. As cultural studies scholar Iain Chambers has argued, "the very idea of a map, with its implicit dependence upon the survey of a stable terrain, fixed referents and measurement, seems to contradict the palpable flux and fluidity of metropolitan life and cosmopolitan movements." In a similar way, religious studies specialist Sam Gill has suggested that "the map-territory metaphor, as powerful and effective as it has been, tends to support the comprehension of territory as static, as stable, as mappable, as graspable from some view." Whether interpreting contemporary "metropolitan life" or ancient religious practices, theorists go astray when they take spatial images, especially mapping metaphors, in ways that understand representations as universal and theorists as static.[9]

In other words, theory as embodied travel resembles the seventeenth-century Japanese poet Matsuo Bashō's wanderings as recorded in his travel account *The Narrow Road to the Deep North* more than the Greek writer Ptolemy's second-century "geography," the product of sedentary observations that claim an omnispective "view of the whole." Ptolemy was challenging another influential interpretation of geography's task—Strabo's "chorography," the oldest tradition of Western geographical inquiry, which aimed to offer only a view of a region. "Now my first and most important concern," Strabo told his readers, "is to try to give, in the simplest possible way, the shape and size of that part of the earth which falls within our map." Strabo suggested that "to give an accurate account of the whole earth and the whole 'spinning whorl'" is not the discipline's function. Both universal geography and regional chorography can be distinguished from local "topography," the representation of a particular city or town: for example, *las pinturas*, the sketches that Amerindian cartographers drew between 1578 and 1584 at the request of Spanish colonial officials in Mexico. Yet even if those *pinturas*, and Native American partial and temporary mappings etched in bark or dirt, challenge the universalistic aspirations of Ptolemy's geography and acknowledge cartography's limited view, to employ mapping metaphors without qualification can still obscure theory's dynamics. Theory as embodied travel is not a stationary view of static terrain. It is not geography or chorography—or even the localized topography of indigenous mapmakers. It is more like "dynography," a term used in medicine to describe the computer-generated representations of blood flow through arteries or of the bodily movements of children with spastic cerebral palsy. But even in that analogy the theorists themselves are still static as their stationary instruments "map" the pathways of fluids or the trajectories of gestures.[10]

That is why, I suggest, it is useful to understand theory as travel—but not as the displacements of voluntary migrants who seek settlement, tourists who chase pleasure on round-trip journeys, or pilgrims who depart only to return home after venerating a sacred site. Theory is purposeful wandering, and, as interpreters of the Japanese poet and diarist have argued, Bashō is an exemplar of wandering (Figure 2). It is not just that there is a "predominance of wayfaring imagery" in his poems and narratives, although there is. Bashō imagined his writing and his life as wayfaring. The seventeenth-century Japanese writer made that point in his first journal, *The Records of a Weather-Exposed Skeleton:* "I set out on a journey of a thousand leagues, packing no provisions. I leaned on the staff of an ancient [the Chinese Buddhist priest Guangwen] who, it is said, entered into nothingness under the midnight moon." As one scholar has noted, a "thousand leagues" is a symbolic number suggesting spatial and temporal immensity, and even though Bashō chose a direction, planned a route, and longed to see this place or that along the way, he understood his treks and his life as wayfaring. Unlike the Japanese writer, theorists might be burdened by *too many* "provisions," and they never step into "nothingness," since neurophysiological processes and culturally patterned modes of perception and affect influ-

2. Baitei Ki (1734–1810), "Bashō with a Deer," Middle Edo Period. Ink and color on paper, 48.9 × 119.1 cm.

ence where they "enter" and what they experience. Yet theorists do lean on "staffs" bestowed by others as they set out in one direction on a journey of uncertain duration toward sites unseen and vaguely imagined, and they negotiate the trail by what illumination they can find along the way. As with Bashō's travel accounts, in which that itinerant included narrative and poems composed on the move about sites along the way, theorists in motion offer partial views of shifting terrain. A theory of religion, as I understand it, is not an omnispective map of the whole offered by a stationary observer. Theory is travel. Here is the image I have in mind. With the peak of Mount Chōkai rising almost 5,000 feet to his right, Bashō walks north from Sakata, traversing the narrow dirt and rock paths that lead to Kisagata, and after "lingering" at that lagoon for several days he sets out again—first on a 130-mile walk to Kaga's provincial capital and then farther south along the coast, as one purposeful journey leads to the next, until there is only the wandering itself.[11]

↦ Positioned Representations

In a second meaning of the term *itinerary*, theory is not only the wandering but its representation. It is, for example, Bashō's narrative of his trip to Kisagata, the lagoon northeast of Sakata: "I followed a narrow trail for about ten miles, climbing steep hills, descending to rocky shores, or pushing through sandy beaches." And it is the poem he composed as he glanced at a tree in the lagoon, a tree that reminded him of a famous Chinese woman who was known for her melancholy beauty:

> Kisagata—
> in the rain, Xi Shi asleep,
> silk tree blossoms.[12]

Theories, then, are *sightings* from sites. They are positioned representations of a changing terrain by an itinerant cartographer. The Greek term *theōria (θεωρία)* is a somewhat redundant compound that combines *theā* (seeing, but also that which is seen, therefore a sight or spectacle) and *horān* (the action of seeing, from the Greek verb "to see").

So the derivative noun *theōria* refers to an observation or sighting. However, as classicist Ian Rutherford points out, the term has nine related meanings. Those meanings, in turn, boil down to four: *theōria* refers to a festival, the traveler to the festival, the travel itself, and the traveler's observations at the festival. To clarify the word's meaning, Rutherford compares it to the Hindi term *darśan,* seeing the gods in a Hindu temple or procession. Yet whether or not we emphasize the term's original religious significance or its intriguing parallels with *darśan*—both as observation at a festival and as philosophical insight— anthropologist James Clifford is right to point out that, at its core, *theōria* refers to the observations of travelers. In that sense, theories are sightings.[13]

It is helpful to understand theories as sightings, I suggest, but only if we keep in mind three cautions. First, as when motorists glance in the rearview mirror, the theorist always has blind spots. Illustrating his point with a passage from Robert Louis Stevenson's story "The Lantern Bearers," William James suggested in a compelling essay that there is "a certain blindness in human beings." Just as the young boys in Stevenson's narrative carried a "tin bull's eye lantern" beneath their topcoats and hidden from the sight of passing pedestrians, so too all humans are unable to notice all that surrounds them. James had in mind "the blindness with which we are all afflicted in regard to the feelings of creatures and peoples different from ourselves," but the theorist's vision is impaired in other ways too. There are sites in the shifting terrain we cannot see, or can only dimly make out. To return to Bashō's narrative, he recounted this sort of experience as he described his journey toward Kisagata and past Mount Chōkai: "just about the time the dim sun was nearing the horizon, a strong wind rose from the sea, blowing up fine grains of sand, and rain, too, began to spread a gray film of cloud across the sky, so that even Mount Chōkai was made invisible." Bashō tells readers that he "walked in this state of semi-blindness" for some time, but then abandoned all efforts at travel and settled there in the impenetrable cloud of sand and rain for the night. Theorists have it worse: they can't wait for the boys to reveal the lantern beneath their topcoats or for the "gray film" to pass from the rising peak. Sometimes the obstructions are not temporary. Observing from my folding chair several rows from the altar at the feast-day mass in Miami, or sitting at my desk to analyze religious practices in other times and places, there was always something I could not see. Some paths are not taken, and my theory, like all others, has blind spots. Theorists are neither omnivagant nor omnispective. They wander only to this place, or that; they see only what that vantage allows. This does not mean, of course, that there is nothing to see from other sites. As Friedrich Nietzsche observed, it is "the immodesty of man" (or woman) to "deny meaning where he sees none."[14]

A second caution is necessary as we talk about theory's positioned representations as sightings: visual metaphors, like all others, have limitations, and the term *sightings* as I use it refers to multisensorial, culturally mediated embodied encounters. Richard Rorty reminded readers of *Philosophy and the Mirror of Nature* that "ocular metaphors" can be unhelpful because they implicitly or explicitly endorse a correspondence theory of knowledge that presupposes that the "eye of the mind" pairs concepts with mind-independent objects. For that reason, Rorty proposes that we get the visual metaphors "out of our speech altogether." The feminist philosopher of science Donna Haraway joins Rorty in warning about the limitations of visual metaphors. She condemns "the god trick"—the illusory presumption that, like a divine being, we can have vision from everywhere and nowhere—and she suggests that visual analogies create the possibility of a disembodied science and philosophy, thereby underemphasizing or overlooking the gritty physicality of human bodies and the artifacts they make. As Rorty's and Haraway's critiques remind us, it was not inevitable that many Western theorists modeled knowledge and representation on seeing. We can imagine the representational or performative tasks of theory as akin to smell, taste, hearing, or touch: we catch the scent of reality, savor morsels of knowledge, hear the universe speak to us, or rub up against things as they are.

In *The Narrow Road to the Deep North*, Bashō engaged all the senses as he wrote about the "cry of the cuckoo," the bite of "fleas and lice," and "the faint aroma of snow." In a similar way, embodied theoretical sightings also evoke all the senses. So Rorty and Haraway are right to note the limitations of visual imagery, but rather than abandon those metaphors I prefer to reimagine them. Theorists' representations, as I understand them, are bodily and culturally mediated processes that include much more than just seeing.[15]

Those representations also are situated, and this is the final caution I want to urge as I propose that we understand theoretical reflections as sightings. To explain what I mean by *situated* let me return to the writings of Hilary Putnam and Donna Haraway. Putnam outlines two fundamental philosophical orientations: externalist and internalist. To highlight spatial motifs, let's call these supra-locative and locative approaches. The *supra-locative* approach presupposes that the interpreter is everywhere at once or nowhere in particular. It presupposes, as Putnam notes, a "God's Eye point of view." However this perspective is framed, it assumes a position beyond any fixed point and outside all categorical schemes. Sometimes called "metaphysical realism," this view suggests that the world consists of some fixed totality of mind-independent objects, and there is one true and complete description of "the way the world is." Truth involves a correspondence between words and external things. Persuasive interpretation, in this view, means that an account corresponds to "the way things are"—either as they are in themselves or as they appear to participants.[16]

The *locative* approach, which I advocate, begins with the assumption that all theorists are situated and all theories emerge from within categorical schemes and social contexts. It only makes sense to talk about reality-for-us, and questions about what's real or true make sense only *within* a socially constructed cluster of categories and an always-contested set of criteria for assessment. Putnam notes that this view—which is akin to coherence and pragmatic theories of truth—holds that truth does not entail "proof" or "justification"; it aims for—to use John Dewey's term—"warranted assertability." Or as Putnam put it in another passage, truth is "some sort of (idealized) rational acceptability—some sort of ideal coherence of our beliefs with each other and with our experiences *as those experiences are themselves represented in our belief system*—and not correspondence with mind-independent 'states of affairs.'" Both the objects and the signs are internal to categorical schemes, so signs make sense only in a particular context as they are used by particular interpreters. Interpretation, then, is not a matter of matching categories and "independent" realities, and there is no single "correct interpretation." Interpretation is not, in sociologist Max Weber's classic rendering, a matter of understanding the mental states or personal experiences of historical or contemporary actors. Theorists do not have access to those "states" or "experiences." They have only the narratives, artifacts, and practices of religious women and men.[17]

In this locative approach there are more or less acceptable interpretations of those narratives, artifacts, and practices, where *acceptable* here means internally coherent and contextually useful. And it means more: a persuasive interpretation is one that would be found plausible by any fair and self-conscious interpreter who engaged in the same sort of research practices—listening, observing, reading, and so on. That, of course, is impossible, so the notion of an acceptable interpretation is always contested and contestable and is always a matter of offering a plausible account *within* an accepted categorical scheme and *within* a particular professional setting, with its scholarly idiom and role-specific obligations. This means that—to borrow Putnam's phrasing—anything does *not* go. We can give reasons for preferring one interpretation over another—including by appealing to professional obligations and pragmatic criteria—though we cannot claim that our account exhausts all significations or corresponds to "external reality" or "subjective states." Putnam notes that "to single out a correspondence between two domains one needs some independent access to both domains." No such "independent access" is possible, since our theoretical sightings are always our account of what we can see—and hear, touch, taste, and smell—from where we stand.[18]

So however self-evident this claim might seem to some readers, it needs to be reaffirmed, because the authorial voice of most academic studies of religion fails to make it clear: as theorists make sense of narratives, artifacts, and practices they are always situated. Further, as Haraway has argued, all reliable knowledge is situated. Extending her analysis, I suggest that self-conscious positioning, not pretenses to universality or detachment, is the condition for making knowledge claims. Both metaphysical realism and cognitive relativism, in different ways, claim to locate the knower everywhere or nowhere. But as I have argued elsewhere, it is precisely because we stand in a particular place that we are able to see, to know, to narrate. Scholars function within a network of social exchange and in a particular geographical location, and in their work they use collectively constructed professional standards. They stand in a built environment, a social network, and a professional community. In this view, theories of religion are sightings from particular geographical and social sites whereby scholars construct meaning, using categories and criteria they inherit, revise, and create.[19]

So I am just this particular theorist—a middle-aged, middle-class, Philadelphia-born white guy of Irish Catholic descent—drawing on the idiom and norms of my profession to offer a disciplined construction of what I can see from where I am. As I have noted, I can't see everything. Culturally mediated objects enter and leave my sensorial and conceptual horizon. The horizon shifts as I do. And my position (including my gender, class, and race) obscures some things as it illumines others. But let me be clear: I am not apologizing. Theorists have been more or less self-conscious and their interpretations have been more or less subtle, but there have been no supra-locative accounts of religion. No theorist has hovered; no interpretation has been ungrounded. All theorists stand in a particular place. Every one of them. The difference? Some interpreters have said so.[20]

Note, for example, that philologist Friedrich Max Müller's theory of religion, which highlighted language and its misunderstanding, took shape at the desk where he translated Sanskrit texts; Karl Marx's analysis of religion as a tool of the economically powerful emerged from his

3. Sigmund Freud's study, with his office desk and patient's couch. Freud Museum, London.

early observations of unemployment and poverty in Trier and his later walks in London's slums; and, surrounded by ancient sculpture and unearthed artifacts from Egypt, Greece, and the Near and Far East, Sigmund Freud excavated the subterranean impulses of the human psyche and framed his theory of religion as neurosis as he sat across from the couch where patients told him stories about fathers, mothers, and unfulfilled desire (Figure 3). So all theory is situated, and offered as an invitation: consider this. All theorists invite readers to see if their account illumines some regions of the religious world that other theories have obscured. If not, toss it. If so, use it, though always recalling the site from which it emerged and the questions it tried to answer.[21]

⤞ Locating This Theory

As I have tried to make clear, this theory—the proposed route, the journey itself, and these representations—began as I tried to answer questions about what I found among transnational migrants in Miami at the annual festival and the Virgin's shrine. As Michel de Certeau argued, we cannot theorize culture, or anything else, "without, first of all, recognizing the fact that we are dealing with it from one site, our own . . . An analysis always amounts to a localized practice that produces only a regional discourse." Not all theorists of culture or religion have agreed with Certeau or tried to self-consciously position themselves. If they address the issue at all, many theorists of religion have followed Morris Jastrow, the important but neglected American scholar of religion, who acknowledged in his 1901 book *The Study of Religion* what he called "the personal equation," but urged colleagues to "keep it in check and under safe control." Those influenced by traditions in the phenomenology of religion have taken a slightly different approach that, in the end, amounts to the same thing as they aim to "bracket" the personal and the local.[22]

In recent decades, however, a number of intellectual trends have pushed interpreters in the humanities and social sciences to think more about their location or position. Feminists have pondered the social effects of male positions of dominance and self-consciously talked about where they stand. Foucault inspired historical analyses of power relations that took seriously how discourses positioned women and men in social space. Cultural anthropologists celebrated a "reflexive turn" in their field as they extended the methodological self-consciousness already a part of their disciplinary legacy. Several traditions in philosophy—including pragmatism and postmodernism—welcomed a similar move to the local and the personal. Drawing on a gardening metaphor that Ludwig Wittgenstein used in a famous passage in *Philosophical Investigations*, Putnam, who has noted his debt to Wittgenstein's linguistic analysis as well as to the pragmatist tradition, acknowledged the interpreter's situatedness while also reminding us that spatial and temporal positions shift: "Recognizing that there are certain places where one's spade is turned; recognizing, with Wittgenstein, that there are places where our explanations run out, isn't saying that any particular place is *permanently* fated to be one of those places, or that any particular belief is forever immune from criticism. This is where my spade is turned *now*. This is where my justifications stop *now*." On very different grounds, confessional and narrative Christian theologians also have found themselves aligned with pragmatists, postmodernists, and others on this issue as they proclaim their own position from within an ecclesiastical community.[23]

Yet situating oneself and one's theory is more difficult than most interpreters have acknowledged. In my ethnography of devotion at the Miami shrine, I tried to say what I could about where I stood, but, as I acknowledged, first-person positionings introduce as many epistemological and moral problems as they resolve. They claim authority just as they seem to challenge it. They do so "by implying that the author has privileged information about his or her own motives and location, persuading the reader that the writer has come clean . . . But what have I not told the reader? What is inaccessible to me? No matter how forthright and vulnerable authors might appear in such confessional passages, more always remains hidden to author and reader." With the geographer Gillian Rose, I challenge the widespread commitment to "transparent reflexivity," the notion that the theorist's position can be easily identified and acknowledged. To return to an image I introduced earlier, theorists always have blind spots—including a certain blindness about where they stand. There is no omnilateral position. So there is no omnispection, and certainly not as we turn the gaze back on ourselves. Our sightings of our own shifting position are always partial. A cloud of sand and rain blows up and obscures our view.[24]

Attempts to locate ourselves, however, are still worth the effort, even if self-conscious positioning will always remain a partially fulfilled ideal. We know more, not less, when theorists eschew pretenses to having "a view from nowhere," when they do what they can to locate the site of their sightings. Theorists owe it to readers to say as much as seems directly relevant—even if blind spots (and unwitting or principled resistance) will mean it will always be too much and not enough.

My theory of religion, which highlights movement and relation and emphasizes the tropes of dwelling and crossing, is positioned in several ways. First, it is culturally located. As observers of all sorts have claimed, the present age seems to be characterized by accelerated movements across time and space. Business leaders talk about instant exchanges in the global economy. Politicians emphasize that nation-states are increasingly interconnected. Communications experts talk about the rapid transnational transfer of media: film, Web sites, electronic mail, and television. Demographers point to the movements of peoples. Artists have traced the same processes: Mông-Lan, the Vietnamese American painter and poet, has suggested in her poem "Trail" that this is an "era of exile." So as Arjun Appadurai notes, "it has now become something of a truism that we are functioning in a world fundamentally characterized by objects in motion. These objects include ideas and ideologies, people and goods, images and messages, technologies and techniques. This is a world of flows." All theories are culturally situated, and this theory, which emphasizes crossing, emerges from a cultural moment in which movement and relation seem important—at least to those with the leisure to reflect on such things and to those who don't find their crossings constrained by racism, sexism, or poverty.[25]

This theory is personally and professionally located too. If it began with observations among transnational migrants in Miami, where I lived and worked, I was not an aging Cuban exile who fled Castro's Cuba in the 1960s or a twenty-something *balsero* who made the perilous journey by raft in the 1990s. I did not grow up speaking Spanish, and I did not share the same ethnic or national heritage. I was raised as a Roman Catholic, so I knew a good deal about the practices I observed, even on my first visit, but I did not attend the rituals because of an enduring personal devotion. I came to the shrine with a notebook and tape recorder. I came from a nearby university as an untenured scholar who was paid to write and teach about religion in the Americas. Even if my social location has changed over time—when I went off to college, our family income was below the federal poverty line—by the time I started the research for my ethnography I was comfortably middle class. My life then, and since, has been briefcases, neckties, department meetings, PTA book sales, and soccer carpools. And that book about Miami's Cubans helped me to get tenure—and a promotion and raise. Even if I chose the shrine as a site for research because the devotions fascinated me, my work there—and it was work—had professional, economic, and social consequences for me, just as this book will. At the shrine and at my desk, I have been fulfilling professional obligations, even if the tasks have given me great joy.

And my professional location mediated my observations in Miami as it has shaped this book on theory. I was not displaced from my homeland, but since age eighteen I have moved more than most of the Cuban exiles I met as I followed programs of study and job opportunities—from Philadelphia to State College to Cambridge to Boca Raton to Palo Alto to Cambridge to Miami to Chapel Hill. Migration, or crossing, was not foreign to me, even if mine was the voluntary displacement of the privileged. When I researched and wrote, I also thought a great deal about travel, since I studied Cuban exiles and Vietnamese refugees. So it is not surprising that I would focus on crossing as a theme. Nor is it surprising that just as Indologist Max Müller alluded to Indian religious traditions as he theorized, many of the examples in this book are drawn from the religions (Christianity and Buddhism), periods (since the eighteenth century), and places (North America and Japan) I know best.

This theoretical sighting emerges from my professional context in other ways. I have listened in on conversations in cultural anthropology about culture and reflexivity, exchanges in philosophy about language and epistemology, and discussions in human geography about space and place, but my graduate training and university appointment is in religious studies. Even if I hope to attract readers with diverse backgrounds and interests, I have inherited questions, categories, and interlocutors from lineages in the academic study of religion and have tried to contribute to an ongoing conversation in my field. Not all scholars of religion offer a theory of religion, but it should not be surprising when one—even a scholar who isn't a philosopher or theorist—is foolish enough to try.

If my observations at the shrine, my academic itinerancy, and my scholarly focus on Latino and Asian transnational migrants made me more attentive to the issues of movement and relation—and the themes of crossing and dwelling—my reading in cultural anthropology, feminist philosophy, and cultural studies nudged me to think about power and position. And the importance of power and position became clearer to me at the start of this theoretical project, as I reflected on the built environment where I do my work. One Wednesday morning in 1999 I walked up the steps to Saunders Hall, where I have my religious studies office. I noticed a man in a blue uniform perched on a ladder near the entrance. Fixing something or other, I thought to myself as I pushed open the door. I had a nine o'clock class that morning, and I was preoccupied with thinking through the assigned reading. But as I walked down the hall, an administrative assistant from our office rushed toward me.[26]

"There's KKK banners all around the building," she said. "I called maintenance to take them down. It's so upsetting. There are even nooses."

Before I went outside to take a look, anger rose in me. Then resolve. We should do something. Hold a forum, get a petition, write an editorial. Something.

But then I learned that it wasn't Ku Klux Klan supporters who had hung the banners and strung the nooses, symbols of the horrors of lynching. We started reading the banners and learned that someone was protesting, not advocating, racial hatred. Someone was angry, we then surmised, that the 1922 building was named for William Laurence Saunders (1835–1891), who in 1871 had been compelled to testify before a congressional committee investigating the KKK. Saunders, who was appointed to the University of North Carolina's Board of Trustees four years later, refused to answer each of the more than one hundred questions posed by members of the Joint Select Committee. To each he replied only, "I decline to answer," a phrase inscribed on his tombstone. And the remaining archival records do not provide incontrovertible answers about his involvement either. Not all the relevant material survived—a newspaper story claimed Saunders ordered a servant to burn a trunk of old papers at his death—but there is enough evidence to conclude that he was a KKK sympathizer. And he might have been, as one historian suggested in 1914, "at the head of the Invisible Empire in North Carolina," even though he probably "never took the oath of membership and hence was, strictly speaking, not a member."[27]

I had learned about Saunders and the accusations of racism in 1994, soon after I left Miami to teach at Carolina. Initially I was stunned, and infuriated. How could they name a building for him? Why didn't someone change that? Does anyone else know? I went to a senior colleague down the hall to learn more.

"Yeah," he told me, "every few years students protest. And then it fades away again."

Well, it shouldn't fade away, I thought. But it did—until the morning of October 6, when I went outside a second time and saw those nooses dangling above the door. At first I agreed with the spokeswoman for the group that hung them (Students Seeking Historical Truth), who told reporters that she organized the protest to change the building's name. Naming it for that KKK sympathizer, she said, "diminishes the importance of Black students. It's like saying what Saunders did is OK." But then as I was walking to Saunders Hall the next week it hit me: I work in this building. I write here. I had argued in print that we should be self-consciously positioned interpreters, but I had forgotten the history of contact inscribed on the landscape, my landscape, this particular place: a university that, like most others I know, has a morally ambivalent past. It was segregated and sexist throughout much of its history. It was home to some leaders who spoke out against social injustice, yet more than half of the students now enrolled—women and people of color— would not have been welcome on campus earlier in the twentieth century. Then I thought of the title of a book I had been reading at the time, a study of the Western Apache Indians: *Wisdom Sits in Places.* That's right, I thought. And that situated wisdom comes not only from cultivating authorial reflexivity but also from excavating the landscape's moral history. We need to know that this is where a slaveholder stood. Women weren't welcome in this classroom. Here—in this very spot— injustice's residue rests. But we should not erase it but mark it, I decided. Agitate for memory. Don't take the name off the building. Instead, enlarge the bronze plaque beside the entrance. Maybe add floodlights. Or two lime neon arrows flashing downward toward the illumined historical marker, so it could serve to remind that, for good or ill, here is where I stand, where we stand, all of us.[28]

So the nooses dangling from the door reminded me again—and apparently I need reminding—that interpreters are situated, and where we stand is morally ambivalent. Further, the theoretical sightings we offer from where we stand negotiate public power, and enact moral principles, just as they construct meaning. Like some other theorists of religion, I leave it to theologians and ethicists, adherents writing within and for religious communities, to adjudicate disputes among traditions' competing moral or metaphysical claims. I am not interested in determining, for example, whether a Hopi picture of the multi-tiered cosmos is right or whether Buddhist moral precepts are adequate. I will leave those tasks to others. Instead, I set out to find a new language that might make more sense of the movement, relation, and positionality I noticed at the annual festival in Miami. I did not try to construct a theoretical platform from which to criticize or celebrate the beliefs, values, or practices of those Cuban Catholics, although I think that my understanding of theories as itineraries, as positioned sightings, might help those who do want to make normative judgments. At the same time, I have come to realize that I cannot pretend that this theory, or any theory, is "morally neutral." My own epistemic and moral values are evident in several passages of this book—for example, as I note the "role-specific obligations" of scholars in Chapter 2, analyze the "compelled crossings" of slaves and the "constrained crossings" of women in Chapter 5, and affirm "pragmatic" criteria for the assessment of theories in the Conclusion. This inscription of values in a theory of religion is not surprising, however, since scholarly interpretations reflect and shape the social, political, and economic order. Theories situate interpreters and readers in social space and tell us who we are. Excavating the moral history of the local landscape brought this home to me again, and in a new way: power, not just meaning, is at stake when we do our theoretical work.[29]

THE PATH TO KISAGATA: BEYOND OMNINAVIGATION AND OMNISPECTION

So the theorist's built environment, personal location, social status, and professional community all shape theoretical work, and theories are sightings from these shifting sites that answer questions about what the itinerant theorist sees along the way. Yet some critics who affirm a deductive-nomological view and remain captured by a picture of theory as an omnispective mirroring of fixed terrain might challenge the view I have proposed here. They may suggest that I have fallen into an uncritical cognitive relativism that offers little help to those trying to understand religion in multiple historical and geographical contexts. But to acknowledge that I stand *here* is not to imply that what I see from that vantage cannot illumine what can be seen in other times and places, even if theory cannot identify universal laws. This theory, like others, asks only: does this provide an illuminating angle of vision as you try to interpret religions in other eras and regions? To acknowledge that sightings negotiate power as well as meaning is to give up any notion of morally neutral or socially disinterested accounts, but it does not mean that self-consciously positioned theories cannot be useful. To say that a cloud of sand blows up as we traverse the path is not to say we are not on the move and cannot offer representations along the way. To say we cannot have a God's-eye view, and to acknowledge blind spots, is not to say we can see nothing at all. It's to say only what all theorists of religion should have said—that we are positioned.

In Chapter 3, I offer a positioned representation that proposes a route—and continues to move toward a dynamic and relational theory of religion. But as most theoretical itinerants do, I first pause to mark the boundaries of the terrain. In Chapter 2, I consider the arguments about whether and how to define religion.[30]

Chapter Two

Religion cannot reasonably be taken to be a valid analytical category since it does not pick out any distinctive cross-cultural aspect of human life.

Timothy Fitzgerald, *The Ideology of Religious Studies*

When everyone around you is demonstrating that no one can walk, it's a good time to get up quickly and start running.

Michel Serres to Bruno Latour, *Conversations on Science, Culture, and Time*

BOUNDARIES

Constitutive Terms, Orienting Tropes, and Exegetical Fussiness

Despite warnings about the futility of efforts to define religion, many scholars still choose to "get up and start running."[1] In this chapter I warm up for the sprint by discussing constitutive terms and arguing for scholars' role-specific obligation to define them. Meeting that obligation, I suggest, means being clear about the type of definition offered and attending carefully to the choice of orienting trope, since definitions imply theories and employ tropes. Interpreters of religion have relied on a wide range of orienting metaphors, and I consider some of the most influential ones as I point to the implications of those choices.

For good reasons, nonspecialists start to doze when definitions come up; scholars of religion, who've heard it all before, exhale a knowing sigh. Not another (doomed) attempt to characterize religion! And there is a long and lofty lineage of scholarly suspicion, even contempt, about definitional attempts. Consider this excerpt from a 1901 article by an influential American scholar of religion, James Leuba, who recorded a familiar complaint: there are lots of definitions and none of them seem to agree.

It has been a favorite custom with [scholars] to put up the concentrated results of their toil with little formulae, commonly called *definitions* of religion. Although they evince most astonishing divergencies, extending even to hopeless contradiction, they will, when considered together and compared with each other, at least warn us away from certain false conceptions which have obscured the view of otherwise clear-sighted men. It must be confessed that the definitions of religion would afford a happy topic for a malicious person bent upon showing the quackery of the Doctors in religion.[2]

I don't think I'm driven by any "malicious" impulses—though readers can decide that for themselves—and I certainly don't think it's "quackery" for scholars to propose definitions, even "astonishingly divergent" and "hopelessly contradictory" ones. On the contrary, I suggest that scholars have a role-specific obligation to define constitutive disciplinary terms: *art* for art history, *music* for musicology, *literature* for literary studies, *culture* for anthropology, *space* for geography, and *language* for linguistics.[3]

"EXEGETICAL FUSSINESS" AS ROLE-SPECIFIC DUTY

Constitutive terms are those that constitute or mark the boundaries of a field of study. Practitioners—artists, musicians, poets, and the pious in the pews—do not have to define these constitutive terms. It is enough that they know how to produce a painting, play the flute, write a sonnet, or recite the Lord's Prayer. However, scholars who have been trained to participate in an academic conversation have a role-specific obligation to reflect on their work—and the constitutive terms of their discipline. They have a professional duty to be self-conscious in their use of central categories—*art, religion, literature,* or *music.* So when poet and literature professor John Hollander composed the poems collected in *The Night Mirror* he was properly focused on his art, but when he wrote *Rhyme's Reason,* his brilliant guide to verse, he rightly also pondered poetry and its "formal structures." When ethnomusicologist John Blacking—who confided to readers that he's also a musician—played Chopin on his living room piano on a Saturday afternoon, he had no duty to ponder whether "humanly ordered sound" was an inclusive enough definition of music. Only when he stepped into his study to write about the *mankuntu* dance song of the Gwembe Tonga of Zambia did he have an obligation to reflect on his field's central category.[4]

But the problems of defining these categories can be so great that some scholars feel unable to meet their role-specific professional duties. In some instances, well-grounded worries about the adequacy of disciplinary idiom have led scholars to silence. The 1980 edition of *The New Grove Dictionary of Music and Musicians,* which had plenty of room in its twenty hefty volumes, included no entry on *music;* the 2002 edition of *A Handbook to Literature* failed to define *literature;* and the editor of the 1997 edition of the *Oxford Dictionary of Art* didn't even take a stab at defining *art.*[5]

And even when scholars do reflect on these categories they often find themselves befuddled. Those struggling with their role-specific obligation encounter the disorienting diversity of previous definitions. As the author of the entry on *religion* in the *Harper Collins Dictionary of Religion* noted, "Defining religion is often held to be difficult. Introductions to the study of religion routinely include long lists of definitions of religion as proof of this." Definers also confront other difficulties, including the constitutive term's alleged inability to include all instances in all times and places: this clan does not seem to have art; those people write no literature; that culture has no word for music.[6]

Some who confront these difficulties eschew definitions but self-consciously reflect on the prior attempts and the conceptual problems. For example, a group of musicologists and philosophers of music who took on the task in an ambitiously titled volume, *What Is Music?*, noted that "the question 'what is music?' has no easy answer." The book's editor suggested, "'music' seems . . . to be a culturally unstable term, likely to remain a contested concept within our own civilization where the term covers a wide range of practices." In the same spirit, the latest edition of the *New Grove Dictionary of Music and Musicians* does include an entry on music (my friends in musicology tell me it's because of the "uproar" generated by its omission from the previous edition), but that standard reference work avoids defining it: "Imposing a single definition flies in the face of the broadly relativistic intercultural and historically conscious nature of this dictionary." The account ends by restating the definitional problem: "It ought to be possible to define music in an interculturally valid way, but the fact that definers inevitably speak with the language and from the cultural viewpoint of their own societies is a major obstacle. Only a few societies have a word whose meaning corresponds roughly to the English 'music'; and it is questionable whether the concept of music in the breadth it enjoys in Western cultures is present in the cognitive maps of all cultures." And other constitutive terms do not seem to be found on all cognitive maps either. After noting the difficulties in discerning whether all cultures have a term or concept for art, the entry in the *Dictionary of Art* makes a similar point: "the question of whether art is or is not . . . an integral part of human society remains undecided."[7]

While discussing attempts to define *geography*, David N. Livingstone explains why faces flush during vigorous disciplinary debates about (apparently) small differences in usage and meaning: "To have command of definition is to have control of discourse. For this reason it is not surprising that *exegetical fussiness* over the precise meaning of terms is characteristic of those apologetic works that aim to fix disciplinary identity." Scholars cannot—and should not—avoid reflecting on the terms that fix disciplinary identity, and it is the academics who use them that get to define them. As religion scholar Jonathan Z. Smith noted, "'Religion' is not a native term; it is a term created by scholars for their intellectual purposes and therefore is theirs to define. It is a second-order, generic concept that plays the same role in establishing a disciplinary horizon that a concept such as 'language' plays in linguistics or 'culture' plays in anthropology. There can be no disciplined study of religion without such a horizon." So even if all interpreters do not have a duty to construct theories and propose definitions—for then what would anyone have to theorize?—our professional obligations nudge us to enter the debate about the meaning and usefulness of constitutive terms. Those of us who claim a lineage in the academic conversation about *religion* should be clear about how we use the term. In that sense, we are called to the task of defining—and to contesting definitions. We are called to offer self-conscious sightings from where we stand, reflexive surveys of the disciplinary horizon. We're called to "exegetical fussiness."[8]

TYPES OF DEFINITIONS: LEXICAL, EMPIRICAL, AND STIPULATIVE

As we get "fussy" about the meaning of terms, we might find that we're appealing to either cartographic or visual analogies: definition is "the setting of bounds or limits" or rendering "an object or image distinct to the eye." And however scholars have defined definition—and some linguists and philosophers have spent a good deal of energy doing precisely that—most note definitions' variety. Among scholars of religion, Robert Baird has presented a helpful typology of definitions. He distinguishes lexical, real, and functional (or stipulative) definitions. For Baird, a *lexical* definition mirrors ordinary usage. It explains "the actual way in which some actual word has been used by some actual person." We might think of this as the dictionary definition. An example might include the long entry from the *Oxford English Dictionary* that documents seven primary uses of *religion* and includes, with each, a chronologically arranged list of quotations from texts that use it that way. So, for example, the fifth definition is: "Recognition on the part of man of some higher unseen power as having control of his destiny, and as being entitled to obedience, reverence, and worship; the general mental and moral attitude resulting from this belief, with reference to its effect upon the individual or the community; personal or general acceptance of this feeling as a standard of spiritual and practical life." Below that definition are ten quotations and citations from texts published between 1535 and 1877, including passages from works by Thomas Hobbes (1651) and Adam Smith (1776).[9]

A *real* definition, which might be labeled an empirical or inductive definition, "is a true statement about things that are." Such definitions offer propositions about the nature of things, and they can be true or false. Truth in this approach often, though not always, means correspondence with objects that are independent of the mind. An example might be found in Rodney Stark and Roger Finke's *Acts of Faith: Explaining the Human Side of Religion.* Although the authors suggest that their sociological theory of religion is not a "*fully* deductive theoretical system," they offer ninety-nine "propositions" and thirty-six "definitions" throughout the book, from assertions that excavate the "micro foundations" of religion to those that help explain how religious institutions transform from sect to church. Consider, for example, proposition six: "In pursuit of rewards, humans will seek to utilize and manipulate the supernatural." Or definition five: "Religion consists of very general explanations of existence, including terms of exchange with a god or gods." In these and other propositions and definitions, Stark and Finke offer proposals about what religion is and how it functions. They offer an empirical definition.[10]

Finally, scholars can propose *stipulative* definitions, which somewhat arbitrarily stipulate "that a certain word means a certain thing." Stipulative definitions cannot be true or false; they can be only more or less useful. The psychologist and philosopher William James decided on this approach near the start of his influential Gifford Lectures, *The Varieties of Religious Experience:*

The field of religion being as wide as this, it is manifestly impossible that I should pretend to cover it. My lectures must be limited to a fraction of the subject. And, although it would indeed be foolish to set up an abstract definition of religion's essence, and then proceed to defend that definition against all comers, yet this need not prevent me from taking my own narrow view of what religion shall consist in *for the purposes of these lectures*, or out of the many meanings of the word, from choosing the one meaning in which I wish to interest you particularly, and proclaiming arbitrarily that when I say "religion" I mean *that*.[11]

In this self-consciously stipulative approach, James says that he offers the definition "for the purposes of these lectures," and italicizes the phrase for emphasis. He acknowledges, without remorse or apology, that his is an "arbitrary" account designed for a particular purpose. And he reminds readers of this a few pages later when he offers his famous definition of religion: ". . .the feelings, acts, and experiences of individual men in their solitude, so far as they apprehend themselves to stand in relation to whatever they may consider the divine." However, scholars usually omit—or at least de-emphasize—the introductory phrase of that sentence: "Religion, therefore, as I now ask you arbitrarily to take it shall mean for us . . ." Note the function of several words here: *I, now, arbitrarily, you, us.* James tried to make clear, then, that a particular scholar was stipulating an arbitrary definition for particular purposes and a particular audience.[12]

One way to clarify the differences between stipulative and empirical approaches to defining constitutive terms is to consider a recent contribution to the ongoing debate over the term *culture* in the field of anthropology. In an imaginative article in *American Anthropologist* four scholars coauthored a piece juxtaposing four positions that, taken together, created a published "conversation about culture." Most important, they reframe the issue of definition in a very helpful way by shifting the question from "what *form* of the concept one might apply" to "*when* to apply the concept." They ask, "Does one lean more toward induction or deduction in applying the cultural concept?" Two of the authors suggest that we introduce the constitutive term only at the end of a study (an empirical or deductive definition); the other two favor proposing a definition at the start of the work (a stipulative or inductive definition). Nomi Maya Stolzenberg, who defends the stipulative approach, acknowledges the "lack of precision" in the term *culture:* "No one could seriously deny that 'culture' is an exceedingly vague and ambiguous term." But, she suggests, "it is precisely because of its lack of precision that culture remains a useful concept, for both anthropologists and those outside the field." Stolzenberg, a legal scholar, suggests that we reimagine *culture* and other constitutive terms and "cease to think of [them] as the name for a thing and come to view [them] instead as a *placeholder* for a set of inquiries—inquiries which may be destined never to be resolved."[13]

CONSIDERING OBJECTIONS TO DEFINITIONS

Whether interpreters have offered lexical, empirical, or stipulative definitions—and empirical definitions have predominated—some religion scholars have challenged any attempt to define the field's constitutive term. Still, as Leuba noted in his 1901 article, there have been many attempts at definition. Eleven years later, in *A Psychological Study of Religion: Its Origin, Function, and Future,* Leuba reprinted a revised version of his essay and listed more than four dozen definitions of religion in an appendix to that volume. Using Leuba's list, and other evidence of the diversity of definitions, some academics have rejected definition altogether on the grounds that scholars have been unable to agree on the meaning and use of the term. This lexical objection, which focuses on linguistic use, is only one of several. A second sort of objection, which focuses on the term's historical origins, suggests that we should abandon the term—and attempts at definition—because *religion* is a Western (and Christian) category that arose (or gained wider usage) in a colonial context. Even if the term has a much longer history, Western missionaries, traders, soldiers, and civil servants advanced its use in a discourse that still informs the academic study of religion. A third objection, closely related to the second, assesses the category using pragmatic criteria and highlights its moral implications. As one interpreter has suggested, the Western term has "mediated the value-charged and deeply inequitable encounters between 'us' and 'them,' the 'West' and the 'Orient,' the present and the past." A fourth objection to defining religion repeats concerns about defining other constitutive terms, like *music:* critics point to its lack of cross-cultural breadth or universal applicability. They note either that the term *religion* is not found in all languages and cultures, or that the announced features of religion are not found in all cultures. This position assumes that all definitions are empirical, and thereby entail true or false claims that can be assessed by considering whether they correspond with a mind-independent state of affairs. It also assumes that "universality" is a reasonable criterion for definitions. Finally, as with art historians who propose that *visual culture* replace *art* in academic conversations, some religion scholars do not object to the view I have supported here—that disciplines employ constitutive terms and we should define them. Instead, they chronicle the limitations of the category *religion* while advocating an alternative(s). So *politics, ritual, soteriology, faith, tradition,* and *cosmographic formations* are nominated as better interpretive categories. Or, in a related approach, religious studies is reimagined as cultural studies, and scholars suggest that *culture* should be taken as the central analytical term.[14]

To consider the final objection first, even if we were to seek alternate categories, none of the proposed alternatives overcomes the other four objections or dissolves definitional problems. *Culture: A Critical Review of Concepts and Definitions,* the classic 1952 work by anthropologists A. L. Kroeber and Clyde Kluckhohn, and many other contributions to the anthropological conversation about that field's constitutive term, shows that *culture* is at least as contested as *religion.* And Timothy Fitzgerald's proposed alternatives—*soteriology, politics,* and *ritual*—are not much better. In *The Ideology of Religious Studies,* Fitzgerald suggests that "religion cannot be reasonably taken to be a valid analytical category since it does not pick out any distinctive cross-cultural aspect of human life." Drawing on several of the standard objections to definition, Fitzgerald argues "for deleting the word 'religion' from the list of analytical categories entirely," and not only because it does not identify a cross-cultural practice and so has no analytical use for those who study, for example, Japan and India, where no term parallels *religion.* The term also deserves to be discarded, Fitzgerald argues, because it is "ideologically charged" since it arose in the context of nineteenth-century European colonization. He proposes that religious studies be reimagined as cultural studies and that we turn to other, less problematic analytical categories.[15]

But those three categories and all constitutive disciplinary terms (including *religion*) have their limits. Consider a few observations about the proposed terms that might at least suggest that they are not self-evidently more adequate, without even highlighting a primary objection—that *religion* has been the primary category used by scholars in this professional conversation since the mid-nineteenth century and cannot be easily replaced. Like the term religion, *soteriology, politics,* and *ritual* also arose in particular social contexts for particular purposes, and they do not seem to have cross-cultural equivalents in all societies. *Politics,* meaning "the science and art of government," comes from a Greek root pertaining to citizens, and it was connected with ancient Greek conversations about citizenship, the state, and (more broadly) the social good. This term is no less idiosyncratic or situated for having had wide influence, and to pencil it in at the top of the religion scholar's lexicon is to evoke certain notions about what religion is and how it functions. The term implies, for example, that to talk about religion is to foreground the collectivity more than the individual and to highlight power more than meaning. Such an approach might be useful. Collectivity and power are important. But it does not mean that this strategy would be free of definitional—or ideological—difficulties.[16]

Ritual, a term of Latin origin that refers to "a prescribed order of performing religious or other devotional service," is a slightly better alternate category, since it seems to make sense of a wider range of practices across cultures and periods. Yet it too arose in a particular cultural context, and, like *politics*, it is not as inclusive as the maligned term *religion*. Anthropologist Roy Rappaport and others who have argued that "ritual is taken to be the ground from which religious conceptions spring" can offer a compelling account of practices. Yet they still confront the difficulties of identifying "religion's most general and universal elements" (for Rappaport, "the Holy") as they also try to find creative ways to illumine traditional religious features that *ritual* ("the performance of more or less invariant sequences of formal acts and utterances not entirely coded by the performers") seems to obscure—for example, artifacts, narratives, and institutions.[17]

And Fitzgerald's third proposed category, *soteriology*, seems even more problematic. It is a Greek term that has been used primarily in Western Christian theology to describe "Christ's saving work" or the "doctrine of salvation." But the Baktaman of New Guinea don't talk much about *soteriology*. Neither do Theravada Buddhist monks in Sri Lanka (Figure 4). And even if some interpreters might respond by suggesting that theoretical terms need not follow vernacular use or that the Buddhists and the Baktaman do share some notion of salvation or, more broadly, some concept of an ultimate goal, we have only returned to the sort of fundamental definitional problems that drove many to befuddlement—or silence. For now we must ask if *salvation* is inclusive enough to make sense of both the Buddhist monk's striving for *nirvāṇa*, the cessation of suffering and release from rebirth, and the Baktaman's hope that their *finik*, spirit, can be transformed through a nonviolent death into a *sabkār*, deceased spirit, that is transported to the land of the dead. We are not far from where we began as we started to ponder the difficulties of the term *religion*.[18]

And this shouldn't surprise us. No constitutive disciplinary term is elastic enough to perform all the work that scholars demand of it. But

4. A Theravadin Buddhist monk bows in homage to an image of the Buddha, who reclines before his entrance into final nirvana. Anuradhapura, Sri Lanka.

that means we should continually refine and revise our understanding of the term for different purposes and contexts, not abandon it. As sociologist Max Weber noted, broad categories—he called them "ideal types"—are theoretical constructs that function as more or less useful interpretive tools. We should not be surprised that they fail to conform to the full range of historical or contemporary cases. And their effectiveness is not challenged when we find some instances that do not seem to "fit"—whether analyzing Shintō in Japan, Hinduism in India, or any other particular cluster of spiritual practices. As the anthropologist Melford E. Spiro has argued, interpretive terms need not be "universal" to be useful: "From what methodological principle does it follow that religion—or, for that matter, anything else—must be universal if it is to be studied comparatively?" The term *religion* has not failed us when we decide it obscures some features we want to highlight. It has directed our attention to practices that we might otherwise have missed. It has prompted further conversation, more contestation. It has done its work. We know something we did not know. We have been reminded— and we always need reminding—that there are other sites that offer other sightings.[19]

If we should not be surprised—or disappointed—by the "discovery" that constitutive terms, while elastic, still do not stretch to cover all we can see from where we stand, we also should not abandon them because our scholarly idiom arose in particular social contexts. All constitutive disciplinary terms—including *music, art, literature, culture,* and *religion*—are located and contested. All arose, and have been used, in particular social sites for particular purposes.

So to return to the five objections to defining religion, only the last— that another term would be better—seems to be without much merit, although the other four objections are not significant enough to abandon the definitional task. First, as critics have pointed out, *religion* has been defined in a variety of ways. Yet definitional variety indicates the term *can* be defined, not that it cannot, since agreement is not necessary, possible, or useful. "It was once a tactic of students of religion," Jonathan Z. Smith argued in challenging Winston King's dismissive claim, "to cite the appendix of James H. Leuba's *Psychological Study of Religion* (1912), which lists more than fifty definitions of religion, to demonstrate that 'the effort clearly to define religion in short compass is a hopeless task.'" But the task is not hopeless, just demanding. Note that the widely consulted religious studies reference work that acknowledged the diversity of definitions still went on to offer one: religion is "a system of beliefs and practices that are relative to superhuman beings." And the entry's author justified the attempt: "the lists [of definitions] fail to demonstrate that the task of defining religion is so difficult that one might as well give up on the task. What the lists show is that there is little *agreement* on an adequate definition."[20]

The second and third objections to definition also seem right, although they too do not preclude attempts to set out the meaning of the term: even if the term has an earlier origin, *scholarly* discourse about religion did emerge in a colonial context, and it has been employed unjustly to marginalize some groups. Many studies, including those by Talal Asad, David Chidester, Donald Lopez, and Richard King, have shown this. But as Chidester notes, that history is not grounds to abandon the term. "After reviewing the history of colonial productions and reproduction on contested frontiers, we might happily abandon *religion* and *religions* as terms of analysis if we were not, as the result of that very history, stuck with them." If, as even Wilfred Cantwell Smith and Timothy Fitzgerald acknowledge, constitutive terms establish disciplinary horizons, religion scholars need such terms. We are "stuck" with them. The disorienting variety, ambivalent history, and inequitable function of definitions only make scholars' obligations to assess previous accounts and to self-consciously redefine the category more complicated—and more morally urgent. Definitions matter.[21]

DEFINITIONS, TROPES, AND THEORIES

Definitions matter, in part, because they offer hints about theories. The widely read reference book I quoted earlier, the *Harper Collins Dictionary of Religion*, notes that "a specific definition of religion usually comes from a particular discipline or theory of religion." I agree that definitions and theories are linked, although I would challenge the misleading causal claim implied in the phrase "comes from," since that phrasing obscures the complex ways that definitions also shape theories. And I would go further. Definitions and theories also intertwine with *tropes*. Definitions, in my view, imply theories and employ tropes. This reciprocal triadic relation involves constant crisscrossing of influences among definition, theory, and trope.[22]

Consider Sigmund Freud's famous definition of religion in *The Future of an Illusion*, which appeared in 1927. Freud had begun his analysis of religion in 1907, with the publication of "Obsessive Actions and Religious Practices," and he continued it in other writings until he died in 1939 at the age of eighty-three. Although his theories have been vigorously and widely challenged, inside and outside the field of religious studies, his lexicon and interpretations have remained influential. For this reason one prominent interpreter said of the psychoanalyst, "Freud is inescapable." I suppose we could try to avoid him, but that would be unwise here since his *Future of an Illusion* usefully illustrates the reciprocal interactivity among definition, trope, and theory. As with most theoretical works on religion, Freud actually employed several tropes in that volume. For example, in a passage that recalls Karl Marx's famous definition of religion as an "opiate," the Viennese therapist suggested that "the effects of religious consolations may be *likened to that of a narcotic.*" But more central to the book's argument than this simile is a metaphor that compares religion to illness, or individual psychological dysfunction. Religion is "the universal obsessional *neurosis* of humanity; like the obsessional neurosis of children, it arose out of the Oedipus complex, out of the relation to the father." As with all definitions to some extent, and especially those for complex cultural practices, Freud reaches for figurative language to establish some contiguity, if not identity, between the *definiendum* (the unknown that is defined) and the *definiens* (the known that is used to define the term). Although I would not agree with much of Freud's explanations of religion's nature and function, I am not criticizing him here for turning to figures. All of religion's scholarly interpreters have done that, and Freud is actually much more self-conscious than many. He ends the paragraph, after going on to suggest that religion, in this approach, becomes "a system of wishful illusions" comparable to amentia (a state of acute hallucinatory confusion), by acknowledging the function and limits of his metaphor: "But these are only *analogies,* by the help of which we endeavour to understand a social phenomenon; the pathology of the individual does not supply us with a fully valid counterpart."[23]

So if Freud self-consciously employed figurative language in his definition of religion, in turn, the definition he fashioned from this primary trope (children's psychological pathology) evokes the outlines of a theory of religion. Even without recourse to the rest of the book—which I think would support this reading—we can tentatively identify several implicit claims in this brief definition. First, since Freud compares religion to a psychological dysfunction, religion's origin is psychic, rather than social, cultural, political, or economic. Second, since it is a "universal" pathology of "humanity," religion seems to be a transcultural form that crosses chronological and spatial boundaries. Third, religion is "like the neurosis of children," so in this simile religious adherents are analogous to children. Fourth, since Freud juxtaposes religion and children, who are not developmentally advanced, it seems to follow that religion represents a lower stage of cultural development. (Freud confirms this in the next sentence: "If this view is right, it is to be supposed that a turning-away from religion is bound to occur with the fatal inevitability of a process of *growth,* and that we find ourselves at this very juncture in the middle of that phase of *development.*") Fifth, since religion arises from "the relation to the father," it must reproduce in some ways that dependent relation (at least as that relation is imagined in a particular model of the family). Sixth, although Freud insists earlier in the book that "to assess the truth-value of religious doctrines does not lie within the scope of the present enquiry," religion seems to be a bad thing. Either, at best, humanity is just going through a stage it will outgrow, or we need to plop humanity on the couch for what promises to be a very long series of therapeutic interventions.[24]

I could go on. I could say more about the outlines of a theory of religion embedded in the tropes found in this one passage, or in many other classic formulations of religion's meaning. You might want to quarrel with this or that in my reading of Freud's definition, but I hope that I have at least established that definition, theory, and trope seem to reciprocally shape each other. I will allude to the relation between definition and theory more below, but so far I have talked about tropes without considering what they are or how they function—or how tropic analysis can be useful in the humanities and the social sciences, especially the study of religion.[25]

As I hinted in my reading of Freud's definition of religion as psychological pathology, tropes are figures of speech that depart from the ordinary form, use, or arrangement of words. They involve figurative, or nonliteral, language. As James W. Fernandez noted in his introduction to *Beyond Metaphor: The Theory of Tropes in Anthropology*, cultural interpreters who have taken figurative language seriously often have highlighted one trope, metaphor. There have been several approaches to the understanding of metaphor. First, some have turned to "the Aristotelian-derived strain of metaphor theory," which "focuses upon the transfer of features of meaning from one domain of understanding to another." A second interpretive tradition is "much influenced by the American critic and philosopher Kenneth Burke . . . [and] concentrates on how experience in culture and position in society are constructed through metaphoric predication." A third approach, which highlights metaphors' effects or uses and challenges the notion that they contain hidden or nonliteral meaning that needs to be decoded, emerges from the philosopher Donald Davidson's 1978 essay "What Metaphors Mean" and has been endorsed and revised by, among others, Richard Rorty and Nancy K. Frankenberry.[26]

As Fernandez and his colleagues suggested, the first two approaches have been most influential, and since the 1980s metaphor theory in the social sciences has focused more on the variety of tropes and their "foundations" in culture. Rhetoricians have identified more than two hundred figures of speech, including simile, symbol, allegory, personification, apostrophe, synecdoche, and metonymy. So Paul Friedrich, one of the contributors to Fernandez's volume, was right to emphasize "polytropy" and to urge scholars to recall the full range of figurative language at play in cultural practices. Yet of the five "macrotropes" that Friedrich identifies—image tropes, modal tropes, formal tropes, contiguity tropes, and analogical tropes—it is analogical language, especially metaphor, that can be especially useful in cultural analysis.[27]

The metaphors that cultural analysts interpret can be direct or indirect. Consider examples from the well-known poem by T. S. Eliot, "The Love Song of J. Alfred Prufrock." "And I have seen the *eternal Footman* hold my coat, and snicker," is a direct metaphor that identifies the divine with an attendant or servant. An indirect metaphor, in which the comparison is implied but not stated, appears in an earlier line: "The yellow fog that rubs its back upon the window panes." This image implies, but does not declare, that the fog is a cat. Or, to use examples from Freud's definition, neurosis is the direct metaphor. He says religion is "the universal obsessional *neurosis* of humanity." And because the next sentence proposes that it is a "neurosis of *children*," the passage also includes an indirect evolutionary or developmental metaphor, as suggested above, that portrays religion as childish, a lower stage of cultural development.[28]

To demarcate religion's boundaries, interpreters of religion have employed many different kinds of tropes. Some have used symbols: Hegel's "consciousness of *God*"; Müller's "perception of the *Infinite*"; and Otto's "experience of the *Holy*." Metaphor, however, is a widely used trope. Although one philosopher has suggested that "a definition must not be expressed in metaphor or figurative language"—one of his thirteen rules for constructing definitions—this seems to be a principle that no scholar who risks a definition can follow. Many contemporary theorists would acknowledge that most language is figurative in some sense, and metaphor is an important figure.[29]

Using metaphor to define metaphor—and, unrepentant, breaking that rule of definition—I suggest that metaphor is a lens and a vehicle. It directs language users' attention to this and not that, and it transports them from one domain of language, experience, and practice to another. In my terms, it prompts new sightings and crossings. As Davidson proposed, it can be helpful to think about "the effects metaphors have on us" and talk about what metaphors do. What do they do? They redirect our attention. Drawing on analogy for their power, metaphors illumine some features of the terrain and obscure others. To use an example from my study of Cuban American devotion at the shrine of Our Lady of Charity, Bishop Agustín Román, the shrine's director, turned to metaphor to address race relations in Miami, a city that had been unsettled by ethnic and racial tension for years. Consider my earlier account of the event:

> In 1994 Román arranged for a bus filled with white Cubans from the shrine to visit the Haitian Catholic Center, where they would participate in a mass and procession on the feast of Corpus Christi. During the ride to Little Haiti the shrine director tried to prepare the Cubans for what they soon would experience: the only white faces in a crowd of several hundred, all eyes on them. And he tried to promote tolerance. Noting the differences in skin color, he turned to an analogy from Cuban foodways to persuade. He reminded the white Cubans—no one needed reminding—of their traditional love for black beans and white rice. Extending that analogy to Cuban history and identity, the shrine director suggested that "*Cuba is beans and rice, black and white.*"

The Cuban leader's metaphor redirected the attention of the white devotees to food, a beloved traditional dish. Cuba is a plate on which black beans and white rice have been mixed. The metaphoric utterance associated language, experience, and practice about food with language, experience, and practice concerning race. As some cognitive scientists have proposed, the metaphor made a "class-inclusion assertion." In other words, the analogy established a grouping or relation between two categories—food and race—and, I would add, between two domains of practice. It highlighted the ways that racial comminglings, like culinary combinations, have been part of Cuban history. Or, to return to the passage from Freud again, the direct metaphor of psychological pathology and the indirect metaphor of evolutionary stages prompt readers to highlight dysfunction and immaturity and obscure the ways that religion might arise from or cultivate mental or physical health and might inspire or reflect a mature engagement with the world.[30]

Metaphor can redirect attention because it functions as a mode of transport. It prompts a linguistic crossing that can create associations, stir affect, and prompt action. The shrine director induced nostalgia, even triggered sense memory, as he used the culinary metaphor to prescribe and transform the white Cubans' behavior when they entered the Haitian church—and after they left. He transferred memories, values, and emotions from the realm of food to the realm of social relations as he talked about black beans. So in this metaphor and in others, more than a single term (*beans, neurosis,* or *children*) is transferred from one use to another, transported from one cultural domain to another. Metaphors propel language—and language users—between frames of reference, to borrow a phrase from physics. Or in Nelson Goodman's terms, there is a "migration of concepts." But metaphor is a reciprocal interactive process. It is not a matter of transferring one static and bounded "scheme" to another. As some interpreters of metaphor have noted, it is the reciprocal and relational *dynamics* of metaphor that characterizes this trope. Victor Turner, for example, suggested that "the two thoughts are active together, they 'engender' thought in their *coactivity.*" So when Freud appealed to the metaphor of children and, indirectly, to the evolutionary model that posits progressive linear "stages" of nature and culture, he put that organic image in dynamic reciprocal relation with the scholarly discourse about religion. In the same way, in that brief passage in Freud's *Future of an Illusion,* a confluence of concepts from depth psychology (obsession, neurosis, Oedipal complex) "migrated" back and forth between a discourse about religious life and a discourse about psychic life.[31]

Analogical language, and this sort of figurative process, is inscribed in many other scholarly definitions of religion. Freud was not the only interpreter of religion to employ tropes. "Key metaphors" (Ortner), "root metaphors" (Turner), "organizing metaphors" (Fernandez), or what I call *orienting metaphors* appear in many other definitions.[32]

ORIENTING METAPHORS: TROPES IN DEFINITIONS OF RELIGION

At least a dozen orienting metaphors have had some influence in the history of scholarly definitions of religion. Most definitions employ more than one of these, so there is no pure type, only hybrid forms that approximate the categories in this taxonomy. And some orienting metaphors have had much more influence than others. Religion has been analogized as: capacity, organism, system, worldview, illness, narcotic, picture, form of life, society, institution, projection, and space.

The first approach—to define religion by identifying it with one or more *psychic capacities*—has been especially popular. In fact, this has been the favorite method of classifying religion's definitions. In some premodern philosophical approaches, interpreters talked about psychological *faculties,* and some (even into the late nineteenth century) posited a distinctive *religious* faculty. Even if the idiom has changed over time, many interpreters have defined religion by emphasizing one or another psychic capacity: believing, feeling, or willing. In other words, there are—as Friedrich Schleiermacher, James Leuba, and many others have proposed—intellectualist, affective, and volitional definitions. For example, religion is *belief* for many scholars, as in the anthropologist E. B. Tylor's famous definition: "the belief in spiritual beings." But the object of belief varies to some extent: religion has been imagined as belief in an ever-living God (Martineau), the superhuman (Tiele), God and spiritual beings (Crawford), humanlike beings (Guthrie), or a world of counterintuitive supernatural agents (Atran). In a related intellectualist approach, not only Guthrie and Atran but several other scholars have applied the findings of cognitive science and have taken *cognition,* and computer processing, as the central metaphor. Volitional definitions, which have exerted less influence, emphasize either moral action (Kant) or ritual action (Rappaport). In a similar way, although sociologist Christian Smith acknowledges the significance of "beliefs, symbols, and practices," the core of his definition emphasizes the ways in which religions are "superempirically referenced wellsprings of moral order." Affective definitions associate religion with a feeling: for example, absolute dependence (Schleiermacher), *mysterium tremendum* (Otto), or hopes and fears (Hume).[33]

Another capacity metaphor is closely aligned with affective definitions: religion is about *experiencing.* Part of the confusion derives from the multiple terms that Schleiermacher employed: he did use feeling *(gefühl)* to mark off religion's distinctive terrain, but also used related terms as well, including intuition *(anschauung)* and experience *(emfindung)*. And the latter has been a central analogy for many definitions. Religion is noncognitive; it does not, as in the Tylorian tradition, make claims about the nature of things. In this view, religion is an experience of the Holy (Otto), the sacred (Eliade), the Infinite (Müller), or invisible things (Jevons).[34]

Some definitions frame religion as desiring or, better, as a *concern*. The philosopher David Hume claimed religion was "an anxious concern for happiness," but in a more influential formulation theologian Paul Tillich suggested that religion was one's "ultimate concern." Other scholars before him anticipated Tillich's approach: religion is a "bearing toward what seems to him the Best, or Greatest" (Stratton) or "the objects, habits, and convictions he would die for" (Bosanquet). And many who have followed Tillich have found "ultimate concern" a compelling analogy, including Robert Baird and John Wilson. As Jonathan Z. Smith notes, Tillich's definition is one of two—the other is Spiro's, which I introduced earlier and will return to later—that "command widespread scholarly assent."[35]

Many influential accounts define religion by pointing to *several* psychic capacities: religion as belief and feeling (Jastrow) or as emotions, conceptions, and sentiments (Tiele). Some definitions that combine intellectualist, affective, and volitional approaches imagine religion not only as *believing* or *feeling* but also as *doing*—by trading on the notion of religion as *will*. Consider James's definition of religion as "feelings, *acts*, and experiences" or Durkheim's account of religion as "beliefs and *practices*."[36]

Other definitions appeal to other orienting metaphors, even if they also might simultaneously appeal to one or another capacity metaphor. Some have appealed to organic tropes, even imaging religion as an *organism*. In a direct metaphor, entomologist E. O. Wilson has talked about "religion as superorganism." In somewhat less direct ways, like

Freud, many scholars since the late nineteenth century have implied an analogy to the development of the individual or the evolution of the natural world (or both). To mention only two famous examples, Tylor spoke of "the natural evolution of religious ideas" and Müller claimed to trace "the origin and growth of religion." Several definitions turn to a term from the natural sciences, *system*, to understand religion. This analogy highlights that religion includes parts that form a whole. It is often interpreted more statically than the meaning of the term in physics, which understands systems as groups of bodies moving in space according to some dynamic law. Applied to the task of definition, religion becomes "a system of willful illusions" (Freud), "a unified system of beliefs and practices" (Durkheim), "a cultural system of symbols" (Geertz), or "a complete system of human communication" (Larson).[37]

And there are other orienting metaphors that have had varying influence. In one formulation that has been affirmed (or assumed) by many scholars in recent decades, religion is *worldview* (Berger and Smart) or *form of life* (Wittgenstein and Larson). Emphasizing the ways that religious language differs from other language, some interpreters have emphasized that religions use *pictures* (Wittgenstein) or, as in Hegel's view, that religions appeal to *vorstellung* or pictorial thought. Emphasizing religion's negative individual or social effects, some have compared religion to an *illness* (Freud) or a *narcotic* (Marx). Some theorists who have been hostile to religion also have, as Van A. Harvey persuasively argued, imagined religion as *projection*. Using the indirect metaphor of a projected beam, Harvey suggests, a number of theorists from Hume and Feuerbach to Horton and Guthrie have turned to this trope. Many beam projection theorists focus on the individual, but other definers of religion have emphasized religion's social or cultural origins and functions. Religion is *society*, in one way or another, for a range of social scientific accounts that began at least as early as Durkheim's *Elementary Forms of Religious Life*, where the French sociologist claimed that religion was "an eminently *collective* thing." Others who have followed in that broad and varied interpretive tradition have defined religion as one or another cultural form, as with anthropologist Melford E. Spiro's influential definition of religion as "an *institution* consisting of culturally patterned interaction with culturally postulated superhuman beings." Finally, just as those who have embraced organic images about "evolution" or "growth" have (wittingly or unwittingly) highlighted change over *time,* there is another tradition of definition that directly or indirectly draws on *spatial* metaphors. Spatial figures are implied in some psychological accounts that focus on the individual and posit "*levels* of consciousness" (for instance, Freud, James, and Jung). Some interpreters (Long and Kaufman) have appealed to indirect spatial images as they talk about religion as "orientation." Spatial metaphors are more explicit, and even more influential, in a tradition of interpretation that goes back to Durkheim and circulated widely in Gerardus Van der Leeuw's *Religion in Essence and Manifestation* and Mircea Eliade's *The Sacred and the Profane.* This approach begins with a distinction between sacred and profane space—or, in Durkheim's phrase, "things set apart."[38]

If these varied tropes intertwine with definitions, the orienting metaphors that authors select also inscribe theoretical commitments, as I tried to show in my analysis of Freud's definition. Metaphors, as I indicated with my analogy of the lens, illumine some things and obscure others. Definitions that highlight a single human capacity (for example, Tylor's religion as *belief*) tend to obscure other components of religion and other aspects of embodied human life. Definitions that foreground the individual—Whitehead's "religion is what the individual does with his own solitariness"—obscure the social, just as collectivist metaphors—Spiro's religion as *institution*—illumine religion's social character but deemphasize its function for individuals. And metaphors have implications. Consider one of the most obvious examples. As other scholars have noted, organic metaphors about the "origin and growth" of religion have been associated with evolutionary models that propose a taxonomy of religions that privileges one tradition and dismisses others as lower "stages" on the cultural ladder. Those taxonomies—primitive and civilized, ethnic and universal, and lower and higher religions—have had negative, sometimes disastrous, moral and social implications. It is much easier to colonize and displace peoples who are aligned with children and imagined as "lower." For this and other reasons, as Turner suggested, "one must pick one's root metaphor carefully."[39]

Scholars, I have argued, have role-specific obligations not only to consider root metaphors—and their implications—but also to enter the debates about how to define the field's constitutive term. We are stuck with the category *religion*, since it fixes the disciplinary horizon, and our use of it can be either more or less lucid, more or less self-conscious. So we are obliged to be as clear as possible about the kind of definition we are offering and the orienting tropes that inform it. Whether we imagine theory as our primary professional work or not, we are called to exegetical fussiness. All of us.

Chapter Three

There are itinerant, ambulant sciences that consist in following a flow in a vectorial field . . .

    Gilles Deleuze and Félix Guattari, *A Thousand Plateaus*

No single word, neither substantive or verb, no domain, or specialty alone characterizes, at least for the moment, the nature of my work. I only describe relationships. For the moment, let's be content with saying it's "a general theory of relations." Or "a philosophy of prepositions."

    Michel Serres, *Conversations on Science, Culture, and Time*

CONFLUENCES

Toward a Theory of Religion

In this chapter, I meet my role-specific obligation to reflect on the field's constitutive term by offering a definition of religion, a positioned sighting that highlights movement and relation. This definition, which draws on aquatic and spatial tropes, is empirical in the sense that it illumines what I observed among Cubans in Miami and stipulative in that I think it might prove useful for interpreting practices in other times and places: *Religions are confluences of organic-cultural flows that intensify joy and confront suffering by drawing on human and suprahuman forces to make homes and cross boundaries.*

This definition, like most others, is hardly transparent. I doubt that, upon reading it, you thought to yourself: Well, thanks for clearing that up. Offering a dense definition of this complex term doesn't end my professional obligations or settle the issue. There is much more to say, and I try to say it in these last three chapters. Attending to each word and phrase, here I explain my choice of tropes and lay out some of the theoretical commitments inscribed in this definition.

Religions. Readers will notice that in my definition I shift from the singular to the plural, marking the boundaries of *religions*, not *religion*. That's not because I want to resist talk about the field's constitutive term, as I hope I've made clear, but rather to emphasize that interpreters—even armchair theorists—never encounter religion-in-general. There are only situated observers encountering particular practices performed by particular people in particular contexts. So even if I suggest that this definition might have interpretive power for the study of religion in a wide range of times and places—though not "universally"—it is never more (or less) than a sighting from one shifting site that might offer an illuminating angle of vision at another site.

Confluences. As I moved back and forth between definition and theory, I pondered which orienting tropes might be most illuminating. I considered the dozen I outlined in Chapter 2, as well as many others. To make sense of what I encountered at the Miami shrine I looked for metaphors, and philosophical and religious frameworks, that highlighted movement and relation.

There are some resources for reimagining religion as dynamic and relational. Philosophical reflections inspired by religious traditions, for example, Buddhism, offer some help. In the *Mahāvastu,* the Buddha affirms that all reality is constantly changing or impermanent *(anitya)* and empty of any enduring and substantial reality *(anātman).* Other Buddhist notions—including dependent co-origination and Indra's Jewel Net—provide resources for thinking about the interrelatedness of all things. The doctrine of dependent co-origination *(pratītya-samutpāda),* which might be described as inter-becoming, traces a circle of twelve interrelated factors that sustain the ongoing flux of human existence through birth, death, and rebirth. The Jewel Net of Indra has been a favorite metaphor for some Buddhists, especially the Chinese Huayan School, who emphasize the "mutual intercausality" among all things in the cosmos. Francis Cook, a Buddhist studies scholar, describes the image and recounts the story about Indra, the Hindu god of rain and thunder, who also appears as a character in Buddhist myth:

> Far away in the heavenly abode of the great god Indra, there is a wonderful net which has been hung by some cunning artificer in such a manner that it stretches out infinitely in all directions. In accordance with the extravagant tastes of deities, the artificer has hung a glittering jewel in each "eye" of the net, and since the net itself is infinite in dimension, the jewels are infinite in number . . . If we now arbitrarily select one of these jewels for inspection and look closely at it, we will discover that in its polished surface there are reflected *all* the other jewels in the net, infinite in number. Not only that, but each of the jewels reflected in this one jewel is also reflecting all the other jewels, so that there is an infinite reflecting process occurring.[1]

In the West, the ancient Greek philosopher Heraclitus did not highlight interrelation, but he has been celebrated for his emphasis on movement. Later Greek texts attribute to him two provocative assertions that have served as foil and inspiration since then: "it is impossible to step into the same river twice" and "all things are in flux." Echoing Heraclitus, and citing Buddhism too, philosopher Friedrich Nietzsche observed that the world is "'in flux,' as something in a state of becoming." In the nineteenth and early twentieth centuries, as evolutionary models that foregrounded linear progressions in nature and culture took hold, other interpreters in a number of fields traced temporal movements through "ages" or "stages." And, as some contemporaries noticed, this meant that scholars had begun to challenge static models. Noting changes in his own field by the 1910s, James Leuba observed "a most consequential change of point of view in contemporary psychology—namely, the adoption of the evolutionary, dynamic conception of mental life as opposed to the pre-Darwinian, static conceptions."[2]

In the twentieth century several other thinkers who turned to mathematics and physics as much as to psychology, biology, and geology rooted their philosophical systems in similar insights. The mathematician and philosopher Alfred North Whitehead, who directly endorsed Heraclitus' view by suggesting that "the flux of things is one ultimate generalization around which we must weave our philosophical system," produced a new lexicon of technical terms—*actual occasion, prehension,* and *nexus*—to replace static and essentialist notions of "substance-quality" with "description of dynamic process." Whitehead acknowledged his debt to another philosopher, Henri Bergson, the Nobel Prize–winning French thinker who proposed *élan vital* as the central category in his dynamic scheme and argued "there is no form, since form is immobile and the reality is movement." "What is real," Bergson suggested, "is the continual change of form: form is only a snapshot view of a transition." Later in the twentieth century Whitehead and Bergson were joined by other theorists with very different interests who also emphasized dynamism and interdependence, including Michel Serres, Bruno Latour, Gilles Deleuze, and Félix Guattari. Communication studies specialist and cultural theorist Brian Massumi, an interpreter of the writings of Deleuze and Guattari, also has advocated a "Bergsonian revolution" that would emphasize "movement" and "relation."[3]

Pointing to terms such as *field, force,* and *chaos,* Massumi has suggested that the most useful concepts for a dynamic and relational philosophical perspective are "almost without exception products of mathematics or the sciences." Yet other contemporary theorists from the social sciences and humanities have come to celebrate movement and relation for different reasons—because they have tried to make sense of transnationalism. The anthropologist Arjun Appadurai has pointed to "global cultural flows." Marcus Doel has noted that geographers "now routinely speak of 'spaces of flows'" to interpret "the flows of money, desire, capital, pollution, information, resources, ideas, images, people, etcetera." Anthropologist Anna Tsing has proposed we speak of *movements*—in the sense of both social movements and the movements of products, ideas, and people. Taking *traveling* as a root metaphor and highlighting the movement of peoples, anthropologist James Clifford has suggested we talk about *translocal culture*. Historian Paul Carter has proposed *a migrant perspective*. In a similar way, cultural studies scholar Iain Chambers has suggested *migrancy* as a useful metaphor, since it "involves a movement in which neither the points of departure nor those of arrival are immutable or certain. It calls for a dwelling in language, in histories, in identities that are constantly subject to mutation." In Chapter 1, as I explored the nature of theory, I emphasized a related theme, itinerancy, and here I have in mind that image, as well as these other Asian and Western resources for putting *religion* in motion.[4]

There are other possible metaphors that signal movement. For example, some religion scholars have turned to the metaphor of a *system*, as I have noted. And in mathematics and the natural sciences, *system* does refer to disorder and dynamics as well as to order and stability. In that idiom we can talk about dynamic systems. Yet the underlying image is still one of distinct parts coming together to form a coherent whole. And, as anthropologist Sally Engle Merry noted about the term *culture*, "classic conceptions of bounded, coherent, stable, and integrated systems clearly are inadequate." To avoid those possible misunderstandings of *religion*, then, I searched multiple academic fields for alternatives to *system*. Bruno Latour's proposal, for instance, has much to offer: "To shuttle back and forth, we rely on the notion of translation or *network*." That term is, Latour argued, "more supple than the notion of system, more historical than the notion of structure, more empirical than the notion of complexity." As Mark C. Taylor has persuasively argued, this image is especially compelling in interpreting contemporary culture, what Taylor and others call "network culture." French sociologist and social theorist Michel de Certeau has offered an even more compelling alternative, one that resonates with scientific idioms but more clearly marks religion as dynamic. "Generally speaking, the cultural operation might be represented as a *trajectory* relating to the places that determine its conditions of possibility." "Thus," Certeau continues, "cultural operations are movements." The English word relates to the French *trajectoire*, "conveying through or over." It takes its meaning here from usage in physics (the path of a wave or body moving under the action of a force) and mathematics (a curve or surface passing through a space). James Clifford tried to make a similar point when he turned to *travel* and *routes* as orienting metaphors for understanding theory and culture. The term *trajectory*, however, folds into it these references to the movement of peoples across boundaries, but is a bit more elastic as it expands to more easily include the artifacts, practices, and forces (agency changing the momentum of a body) that cross temporal and spatial boundaries.[5]

These interpretive categories—*network, system, movement, migrancy,* and *travel*—each have some advantages, and I use Certeau's *trajectory* as a synonym to point to religions' dynamism. I decided, however, that two other orienting metaphors are most useful for analyzing what religion is and what it does: spatial metaphors (*dwelling* and *crossing*) signal that religion is about finding a place and moving across space, and aquatic metaphors (*confluences* and *flows*) signal that religions are not reified substances but complex processes. I say more about those spatial metaphors below. Here I analyze the first key term in my definition: *confluences*.

The metaphor, taken from physics, suggests that religions are *flows*—analogous to movements of electric charges, solids, gases, or liquids. If we are trying to formulate a theory that accounts for the dynamics as well as the statics of religion, I suggest, it can be especially helpful to turn to fluid mechanics and aquatic metaphors, applying what Gilles Deleuze and Félix Guattari called a "hydraulic model" from the "itinerant, ambulant sciences." As with scientists who study hydrodynamics, interpreters of religion "follow a flow in a vectorial field." Or to turn to Bruno Latour's explanation of his actor-network theory, which he designed to interpret both natural forces and cultural forms, we need "a theory of space and fluids circulating." So the picture of religious history that I'm drawing is not that of self-contained traditions chugging along parallel tracks. To return to the aquatic metaphor, each religion is a flowing together of currents—some enforced as "orthodox" by institutions—traversing multiple fields, where other religions, other transverse confluences, also cross, thereby creating new spiritual streams.[6]

If this aquatic metaphor avoids essentializing religious traditions as static, isolated, and immutable substances, and so moves toward more satisfying answers to questions about how religions relate to one another and transform each other through contact, it also allows a preliminary answer to the question about how religion relates to economy, society, and politics. This question has attracted scholars' attention since the nineteenth century: is religion *sui generis?* Is religion "of its own kind"? As with most questions, the answer depends on what we mean. If we are asking if scholars are justified in marking religion's boundaries by defining and theorizing their field's constitutive term, then religion is *sui generis* in that weak sense of the term, as are other constitutive terms—culture, space, music, and literature. However, I reject strong versions of the *sui generis* argument: humans do not have a distinct "faculty of faith," as Max Müller claimed; "special revelation" does not set some religions apart, as Hendrik Kraemer argued; the feeling of the "numinous," as Rudolf Otto proposed, does not make religion "qualitatively *sui generis.*" At the same time, religions cannot be reduced to economic forces, social relations, or political interests, although the mutual intercausality of religion, economy, society, and politics means that religious traditions, as confluences of organic-cultural flows, always emerge from—to again use aquatic images—the swirl of transfluvial currents. The transfluence of religious and nonreligious streams propels religious flows.[7]

If this talk about *confluence* and *transfluence* opens new angles of vision—and I think it does—it is important to acknowledge that there are limits to the interpretive elasticity of the metaphor *flow.* Tsing has suggested that we replace *flow* with *movement,* because the former does not seem to call our attention to the personal, and she wants to highlight social movements. So perhaps here is a blind spot, or at least a site along the theoretical trail where the wind blows up a cloud of sand and rain. While terms like *confluence* encourage interpreters to offer sightings that attend carefully to the movements of artifacts and institutions—impersonal forces—we need to continually remind ourselves to also keep our eyes fixed on the human forms crossing the landscape, whether they are lit by noon's glow or obscured in cloud.[8]

Arjun Appadurai, who has talked about "cultural flows," introduced the term "ethnoscapes" to highlight the movements of human forms across the landscape, and we can play with his theoretical terms to introduce another category that can be helpful in the analysis of religion's dynamics. Appadurai understood the "five dimensions of global cultural flows" as distinct and dynamic "imagined worlds": (1) ethnoscapes, (2) mediascapes, (3) technoscapes, (4) financescapes, (5) ideoscapes. Appadurai proposed this scheme to interpret recent globalizing patterns, and to challenge Immanuel Wallerstein's less complex and more static notion of "world systems." These five terms illumine the transnational flow of peoples, technologies, media, and capital, but offer little aid in interpreting religions, unless we suggest that religion is nothing more than ethnicity, economy, or ideology. So, I suggest, a parallel image that points to *religious* flows might be useful: we can talk about religions as *sacroscapes*. Those who think definitions grounded in notions of the *sacred* are vacuous or circular should be relieved to find that it is not a central term in my account. The prefix "sacro" does not imply any metaphysical claims. It does not imply, with Eliade, that religion involves "hierophanies" that mark some spaces as distinct. And it does not function—as *sacred* does in some definitions—to distinguish religion from other cultural forms. As I will note below, other phrases in my account—*suprahuman forces* and *ultimate horizon*—do that interpretive work.[9]

Yet using this term *sacroscapes* only helps if we have aquatic and not terrestrial analogies in mind. Sacroscapes, as I understand these religious confluences, are not static. They are not fixed, built environments—as the allusion to landscape in the term might imply—although religions do transform the built environment. I have in mind much more dynamic images. Imagine the wispy smoke left by a skywriter, the trail of an electron, the path of a snowball down a steep icy hill, or the rippled wake left by a speeding boat. Whatever else religions do, they move across time and space. They are not static. And they have effects. They leave traces. They leave trails. Sometimes those trails are worth celebrating: not only Bashō's *Narrow Road to the Deep North*, but also the annual dancing procession to honor Saint Willibrord that has wound through the cobblestone streets of Echternach, Luxembourg, at least since the mid-sixteenth century, or Abū 'Abdallah ibn Battuta's fourteenth-century wanderings from Fez to Peking and the tracings he left behind in his *rihla*, the multivolume account of that Muslim's twenty-nine years of travel. Sometimes trails are sites for mourning: the paths worn away by Jews fleeing the medieval Spanish Inquisition or the Cherokee's westward "trail of tears," prompted by the United States' policy of forced "removal," which was supported by a taxonomy of religions that classified indigenous peoples as "lower," as heathens and barbarians (Figure 5). So this term, sacroscapes, invites scholars to attend to the multiple ways that religious flows have left traces, transforming peoples and places, the social arena and the natural terrain.[10]

Organic-cultural flows. If religions can be imagined as flows, what kind of flows? I suggest that these flows are spatial and temporal and—as this phrase in my definition signals—organic as well as cultural. These flows involve, as I will explain, both neural pathways in brains and ritual performances in festivals.

Religious flows—and the traces they leave—move through time and space. They are horizontal, vertical, and transversal movements. They are movements through time, for example, as one generation passes on religious gestures to the next: this is how we do it, this is how we offer *pūjā* to Vishṇu or make the sign of the cross. And religious flows move across varied "glocalities," simultaneously local and global spaces, as for example when missionaries carry their faith from one land to an-

5. Jerome Tiger (1941–1967), "Untitled, Trail of Tears," 1967. Oil on canvas, 17 × 23½ inches. A representation of the forced removal of the Cherokee nation in 1838–39 by a twentieth-century Creek-Seminole artist.

other. In other words, flows, or sacroscapes, are historical as well as geographical. They change over time and move across space. To signal this, I turn to adjectives I coined in *Our Lady of the Exile*—*translocative* and *transtemporal*—and a term I have borrowed from literary theorist Mikhail Bakhtin, *chronotopic.* Sacred flows cross space-time. In the analysis that follows there is always the implied hyphen, even if I appeal more to spatial than to temporal tropes.[11]

Religions also are simultaneously individualistic and collective. We should combine the perspectives of, for example, William James and Emile Durkheim. As philosopher Charles Taylor noted in his analysis of "the Jamesian view of religious life," James claimed that "there are people who have an original, powerful religious experience, which then gets communicated through some kind of institution; it gets handed on to others, and they tend to live it in a kind of secondhand way." In this view, institutions play a "secondary role." And, at least in his *Varieties of Religious Experience,* James acknowledged but minimized the ways that culturally shared linguistic categories and institutionally transmitted practices shape individual experience. In the same way, as reviewers began to note soon after *Elementary Forms* first appeared, the Durkheimian view "prejudices the investigator in favor of the social elements in religion and at the expense of the individual elements." Here too an inclusive definition answers an either-or question with a both-and. We, once again, invoke the hyphen. Religions are always both solitary and social.[12]

And there are other hyphens to invoke: *mind-body* and *nature-culture.* To say that religions are individual as well as collective does not go far enough, since that formulation does not highlight the ways that those individual processes are biological as well as cultural. To signal this, I talk about religions as *organic-cultural* flows, but that does not mean I agree with accounts that reduce religion to *only* neurons firing. Religions, and other cultural forms, are about neurons firing, but no satisfying account of what they are and what they do can stop there. So the anthropologist Dan Sperber was right when he suggested that interpretations of cultural trajectories like religion cannot ignore "the micro-mechanisms of cognition and communication." At the same time, interpreters cannot obscure or minimize the ways that macro-cultural processes are at work in the religious lives of women and men. For that reason, while I think we can learn a great deal from recent theories that draw on neuroscience and cognitive science—some of them self-consciously extending Sperber's insights—sometimes they shift the focus too much toward individual neurophysiological processes associated with, for example, perception, inference, and memory. Many of those theorists—including Harvey Whitehouse, E. Thomas Lawson, and Robert McCauley—share a presupposition found in the work of some earlier interpreters, like E. B. Tylor. It is a premise that has been lucidly articulated by a contemporary cognitive theorist, Pascal Boyer: "The explanation for religious beliefs and behaviors is to be found in the way all human minds work." As a corrective to theories that obscure those individual micro-processes, this perspective is helpful, but I think we need to find other ways to emphasize that religions involve both biological and cultural processes.[13]

It is impossible to disentangle the threads that embed persons in cultures. As anthropologist Clifford Geertz has argued, we cannot expect to produce a "synoptical view" of mind and culture. Drawing on work in a wide range of disciplines, we can continue to ponder the "social habitation of thought" and the "personal foundations of significance." The best we can say is that mind and culture co-evolved, and that they are—to use Geertz's apt phrase—"reciprocally constructive." Religion scholars, in turn, can only do their best to acknowledge the complex interactions of *organic constraints* (neural, physiological, emotional, and cognitive) and *cultural mediations* (linguistic, tropic, ritual, and material). The cognitive anthropologist and psychologist Scott Atran turned to the metaphor of landscape to make a similar point. He suggested that we imagine humankind's evolutionary history "as a landscape formed by different mountain ridges." There are some "well-trodden, cross-culturally recurrent paths in the basin of this evolutionary landscape." Religion, as one set of paths in the landscape's drainage basin, "results from a confluence of cognitive, behavioral, bodily, and ecological constraints that neither reside wholly within minds nor are recognizable in a world without minds." This model is useful in some ways. For example, Atran signaled the importance of emotional processes as well as cognitive processes and social interaction, by proposing that we consider each of those as a mountain ridge that channels human experience toward religious paths. Also, for Atran, the landscape "canalizes" but does not determine religious development.[14]

Yet because the rate of religious change can be much greater than the long, slow geological alterations in "ridges" and "basins," I think it is more helpful to turn again to aquatic metaphors and consider the interaction between *constraining organic channels* and *shifting cultural currents*. This surfaces two important presuppositions of my theory: (1) humans are bipedal mammals with embodied physiological, cognitive, and emotional processes that limit—but do not determine—the range of interactions with other humans and the environment; and (2) despite notable continuities across cultures and periods, religions have diverged in important ways, just as other cultural trajectories (for example, music and art) have varied. So religions can be imagined as a confluence of flows in which organic channels direct cultural currents. This way of putting it, however, seems to make the organic more primary. But metaphors fail. I don't intend that. I mean to make only this modest, but often overlooked, point: as embodied beings produced by organic processes as much as by cultural practices, humans have certain neurological and physiological constraints on how they interact and how they transform their environment. However malleable human brains might be, they work in certain ways. Human eyes are positioned in the front of the body. And so on. Organic and cultural processes combine in complex ways. I will return to this point in the next chapter as I discuss organic and cultural processes at work in spatial and temporal orientation; for now it might help to illustrate by referring to Figure 6 and draw on the case of Cubans in Miami. We might say, then, that re-

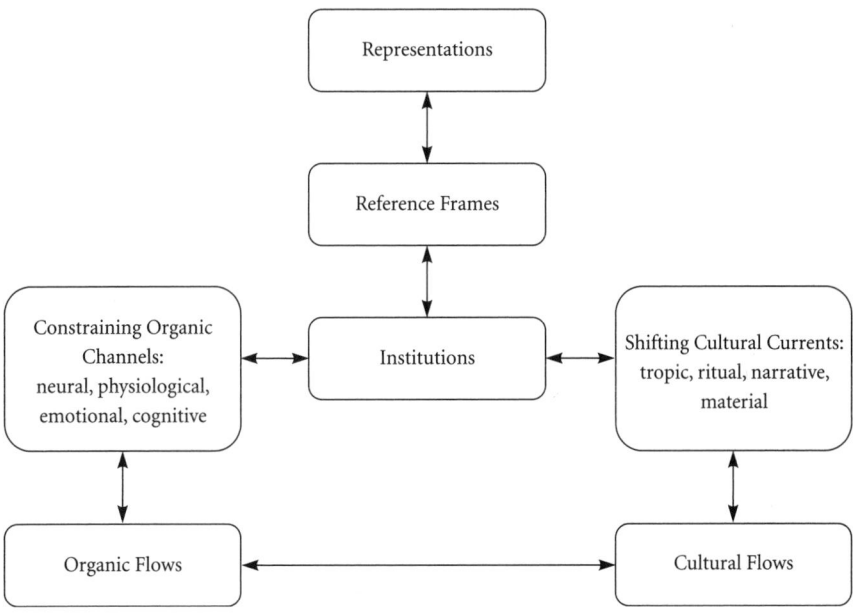

6. The confluence of organic and cultural flows in religions.

ligions are processes in which social institutions (the shrine's confraternity) bridge organic constraints (hippocampal neural pathways and episodic memory processes) and cultural mediations (the symbol of Mary and the metaphor of exile) to produce reference frames (the Cuban American community as diaspora and the shrine as diasporic center) that orient devotees in time and space. As Figure 6 signals, those reference frames yield a wide range of verbal and nonverbal representations that, in turn, are institutionally, ritually, and materially transmitted— and enfolded back into the complex bio-cultural process.

So I not only reject theories that fail to acknowledge the role of bodily processes, but I also reject definitions that identify religion with a single psychic capacity. Instead, on this point I align myself with Jastrow and James, who identify multiple capacities. I acknowledge that religion shapes and is shaped by cognitive *(beliefs)*, moral *(values)*, and affective *(emotions)* processes. In mentioning affective processes I acknowledge that religions help determine what humans want and how they feel. Believing and valuing are part of religions too, as the devout offer assertions about the nature of things and prescribe moral codes to guide conduct. In adding *tropes* I suggest that religions, like theorists of religion, provide orienting tropes—including metaphors, similes, myths, allegories, personifications, and symbols—that function as figurative tools for making and remaking imagined worlds. It is not that the religious are privy to some inaccessible or hidden meaning through their use of tropes or that tropes are unique to the religious realm. Tropes are pervasive in many areas of human life, from poetry and art to science and technology. Yet it is not surprising that the religious would turn to tropes, especially analogical utterances, to talk about suprahuman forces and ultimate horizons, since those defining features of religion are at least as difficult to represent as sentiments like love or concepts like relativity. Further, as part of religions' shifting cultural currents, tropes can also function as one source of change in the history of religions, as new metaphors redirect the attention of adherents. In some ways, *institutions* can function as agents of change as well. Like many anthropologists and sociologists, I note that religions take social form in one way or another and are passed on to future generations by institutions like the family, the school, the monastery, the church, and the temple. They transmit—and transform—traditions. Although this is not explicitly noted in the most influential definitions, I also suggest that *artifacts* anchor the tropes, values, emotions, and beliefs that institutions transmit, and that the religious create artifacts and prescribe procedures for their use—from domestic furnishings and ordinary dress to ritual objects and sacred buildings. Making and using artifacts are *practices,* and as many theorists have noticed, religions are performed. The religious prescribe and enact a wide range of embodied practices, including culturally patterned practices or rituals—for example, praying, bowing, reading, singing, fasting, dancing, meditating, or chanting.

To say that religions are organic-cultural flows, then, is to suggest they are confluences of organic channels and cultural currents that conjoin to create institutional networks that, in turn, prescribe, transmit, and transform tropes, beliefs, values, emotions, artifacts, and rituals.[15]

But why do these religious flows exert such a hold on devotees, and how are sacroscapes distinguishable from other cultural trajectories? The next two phrases in the definition—*intensify joy and confront suffering* and *human and suprahuman forces*—propose answers to those questions.

Intensify joy and confront suffering. This phrase reaffirms what I have suggested above in my analysis of religious flows—that religion involves emotion. Recent research on emotion in a number of fields—from neuroscience to anthropology to philosophy—varies on the question of whether it is an organic universal process or a culturally relative practice. Scholars who tend toward the view that emotions are cross-cultural universals have identified sentiments that seem to be labeled and expressed in multiple times and places. Building on Charles Darwin's classic study *The Expression of Emotion in Man and Animals*, Paul Ekman has claimed that there are six common human emotions; using an analysis of language, Anna Wierzbicka has counted eleven "emotional universals." Scholars who lean toward the other end of the continuum point to the cultural and historical variations in the ways that humans label and experience emotions. They emphasize the variety of culturally constructed and historically variant "feeling rules": for example, Jean Briggs's ethnography of the Utku Eskimo suggested they do not have an equivalent of *anger,* and studies of the Ifaluk of the Caroline Islands proposed that *fago,* an emotion that combines compassion, love, and sadness, has no obvious parallel in other cultures.[16]

My own view again invokes the hyphen. Although a convincing synthesis has not yet appeared, it seems that emotions are *organic-cultural* processes that have a biological basis but vary across cultures. Neurological and physiological processes set certain constraints, but cultural practices—including religious practices—generate emotional idioms and rules that frame affective life. Religions label, prescribe, and cultivate some emotions and obscure, condemn, and redirect others. For example, in some forms of Christianity regret—framed as guilt for sin—is valued as a necessary condition for any genuine turning of the heart to God; on the other hand, Sōtō Zen Buddhists might be told to notice the arising of regret—and all other emotions—but exhorted to put it out of mind by returning to focus on the breath. So even when traditions name similar emotions they encode them differently. Affect also varies within religious traditions and across time. It would not be too much of an exaggeration to say that Cuban American Catholicism at the Miami shrine during the 1990s was most fundamentally about sadness. As many devotees signaled to me as their eyes filled with tears or as they actually began to cry, their piety was about the naming and overcoming of the sadness prompted by the dislocation of exile. In that sense, the emotional coding of religious practices among Cuban American Catholics might have more in common with the piety of other diasporic groups than with that of other Catholics in other times and places. And religions mediate a wide range of emotions—not only sadness and joy but also Schleiermacher's absolute dependence and Kongzi's filial sentiments as well as shame, love, anger, contentment, awe, and fear. To suggest that religions *intensify joy and confront suffering,* then, is shorthand for saying this: they provide the lexicon, rules, and expression for many different sorts of emotions, including those framed as most positive and most negative, most cherished and most condemned.[17]

In that sense, this phrase not only reaffirms that religions are about emotion as much as cognition, feeling as much as thinking, but it also points to why religions are satisfying to adherents. I don't speculate about the "origin" of religion, a long-standing preoccupation of religion's interpreters. If we mean by that term a temporal starting point, I assiduously resist all attempts to speculate about origins. I am unapologetically agnostic on that historical issue, and leave it to archeologists, evolutionary biologists, and others with longer memories and different skills. Instead, I am concerned here only with what grips the religious. I want to know why devotees turn to religion and what it does for them. There are some answers from within traditions, of course. What do you mean what grips us, a Pentecostal might ask? It's the saving power of the Holy Spirit. And that is an answer that interpreters need to consider. As theorists move beyond that circle of Pentecostals to consider other religious women and men, however, they are driven to frame the question—and the answer—in ways that cross traditions and cultures. So why do religions—not only Christian Pentecostalism but other traditions as well—exert their power in the lives of adherents? My short answer: religions intensify joy and confront suffering.[18]

This deceptively simple phrase enters a conversation about religion's function, and it offers a no and a yes. On the one hand, it conditionally affirms the long tradition of interpreters who have suggested that religions are responses to evil. The philosopher David Hume, for example, proposed that religions—at least polytheistic traditions—spring from "ordinary affections of human life." They deal with humans' "incessant hopes and fears." What kind of hopes and fears? For Hume, those include "the dread of future misery" and "the terror of death." Many Western interpreters who followed the eighteenth-century Scottish philosopher have concurred, including Freud. Max Weber, who put a slightly more positive spin on it, suggested that religions deal with the "imperfection of the world." Using a term taken from Christian theology, the German sociologist proposed that religions offer theodicies, or explanations for evil. Following Weber, the American sociologist Peter Berger has made a similar point. He has suggested that in religions "the sacred order of the cosmos is reaffirmed, over and over again, in the face of chaos." These interpreters, and others, are right in suggesting that religions interpret and ease suffering: disease, disaster, and death.[19]

However, as the feminist philosopher of religion Grace M. Jantzen has argued, this Western tradition of theorizing has overemphasized these imperfections in accounting for the meaning and function of religions. Jantzen has suggested that "much of traditional philosophy of religion (and western culture generally) is preoccupied with violence, suffering, and death and built upon mortality not only as a human fact but as a fundamental philosophical category." But, she asks, "what if we were to begin with birth, and with the hope and possibility and wonder implicit in it?" So, for Jantzen, natality is as important a category as mortality. Confirming Jantzen's reading of Western theorizing, Berger suggests that "the power of religion depends, in the last resort, upon the credibility of the banners it puts in the hands of men as they stand before death, or more accurately, as they walk inevitably toward it." Yet before men—and women too—started to walk toward death, they had to crawl, and before that they were born to a mother. The birth process involved pain as well joy, but it is important to recall that religions function to name and intensify those joys, even if that is not all they do. There is some truth in Hume's claim that humans are "much oftener thrown on their knees by the melancholy than by the agreeable passions." When good things happen, we are just getting our due; however, when bad things happen, that seems to require some explanation. Further, some humans have more suffering to confront: the poor, the ill, the abused, and—remembering the Cubans journeying to Miami and the Cherokee along the Trail of Tears—the displaced. Yet even if Max Müller went too far in emphasizing humans' encounter with the sun and the stars, natural wonders—comets, rainbows, and births—also are part of the experience of the world. Religions provide ways for humans to imagine and enhance the joys associated with the encounter with the environment and the transitions in the lifespan. Humans want something to say and do in the face of wonder. Religions provide that idiom and transmit those practices. They celebrate not only birth but also marriages, harvests, and the rising and setting of the sun. Religions do confront "the terror of death," as they also interpret and ease the sufferings of life, from tsunamis and plagues to famines and disease. But, as most theorists have failed to emphasize, religions confront—to revise Weber's terms—the world's perfections as well as its imperfections. Religions are about enhancing the wonder as much as wondering about evil.[20]

Human and suprahuman forces. Although there can be no intransient boundary between the religious and the secular since that border shifts over time and across regions, satisfying theories of religion say something about what distinguishes religions from other cultural forms. For that reason, I add another phrase—*human and suprahuman forces*—to note that adherents appeal not only to their own powers but to suprahuman forces, which can be imagined in varied ways, as they try to intensify joy and confront suffering. Concurring with Durkheim but not Spiro, I use the term *suprahuman* to avoid narrower alternatives—such as *God, gods,* or *spiritual beings*—and to respect the multiple ways that those forces are imagined. The classic example is Buddhism, which in most formulations does not affirm theism—the belief in a personal creator of the universe—but in devotional life does appeal to human and suprahuman beings—bodhisattvas and buddhas—for aid in treading the religious path. I include reference to *human* forces because some traditions imagine the suprahuman as imbedded in the human in some way and to some extent: for example, in some Christian interpretations of *imago dei* (the image of God) and some Buddhist views of *tathāgatagarbha* (the embryo of the Tathāgata, or Buddha-nature). So to include Buddha-nature—as well as the Neo-Confucian *li* (principle) and the Daoist *dao* (way)—I talk about *forces* rather than beings, since not all lineages in all religions personify the suprahuman, despite some interpreters' arguments for the ubiquity of anthropomorphism.[21]

Make homes and cross boundaries. Shifting from aquatic to spatial tropes, this phrase, which is the heart of my theory, says more about *how* the religious draw on human and suprahuman forces to intensify joy and confront suffering. If aquatic metaphors can be helpful for putting religion in motion, spatial images, while still too static as they have been employed, offer promise for making sense of the practices of transnational migrants at the Miami shrine and for interpreting other traditions at other sites. The tentative definition I offered in my ethnography of devotion at the Cuban shrine was a good starting point, although only that: religions, I suggested, are spatial practices. "Religious women and men are continually in the process of mapping a symbolic landscape and constructing a symbolic dwelling in which they might have their own space and find their own place." Even if I now think that definition is more narrow and less useful than the one I have proposed here, I remain convinced that *place* is a useful orienting metaphor. And as I was just beginning to work out when I wrote that earlier book, two other spatial images—*dwelling* and *crossing*—are helpful terms to add to the interpreter's lexicon.[22]

Religious women and men make meaning and negotiate power as they appeal to contested historical traditions of storytelling, object making, and ritual performance in order to make homes *(dwelling)* and cross boundaries *(crossing)*. Religions, in other words, involve finding one's place and moving through space. One of the imperfections the religious confront is that they are always in danger of being disoriented. Religions, in turn, *orient* in time and space. As Charles Long noted in a highly suggestive but mostly overlooked stipulative definition, "For my purposes, religion will mean orientation—orientation in the ultimate sense, that is, how one comes to terms with the ultimate significance of one's place in the world." So, as long as we keep in mind the cautions I noted in Chapter 1 about the limits of cartographic metaphors and as long as we put the cartographers, the terrain, and the representations in motion, we can understand religions as always-contested and ever-changing maps that orient devotees as they move spatially and temporally. Religions are partial, tentative, and continually redrawn sketches of where we are, where we've been, and where we're going. Unlike most life forms—although certain mammals might be less dissimilar than some might imagine—humans require orientation that genetic coding and neurophysiological processes alone cannot provide. Religions, then, survey the terrain and make cognitive maps—and sometimes even graphic representations of space. In other words, as I argue more fully in the next chapter, they situate the devout in the body, the home, the homeland, and the cosmos. Religions position women and men in natural terrain and social space. Appealing to supranatural forces for legitimation, they prescribe social locations: you are this and you belong here. You are in this clan, and you are an uncle. You are a member of this caste. You are a slave, and the gods approve. You are Tibetan, Israeli, or Cuban. Religions mark this place as unlike others. Religions say: take off your shoes before you enter here. Religions say: walk no farther than this on the Sabbath, or that mountain is where the gods live, or face this way when you pray. In these and other ways, religions help the pious to find a place of their own. Religions, in other words, involve homemaking. They construct a home—and a homeland. They delineate domestic and public space and construct collective identity. Religions distinguish us and them—and prescribe where and how both should live. Put this on the threshold of your home to signal who you are. Mark your bodies with clay every morning. Don't eat pork. Do this, but not that, when you lie down to sleep, and sleep only with this person, not that one. Homemaking extends even to the cosmos, the space beyond the home and the homeland. The religious not only set aside sacred sites on the earth, but they also survey celestial and subterranean worlds. They say: you came from the underworld or you were formed by the copulation of these two deities. They say: when you die, if you have lived and died properly, you will go where you truly belong. You will live among the ancestors. You will dwell in the house of the Lord. Finally, religions promise, you will be home.[23]

But the religious are migrants as much as settlers, and religions make sense of the nomadic as well as the sedentary in human life. They involve another spatial practice—*crossing*. As I argue in Chapter 5, religions enable and constrain terrestrial, corporeal, and cosmic crossings. Religions enforce socially constructed spatial codes. Make this pilgrimage to the holy city before you die. Women cannot enter this part of the temple. Religions also cross the limits of embodied life. As I have suggested, religions not only point to the wonder of the world and mark the joyful transitions of life—for example, in marriage ceremonies and initiation rituals—but also confront suffering. As one Jain text puts it, "the skulls of dead men, with deep caves for eyes, horrid to see, address the living." And in religions the living offer their reply. But religions do more than point to suffering. They offer solutions that enhance joy. And even where "solutions" don't seem possible—death, for instance—they provide means to traverse those boundaries anyway. They say: the limits are not really there. Or they uncover a concealed and overgrown path: here's a way over, under, through, or around.[24]

Religions mark and traverse not just the boundaries of the natural terrain and the limits of embodied life but also the *ultimate horizon*—a phrase that, with *suprahuman forces,* distinguishes religious and nonreligious cultural forms. Just as the phrase "make homes" in my definition is shorthand for saying that religions situate followers in the body, the home, the homeland, and the cosmos, the phrase "cross boundaries" indicates three kinds of crossings—terrestrial, corporeal, and cosmic. Most important for delineating religion, religions mark and cross the *ultimate* horizon of human life. Other cultural trajectories—for example, art, music, and literature—can mark and traverse the boundaries of the natural terrain and the limits of embodied life. Those other cultural forms, however, usually do not appeal to superhuman forces or map cosmic space—and they do not offer prescriptions about how to cross the ultimate horizon.[25]

As I am using it, the term "ultimate" refers to the most distant, not the proximate or penultimate, limit of life. It is the imagined beginning and end, or (for religions with a nonlinear notion of time) the cyclic process that constitutes existence. It is the end or aim that participants take as most important. So, for example, in forms of Christianity the ultimate horizon has been imagined in varied ways—including as *heaven* or as the *Kingdom of God.* As with Christians, adherents from the same tradition, and the same time and place, can mark this boundary differently. Some devotees of Kṛṣṇa in contemporary India might imagine the most distant horizon as *mokṣa,* or release from the cycles of birth, death, and rebirth; other devotees might emphasize devotion (*Kṛṣṇa bhakti*) as its own end or envision a better rebirth as the practical limit of their religious imagining. In a similar way, some practitioners of Jōdo

Shinshū in Japan might focus their attention on rebirth in Amida Buddha's Pure Land in the West, even if they also might acknowledge that ultimately their goal, though not in this lifetime, is *nirvāṇa* and the cessation of desire and, therefore, rebirth. Yet in marking an ultimate horizon through narrative, ritual, and artifact, the religious distinguish the most distant from more proximate ends, for example the desire for sustenance, sex, fame, or power. As Tillich noted—and I try to approximate some of the interpretive reach of his definition—sometimes what is taken as ultimate might not be the spiritual horizons mapped by canonical texts or charted in temple rituals. The brilliance of Tillich's account is that it allows interpreters to consider practices connected with institutions that are not usually taken as "religious": for example, Maoism, Nazism, twelve-step programs—and the flag-waving nationalism constructed ritually at the Cuban Catholic feast-day celebration in Miami. At the same time, I concur with critics who have argued that Tillich defines the religious so broadly that his account has difficulty performing one of definition's central tasks—delineating what is *not* religious.[26]

So religion is about settling in and moving across, and the latter preposition—*across*—announces the most central theoretical commitments encoded in the two indirect spatial metaphors that distinguish my account. This theory is, above all, about movement and relation, and it is an attempt to correct theories that have presupposed stasis and minimized interdependence. In this chapter, I have already celebrated movement in my "fussy" exegesis of *confluence* and *flows,* so let me say more about the other key metaphor announced in the preposition *across:* relation.

Definitions (and theories) of religion have focused more on some parts of speech than others. Most have taken religion as a noun, a substantive thing corresponding to a linguistic label. I agree with theorists who have challenged the emphasis on nouns. Wilfred Cantwell Smith rejected the noun *religion* but accepted the adjective *religious*. He argued that attention to adjectives might yield interesting theoretical results: "That adjectives may come closer to describing reality than do nouns, especially in the personal realm, is perhaps an important philosophical orientation." Highlighting a different part of speech, anthropologist Malory Nye proposed that we imagine religion as practice and emphasize verbs instead of nouns. We should, Nye suggested, talk about *religioning,* not religion.[27]

I agree with Smith that adjectives are more useful than nouns as linguistic tools for theory; and as I suggested in my celebration of movement and my analysis of religion as a spatial practice, I am even more inclined to emphasize verbs as we try to make sense of religion. I have claimed that religions involve *dwelling* and *crossing,* thereby appealing to a verbal form, the gerund. Gerunds are the present participle form of a verb used as a noun. They are absent from French and infrequent in German, but occur in many Semitic and Indo-European languages. They are common in English, usually in words ending in -*ing.* As the religion scholar Gustavo Benavides has pointed out, there has been a "predominance of gerunds in the titles of academic books published in English" in recent decades. Consider Smith's *Imagining Religion* and McCutcheon's *Manufacturing Religion.* Benavides endorses this turn to the gerund to some extent, since it helps scholars free themselves "from the allure of reification." However, he offers a warning as well: "But it is also worth considering whether the relentless processual emphasis, embodied in the gerund, is not likely to distract scholars of religion from seeking to identify the building blocks, the constants, the recurrent features of religion. In other words, while it is important not to succumb to reification, it is also necessary to keep in mind that the rejection of hypostases can itself be reified." Taking Benavides's warning to heart, I have tried to emphasize process—and verbal forms—without being "distracted" from the role-specific task of identifying some transcultural—though not universal—"features" of religions.[28]

And, I propose, it is also useful to foreground prepositions as we make our way toward a theory of religion, since prepositions signal relation. As Michel Serres, the philosopher of culture and science, argued in a published conversation with Bruno Latour, "traditional philosophy speaks in substantives or verbs, not in terms of relationships . . . Instinctively, that's what you are asking me—that what's always demanded from a philosopher. What is your basic substantive? Is it existence, being, language, God, economics, politics, and so on through the whole dictionary." Some philosophers of religion have acknowledged relationality and coined helpful terms—Whitehead's *principle of relativity*, which suggests that every item in its universe is involved in the *concrescence*, or becoming, of an *actual occasion*—but few have highlighted prepositions as explicitly as Serres, as I noted at the start of this chapter. And I think he is right in being "led by fluctuations" and "following the relations." He is right in calling for a "philosophy of prepositions." In turn, my definition of religion moves toward a verbal and prepositional theory. As spatial practices, religions are active verbs linked with unsubstantial nouns by bridging prepositions: *from, with, in, between, through*, and, most important, *across*. Religions designate where we are *from*, identify whom we are *with*, and prescribe how we move *across*. Emphasizing movement and relation, in the next two chapters I consider religion's spatial practices—dwelling and crossing.[29]

Chapter Four

For my purposes, religion will mean orientation—orientation in the ultimate sense, that is, how one comes to terms with the ultimate significance of one's place in the world.

Charles Long, *Significations*

I'm not saying there are no locales or homes, that everyone is—or should be—traveling, or cosmopolitan, or deterritorialized. This is not nomadology. Rather, what is at stake is a comparative cultural studies approach to specific histories, tactics, everyday practices of dwelling *and* traveling: traveling-in-dwelling, dwelling-in-traveling.

James Clifford, *Routes*

DWELLING

The Kinetics of Homemaking

Even if the religious practices of first-generation Cuban exiles and other migrants seem to focus on remembering an earlier crossing and imagining a future one, they are about being in place as much as about moving across space. Consider my account of the 1973 consecration ceremony in Miami:

> More than ten thousand Cuban exiles gathered on a chilly Sunday afternoon in 1973 to dedicate the new shrine of Our Lady of Charity in Miami—waving flags, singing songs, and chanting petitions to the national patroness. After six years of work, the committee of laity and clergy that had assumed responsibility for planning and constructing the building had managed to raise $420,000, mostly in small donations from recent exiles who could not afford it. The conical-shaped concrete structure,

which they had toiled so hard to build, rose ninety feet above the crowd. Over the portal was a tiled image of Our Lady of Charity; perched on the rear were busts of two influential nineteenth-century Cubans. The focus inside was the pedestaled fifteen-inch statue of the patroness, the one that had been smuggled out of Cuba in 1961. In front of her stood the marble altar and the steps that led down to the circular interior. There only two hundred and ninety chairs (replicas of *los taburetes,* traditional Cuban stools made of wood and leather) awaited the Virgin's devotees in the small shrine. No one knew then that on many nights four or five hundred Cubans, with more spilling out down the steps, would crowd into that small space, pressing close to the patroness. Only the throng outside for the dedication that day signaled how important this shrine would become for Cubans in the diaspora.[1]

The consecration of that important shrine was a translocative and transtemporal ritual attended by migrants who longed to return to the homeland, but it was as much about settlement as about migration (Figure 7). Emplacement was as significant as displacement. It was about locating devotees in a religious-nationalist historical narrative and situating them in social space and the natural landscape. To use historian of religion Charles Long's language, this religious practice provided "orientation": it helped the religious establish their place in the world. The diminutive statue of the national patroness had been smuggled out of Cuba, but Our Lady of Charity had found a new home at the shrine. The chairs, the songs, the busts, and the prayers would have been familiar to relatives back on the island, but those artifacts and rituals also signaled a new start, even if devotees' focus continually shifted back and forth from the homeland to the new land.

In other words, to apply and revise James Clifford's understanding of the term, the consecration ceremony was about *dwelling.* To dwell, dictionary definitions suggest, is "to abide for a time in a place, state, or condition." It is "to inhabit." Note that dwelling is always "for a time"; it is never permanent or complete. Note also that the English verb *dwell* is

7. Dedication of the Shrine of Our Lady of Charity in Miami on December 2, 1973.

related to a Sanskrit root meaning "to mislead or deceive." The deception involved in understanding dwelling, I suggest, is that it appears to be static. It appears to imply the absence of action. Dwelling, however, is a gerund, a verbal noun, and that signals something important: dwelling, like crossing, is doing. Dwelling, as I use the term, involves three overlapping processes: mapping, building, and inhabiting. It refers to the confluence of organic-cultural flows that allows devotees to map, build, and inhabit worlds. It is homemaking. In other words, as clusters of dwelling practices, religions orient individuals and groups in time and space, transform the natural environment, and allow devotees to inhabit the worlds they construct. As the above account of the consecration indicates, finding a space and making a place involves a great deal of activity. Before the ceremony devotees were donating, planning, and constructing; at the consecration, which established the shrine as the Virgin's new home and provided the exiles with a new religious site, devotees were singing, waving, and chanting.[2]

An imperfect analogy from physics might help to make the point that dwelling is as much an active process as crossing, settling as much an activity as migrating. Consider the distinction between accelerated and unaccelerated motion. Both terms imply movement, even though accelerated motion signals that forces acting on a body *change* its velocity, and unaccelerated motion indicates that the motion is at a *constant* velocity. It's the difference between the motion involved when an intergenerational carload of Cuban devotees turns out of the driveway in Little Havana and the motion involved when that same car is moving along the highway at a steady velocity on its way to the shrine. In both instances, the car is in motion, and the passengers have the capacity to discern that both stages of the journey involve movement, though they're of different kinds. Psychophysiological studies have shown that the human visual cortex has two distinct pathways for the detection of accelerated and unaccelerated motion. Some cells are sensitive to accelerated motion; others detect unaccelerated motion. No evidence suggests that the middle temporal visual area of the human brain—even the brains of religion scholars—affords any special advantage in detecting the kinetics of religion. Nonetheless, I want to suggest that in interpreting the Cuban consecration in Miami, and religion in other times and places, it is helpful to draw on both "pathways" and cultivate more sensitivity to the complicated dynamics of religious practice, attending to both kinds of motion. The analogies from physics and physiology might not be perfect, but they point to the ways that dwelling, like crossing, involves movement.[3]

In this chapter I consider the kinetics of dwelling. I first discuss how religion as dwelling orients devotees in time and space and, so, functions as watch and compass. Second, I note that this spatial and temporal orientation involves both organic processes and cultural practices. Finally, I argue that the "autocentric" and "allocentric" reference frames that emerge from these processes and practices allow the religious to map, construct, and inhabit ever-widening spaces: the body, the home, the homeland, and the cosmos.

In that last section, and along the way, I draw on examples not only from the shrine in Miami but also from diverse cultural contexts, and before I continue on this theoretical journey it might be helpful to explain why I do this. If theory is a positioned sighting, as I suggested in Chapter 1, then why do I wander so far as I accumulate illustrations from other religions in other times and places? The short answer: this theory emerges from a particular site, the shrine, but I think it has applications beyond that site. As I noted in the last chapter, my definition is both empirical and stipulative, and the theory, which explicates and expands that definition, attempts to illumine what I encountered in Miami as it also offers angles of vision on religions in other cultures and periods. To put it differently, what follows in my analysis of dwelling (and, later, crossing) is a positioned sighting from not only the shrine but also the study. I wrote this book in my office, surrounded by shelves and shelves of books, and not far from a university library with even more shelves. I did not consult all those books, of course. I walked the office bookcases and the library stacks with questions in mind, questions produced by interactions at the shrine and conversations in the academy. Why, then, do I cite some examples from some passages in some books and not others? Because I decided they might be helpful in this theoretical itinerancy, this thought experiment, this attempt to see if motifs and metaphors that emerged for me at the shrine might make sense of practices in other times and places.

Toward that end, I select examples from varied cultures and multiple periods as I try to persuade readers by being amply illustrative rather than propositionally argumentative. After all, it would be difficult to convince anyone that this theory has some interpretive reach if I restricted myself to examples from the Miami shrine. Yet comparative thematic analysis always risks the criticism that it is ahistorical. It seems to uproot practices from their native soil and plop them down where they don't belong. That's true, of course. And in my other historical and ethnographic work I have spent a good deal of time fingering fibrous roots that descend in complicated patterns into native soil. In my study of Buddhism I kept close to the ground, analyzing the historical shifts in terms of the beliefs and values of Victorian America; in my ethnographic study of Cuban American Catholics, I rarely ventured beyond the circular parking lot of the Virgin's shrine. But in this book, I traverse a wider landscape in order to see if this theoretical wandering might yield something of interpretive value. Doing so requires that I rely on histories, translations, and ethnographies from many colleagues, who offer interpretations of the sites along the way. It could not be otherwise. Theorizing—even positioned theorizing—can't stay put. It has to move, and in what follows, I move—back and forth between the shrine and the study, between the historical particular and the transcultural theme, between positioned questions and tentative answers. The primary criterion for the assessment of all this transtemporal and transcultural traversing, I suggest, is not whether I have fully represented the complexities of each case I cite. I haven't. It's this: do these interpretive transmigrations produce categories and prompt questions that allow more illuminating sightings at other sites? I think they do, and to begin to make my case I first consider some of the ways that religions provide orientation.

RELIGION AS WATCH AND COMPASS

Some religion scholars have explored the gritty particulars of religious orientation, but philosophers and theologians have talked about orientation—and the concomitant disorientation—in more abstract terms. In his "Lecture on Ethics" the philosopher Ludwig Wittgenstein told a Cambridge audience about a defining experience: "I believe the best way of describing it is to say that when I have it *I wonder at the existence of the world*. And I am then inclined to use such phrases as 'how extraordinary that anything should exist' or 'how extraordinary that the world should exist.'" The Christian theologian Paul Tillich described a similar experience by noting that "the ontological question," the question of being-itself, "arises in something like a 'metaphysical shock' in the question, 'Why is there something; why not nothing?'" Even if some philosophers and theologians have framed the problem of religious orientation and disorientation in this way and some creation myths seem to answer metaphysical questions they have posed, it is difficult to know how many religious women and men have shared that experience of "metaphysical shock." As the cognitive theorist of religion Pascal Boyer has argued, citing an ethnography of the Kwaio people in the Solomon Islands, "the origin of things *in general* is not the obvious source of puzzlement that we may imagine." Boyer suggested that the Kwaio myths "assume a world where humans gave feasts, raised pigs, grew taro, and fought blood feuds," and what matters to people are *particular* instances in which the usual activities are disrupted. I would put it slightly differently: some people might sometimes pose Tillich's ontological question, but it is more common for individuals to ask more positioned and relational questions: Where do *I* belong? How did *we* get *here?* As far as I can tell, devotees at the shrine—and most people in most cultures—do not seem to be consciously aware of metaphysical shock, though they might have a fleeting experience of it, for example when encountering life's painful or joyful boundary moments: disease and death or recovery and birth. To be more precise, none of the hundreds of pilgrims I interviewed at the Miami shrine talked about being-itself. No one told me they wondered why there was something instead of nothing, though it's not the sort of thing that might come up, even when talking to someone who gets paid to think about such things. Almost every day during the five years I did fieldwork at the shrine, however, devotees reminded me in one way or another—a teary story about the hurried journey to South Florida or a ritual expressing longing for an imagined past—that the displacement of transnational migration had disrupted their sense of time and place.[4]

They did not have their bearings, and, as I suggested in *Our Lady of the Exile*, devotion at the Miami shrine can be seen as diverse attempts to situate Cuban migrants temporally and spatially. Consider the ways that the shrine's mural imagined a past and future and situated pilgrims in a present that, though painful, had some meaning (Figure 8). The 740-foot painting by the Cuban exile Teok Carrasco is wider at the base and narrower at its zenith, rising 36 feet from the sanctuary floor. It was begun in July 1974, and consecrated on the patroness's feast day in 1977. The painting evoked strong emotions among Cuban pilgrims, I learned, because Carrasco had managed to combine religious devotion and nationalist sentiment in a visual narrative that recounted the Cuban past. Carrasco saw himself as a historian: "It is my job as a painter to bring history to life." And the mural, *The History of Cuba at a Glance,* told the story of the Cuban nation from the voyages of Columbus (in the lower left corner) to the journeys of exiles (in the lower right corner). Overlooking the ill effects of colonization and evangelization, the painter narrates several centuries of the homeland's history, and on the mural's right side, which recounts the nineteenth and twentieth centuries, Cuban history marches triumphantly and inevitably toward the successful wars for independence, with religious, cultural, and political leaders all playing their role. Bringing the story to a close in the lower right side of the mural, the Statue of Liberty points skyward, and a boat filled with exiles who will not make it to shore alive floats in the sea between the island and the American coast.[5]

Just as the mural offers a narrative of collective history that positions the exile in a longer time frame, the shrine's cornerstone orients devotees geographically. The building committee, which included the Cuban American architect José Pérez-Benitoa, Jr., and seventeen lay members, transformed the exilic sense of space in its design for the cornerstone. The six-sided concrete object, which rests in a triangulated space created at the altar's base, maps the natal terrain onto the Miami shrine. Affixed on each of its six sides are samples of soil and stone from the six prerevolutionary Cuban provinces. Those fragments were mixed with water taken from a raft on which fifteen refugees died at sea. The home-

8. Interior of the Shrine of Our Lady of Charity in Miami, 2005. A devotee, who holds yellow flowers for the Virgin, kneels as she looks up at the illuminated statue. Immediately in front of the woman is the altar, which is covered with a white cloth that conceals the six-sided cornerstone beneath it. In the background is the mural "The History of Cuba at a Glance."

land's regional divisions, recent history, marine environment, and native soil are all represented in that artifact, which bridges the homeland and the new land and establishes the site on Biscayne Bay in Miami as simultaneously Cuban terrain and American land.[6]

Other religions function in similar ways, as a Muslim pocket watch usefully illustrates (Figure 9). Concentric circles of calligraphy adorn the polychromatic exterior of this brass pocket watch, which was manufactured in Switzerland and decorated in India in the late nineteenth century for Sheikh Hadji Rahim Bakhsh, a Shī'ī Muslim gem merchant from Ludhiana, a market town in North India. It has an Urdu inscription and Arabic prayers and verses addressed to the five holy persons of Shī'ism. The interior includes a clock to determine the time for daily worship *(ṣalāt),* which Islamic ritual prescriptions suggest should be performed at dawn, noon, mid-afternoon, sunset, and night. The compass in the stem also helps to discern the direction of prayer toward Mecca. Although Shī'ī prayer differs from Sunni prayer in some ways, all Muslims face toward the Ka'ba in Mecca during daily worship, and so the compass orients the devotee in space.[7]

The mural, the cornerstone, and the pocket watch orient both individuals and groups. Bakhsh, the late-nineteenth-century Muslim who consulted the watch and compass to mark the time and direction for worship, belonged to a North Indian Shī'ī community that recorded and transmitted the prescribed practices—washing, bowing, prostrating, kneeling, and standing—and passed on oral and written narratives about the holy persons of Shī'ism and the sacrality of the Ka'ba. In the same way, the Cuban devotee kneeling at the shrine's altar on a Saturday afternoon in 2005 to petition the Virgin learned the words and gestures of prayer in her home and in the church, and was part of a community that imagined its history and geography using shared symbols (Mary) and metaphors (exile) that were inscribed in artifacts like the mural and the cornerstone (see Figure 8).

Spatial and temporal orientation is not only individual as well as collective; as I noted in Chapter 3, it involves organic as well as cultural

9. Watch and compass, late nineteenth century. North Indian and Swiss; brass, enamel, silver overlay, and glass. $2\frac{3}{4} \times 1\frac{7}{8}$ inches.

processes. Depending on the position of the interpreter and the scale of the analysis, religions can be alternately, or simultaneously, about neurons firing and institutions working. My emphasis in this chapter—and throughout the book—is on the cultural. I leave it to others with more expertise in the life sciences and the behavioral sciences to explore that intersection where neural pathways meet cultural trajectories. As I did in Chapter 2, here I just want to signal that I remember it is always *embodied* beings who do the orienting, even if culturally constructed tropes, collectively enacted rituals, and socially produced artifacts play a decisive role in that process. So even though I intend this only as a gesture toward a fuller analysis—and a commitment to seek illuminating tropes and perspectives wherever we can find them, including the natural sciences—I want to say a bit about how organic and cultural forces interact as religions function as both watch and compass.

Biological and Cultural Clocks

The human central nervous system continually receives information that is important for spatial and temporal orientation. The neurophysiological processes involved in human perception and representation of time are not as well understood as the processes for the perception and representation of space. Much of the research, however, suggests that the basal ganglia, the frontal cortex, and the cerebellum are the areas of the brain most directly involved in human perception of temporal intervals. Recent studies of the psychophysics of temporal cognition have prompted several theoretical models, including the Scalar Timing Theory, which turns on the metaphor of an "internal clock" and suggests that this clock system, which allows humans to make judgments and decisions about time, includes a pacemaker, a switch, and an accumulator. On this model, the "pacemaker" emits pulses with a mean rate that pass through a "switch" on their way to an "accumulator." Whatever direction future research leads, it seems likely that cognitive scientists will continue to think that varied and complex neurophysiological processes set some constraints on the human perception and representation of time.[8]

Yet those neurophysiological processes are not the whole story. Brain-minds are embedded in cultures, and the perception and representation of time involves a wide range of cognitive, emotional, and cultural processes. Even if there appear to be some cross-cultural constants about how humans process stimuli to form judgments about intervals, in representations of temporal passage—from the momentary to the epochal—a cultural clock interacts with the biological clock. Those culturally constructed processes for marking time, which are much more fluid than the clock metaphor allows, are continually being made and remade by the influence of multiple extra-individual forces and practices, including religion. It is not clear to what extent religions as organic-cultural flows shape microlevel judgments about small intervals—how did religion influence the perception of time as a devotee at the consecration ceremony whispered a prayer to the Virgin?—but religious practices are part of the confluence of forces that shape judgments about larger temporal scales. As with the Muslim watch and compass, religions measure time in midrange intervals—a day is this long and you pray at these five times during the day—and they establish annual calendars ritually, artifactually, symbolically, and mythically. For example, devotees from the same Cuban municipality visit the shrine for a weekday mass on the same day each year, and most exiles anticipate Our Lady of Charity's feast day on September 8. In that feast-day celebration organic constraints (memory processes) channel the recording and transmitting of cultural forms (ritual actions) as the annual rites' smells and bells—or, to use the language of some cognitive theorists, high sensory pageantry and low performance frequency—increase the chance that participants will draw on "flashbulb" or episodic memory systems to record the event. If cognitive studies of memory are right, this, in turn, will enhance the participants' ability to remember the ritual and to use it to mark the year—and the years. As confluences of retrospective and prospective practices, religions—including some forms of Cuban American Catholicism—also look back to distant pasts and imagine distant futures. God created the world; the cross came to the island with Columbus; next year we will have Christmas dinner in Havana; when I die I will go to heaven. Culturally constructed, recorded, and transmitted forms—the symbols *God, cross,* and *heaven* as well as the narratives that frame them, the emotions that encode them, the artifacts that anchor them, and the rituals that convey them—mediate devotees' experiences and representations of time.[9]

⤞ Neural and Cultural Compasses

Humans' perception and representation of space also involves multiple processes—including the interaction of neural, psychological, and figurative processes. Spatial cognition emerges from the confluence of perceptual experience, emotional coding, and cultural forces. Research in cognitive science—cognitive psychology, neuropsychology, neuroimaging, and neurophysiology—has pointed to two modes of spatial cognition associated with distinct regions of the brain that, in turn, correspond to two forms of spatial representation. Using terms introduced by the psychologist Trigant Burrow in 1927, cognitive scientists have distinguished *autocentric* (self-centered) and *allocentric* (object-centered) spatial representations or reference frames. Autocentric frames of reference involve the parietal neocortex, draw on cognitive processes involved in action and attention, and orient humans in the immediate environment. In this sort of representation, space is framed in terms of the embodied subject, who constructs a spatial model from extensions of the three body axes—the head-feet axis, the front-back axis, and the left-right axis. A kneeling devotee at the Miami shrine, for example, might say that the image of Our Lady of Charity is *above,* or that the Saint Lazarus statue stands to her *right.* In contrast, allocentric reference frames involve the hippocampus and adjacent cortical and subcortical structures, concern large distances and long-term spatial memory, and aid humans in orienting and navigating space beyond the body and the immediate environment. Allocentric framing relates locations to each other and to environmental landmarks. There is no privileging of the subject's position, and no location to which all others are related. Space is represented allocentrically in terms of fixed, not relative, points—for example, north, south, east, and west—and many researchers have appealed to the metaphor of the "cognitive map" to explain this mode of spatial perception and representation, although the psychologist Barbara Tversky has argued that "cognitive collage" is a better image, since these allocentric representations are put together unsystematically and involve multiple media. For example, twentieth-century exiled Cuban devotees constructed allocentric representations—cognitive maps or collages—when they told me that their homeland is *south*. That nineteenth-century Muslim in North India used his compass to discern that Mecca was *west* as he placed his prayer rug on the floor for the midday prayer.[10]

Even if research in neuroimaging and neurophysiology has shown some remarkable continuities in the perception and representation of space and even if most cognitive scientists agree that spatial terms are prominent in language and cognition, some recent studies in psychology, anthropology, and linguistics suggest that there is a good deal of cross-linguistic variation in spatial semantics and symbolization. Most languages have a root meaning "where?," and most linguists agree that cross-cultural patterns are evident. They point to autocentric and allocentric reference frames, although some rename them *relative* and *absolute*. And linguists add a third type of spatial representation, *intrinsic*, which subdivides the ground and locates the figure by relating it to one part of the ground. For example, a Cuban devotee might say that the image of Our Lady of Charity is "in the front of the shrine." Here the spatial representation is not oriented according to fixed points on a map and does not designate a site relative to a speaker; rather, it identifies the figure in relation to a part (the front) of the ground (the shrine). Not all languages use all three linguistic frames of reference. Many culturally constructed linguistic systems make no regular use of autocentric or relative frames of reference—and would have no way to say, for instance, "the image of the Virgin is above"—and even if they do represent space autocentrically, the relational terms do not always follow the same pattern. For example, Japanese conflates *on* and *over* in ways that English does not. Many languages use allocentric frames of reference to designate almost all locations or motions, but those map-like schemes also are diverse. As one specialist in psycholinguistics notes, the Inuit use prevailing winds as the source of their spatial representation and identify up to sixteen directions around the compass, with subdivisions down to 22.5 degrees. In this and other examples, even the "fixed" directions of cognitive maps vary. It is at this point in the analysis that it becomes clear that spatial orientation, like temporal orientation, is a cultural as well as a biological process. If recent research proves right in the long run, hippocampal and parietal neural processes seem to set some constraints on the forms of spatial representation, but there is a good deal of variation across languages and cultures.[11]

Religions are among the cultural trajectories that help construct spatial frames of reference as institutions record and transmit tropes, artifacts, and rituals that encode representations. In particular, tropes—especially analogical utterances—seem important. Even though I understand tropes differently from some theorists, it is important to note that other interpreters have acknowledged their significance. The philologist and religion scholar F. Max Müller suggested that analogical thinking—making comparisons between unlike things—was at work in religious development. Humans, according to Müller, enjoy a "mental faculty" that "enables man to apprehend the Infinite under different names, and varying guises." Religion "grows" as humans attempt to capture this vague sense of the Infinite derived from their encounter with nature in analogical language, often applying terms for the most "exalted" things in their experience—solar phenomena. Rejecting Müller's "naturism" (and Tylor's "animism"), Emile Durkheim still left some room for analogical representation in religion. Tribal traditions, he argued, turned to comparisons with animals and plants in totemic beliefs and practices. They used "physical emblems and figurative representations" to create a sense of the unity of the clan. In fact, Durkheim proposed, "social life is only possible thanks to a vast symbolism." The sociologist Max Weber considered the role of "analogical thinking"—especially simile—but he argued that it originated in magic, not religion, and that devotees later "rationalized" it into symbolism in the religious realm. To offer a final example, in his theory of religion as anthropomorphism, anthropologist Stewart Guthrie, like Freud, highlighted the role of personification.[12]

Yet other tropes—including other forms of analogical cognition—mediate religion as well. Metaphors, as I have suggested, are especially important, even though I would not go as far as Müller in suggesting that "the whole dictionary of ancient religion is made up of metaphors." Yet metaphors do mediate representations of space in ancient and not-so-ancient religions, as most theorists have failed to emphasize. For example, Durkheim, who said as much about spatial representation as any interpreter, brilliantly pointed to the role of emotion—or "affective colorings"—when he noted that regions are associated with affect. Anticipating the distinctions that cognitive science would draw between autocentric and allocentric spatial representations, Durkheim also noted that "to have a spatial ordering of things is to be able to situate them differently: to place some on the right; others on the left, these above, those below, north or south, east or west, and so forth," but he obscured metaphor's role in this "spatial ordering." As I suggested before, metaphors function by propelling users between cognitive and emotional domains, as when we map language (and the concomitant inferences and sentiments) from the medical domain onto language about computers in the statement "my computer has a virus" or when we draw on networks of inferences from family relations to imagine the gods as "father" or "mother." This cognitive-affective fluidity, or metaphoric domain crossing, is one important source of cultural creativity and religious innovation—and it shapes spatial representation. As with some forms of Judaism and African American Christianity, for example, it is difficult to overemphasize how much the biblical metaphor of exile—*el exilio*—framed and transformed Cuban Americans' representations of where they are and where they are going. As the Virgin's devotees at the shrine told me again and again, they saw themselves as a people displaced from their homeland and destined to return again, and they inscribed that exilic metaphor in a wide range of stories, artifacts, institutions, and rituals that mapped space in terms of the difference between here and there, Havana and Miami, the homeland and the new land.[13]

Yet even if that metaphor was important, it was only one cultural trajectory in the crisscrossing flow of biocultural processes that created and re-created religious homemaking. Turning to allocentric and autocentric frames of reference produced at the intersection of neural pathways and migratory routes, Cuban Americans understood themselves as *far* from relatives and *north* of the island. For them, the exilic metaphor co-mingled with biblical narratives and familial memory in accounts about leaving and returning. That metaphor also intertwined with another trope, the symbol of Our Lady of Charity, which was anchored materially in the shrine's diminutive statue. It was a nationalist symbol that triggered powerful emotions—including sadness—in translocative and transtemporal rituals associated with institutions like the (uprooted) family and the (diasporic) church.

So far I have argued that religions function as watch and compass and that organic and cultural processes interact in temporal and spatial orientation, but there is more to say about the kinetics of dwelling practices. Cubans at the Miami shrine and the religious in other periods and places, I propose, use autocentric and allocentric reference frames to map, construct, and inhabit four ever-widening spaces, or, to signal that spatial and temporal orientation intertwine, what we might call four *chronotopes:* the body, the home, the homeland, and the cosmos. Highlighting cultural more than organic processes, I suggest that religiously formed bodies function as the initial watch and compass, but religious women and men construct habitats, intimate spaces for dwelling, and inscribe those homes with religious significance. Moving beyond those intimate spaces and the kin who inhabit them, individuals and groups draw on religion to negotiate collective identity, imagine the group's shared space, and—in the process—establish social hierarchies within the group and generate taxonomies of others beyond it. So the homeland, which might be as small as a river valley and as large as a colonial empire, is not the largest space in religion's figurative world. Religions also imagine the wider terrestrial landscape and the ultimate horizon of human existence—the universe and the beings that inhabit it.[14]

THE BODY

Religion begins—and ends—with bodies: birthed bodies and dead bodies; polluted bodies and purified bodies; enslaved and freed bodies; bodies that are tattooed, pierced, flagellated, drugged, masked, and painted; sick bodies and healed bodies; gendered bodies and racialized bodies; initiated and uninitiated bodies; bodies that are starved and fed, though fed only *this* way; exposed bodies and covered bodies; renounced and aroused bodies, though aroused only *that* way; kin bodies and strangers' bodies; possessed bodies and emptied bodies; and, as humans cross the ultimate horizon of human existence—however that horizon is imagined—bodies that are transported or transformed.

So bodies cross and dwell. They cross not only that ultimate horizon but many other boundaries as well, as I argue in the next chapter. Here I focus on the ways that spatial and temporal orientation begins with the body, which, since distance and sequence initially are represented autocentrically, is the first watch and compass. Even if humans have unconscious circumspatial awareness, a hidden capacity for sensate inferences about the world that confronts the body on all sides, and even if some traditions represent the body allocentrically by using tropes to compare the body to the landscape or the cosmos—for example, in terms of the cardinal directions—corporeal axes constrain (but do not determine) spatial and temporal orientation. The cultural geographer Yi-Fu Tuan has argued that "vertical-horizontal, top-bottom, front-back, and right-left are positions and coordinates of the body that are extrapolated onto space." Considering temporal as well as spatial orientation, sociologist Alfred Schutz made a similar point when he suggested that a human is "primarily interested in that sector of the world of his everyday life which is within his scope and which is centered in space and time around himself." He continued: "The place which my body occupies within the world, my actual Here, is the starting point from which I take my bearings." In this sense, the body is the *actual Here* that surveys other spaces, both close and distant; it is the *actual Now* from which humans narrate the past and imagine the future. Drawing initially on this sort of autocentric framing, religions record, prescribe, and transmit figurative language and embodied practices about food, sex, health, drugs, dance, trance, gesture, and dress that position the body in time and space.[15]

Religions construct the body as watch and compass by figuring, regulating, and modifying that organic-cultural form. First, they use figures or tropes to imagine the body in a variety of ways. The religious turn to myths about the origin of the human body—which often intertwine with stories about the universe's origin—and they draw on analogical language to represent the corporeal form. One famous Buddhist text, for example, imagined the body as a chariot. In the *Questions of King Melinda*, the Buddhist Nāgasena explains the nature of the embodied person as a confluence of multiple forces or an aggregation of multiple parts by employing a metaphor from modes of transport. Just as the term *chariot* is only a conventional designation for multiple parts—pole, axle, and wheels—personal names are imperfect designations for the confluence of embodied processes: the five *skandhas* and thirty-two parts of the body. Some passages in the Hebrew Bible propose that embodied humans resemble the divine: "So God created humankind in his image." The likeness suggested here is not imagined as similar physical appearance but as a parallel in relationship and role: humans are like divine children just as Adam also fathered a child "according to his image" and humans, like God, have "dominion" over the earth. In this analogy, the embodied person is imagined in relation to benevolent cosmic forces—the divine creator. Other narratives, from the Zoroastrian tradition, use martial images to imagine the body as battleground between cosmic forces of good and evil. The body is a symbol of the integrity of the world order of Ahura Mazdā, the good creator, against the chaos of Angra Mainyu, the hostile spirit. Turning to a simile, an important Zoroastrian text suggests that the devout "makes his body *like a fortress*" and thereby "does battle" against the demonic forces that threaten to enter.[16]

Second, as in this Zoroastrian example, religions mark boundaries that exclude as much as they enclose. They chart the cosmos, patrol the borders, and fence the home, but they also monitor bodily orifices and habituate sensory processes. For example, just as Zoroastrians have engaged in multiple practices to protect and purify the body, some Jain monks have worn masks over their mouths to avoid inadvertently ingesting an insect or some other small living being; some Seventh Day Adventists have followed Ellen Gould White's *Counsels on Diet and Food* by eating a lacto-ovo-vegetarian diet of fruits, grains, nuts, and vegetables; some evangelical Protestants have cited scriptural authority as they condemn homosexual bodily contact and even try to re-habituate the sensory processes of those who are willing to allow the divine to transform their sexual urges.[17]

Finally, religions do not only represent and regulate the body; they alter it. As religion scholar William LaFleur has noted, traditions fall on a continuum from prescribing acceptance to prescribing modification, even if most religions do seek to modify the body in one way or another. Some embodied practices—or, in Marcel Mauss's phrase, *bodily techniques*—do not change the body much: for instance, not only Adventists practicing vegetarianism and Jains wearing masks but Catholics baptizing babies and Baktaman painting faces. Other practices transform the body more drastically, even intrusively and permanently: circumcision, flagellation, and tattooing. Among them are gendered and racialized practices that carry religious sanction and involve violence: African American lynchings in Mississippi or female clitorectomies in the Sudan. All these spiritual practices alter the corporeal form in some way, even if only temporarily, and they simultaneously situate individuals and groups in time and space. Ellen White's dietary prescriptions, for instance, determine what happens in domestic space, the kitchen, just as vegetarianism situates followers in social space, setting them apart from the carnivorous within that Christian denomination and in the wider society. At the same time, vegetarianism positions Seventh Day Adventists temporally, since they believe that those culinary practices constituted humanity's "original" diet and, therefore, that it best prepares them for Jesus' return and the world's consummation.[18]

As the example about Adventist food practices indicates, religions position the body in relation to other chronotopes—including the home, the homeland, and the cosmos. Religions position bodies, first, within the home: they not only organize the interior spaces but also prescribe embodied practices for those sites: sleep only with your spouse in the bedroom, and—as with some Adventists and many Buddhists—don't eat meat in the kitchen. Or, as with many Jews and Muslims, eat only meat that has been slaughtered and prepared in this way. Some artifacts and rituals extend the boundaries of domestic space and kinship networks, as when Cuban American devotees at the shrine wear Marian medals given to them at home by their mothers. Bodies also signal collective identity, as when nomads tattoo their bodies with the animals that symbolize their clan, and bodies situate individuals in national space by affirming—or rejecting—the homeland, as when exiled Cuban American women wearing yellow, the national patroness's color, wave, sing, and weep as the Virgin makes her way to the altar during the annual feast-day celebration. Dress can negotiate national identity in other ways: eastern European orthodox Jewish women in late-nineteenth-century America wore wigs, shawls, or scarves that reaffirmed Old World affiliations—and embarrassed their daughters who were eager to acculturate to Victorian Protestant customs. In a similar way, the dress of the Eastern Dakota in the mid-nineteenth century alternately accommodated and resisted the Euro-American Protestant missionaries' exhortations not only to accept Christ but to signal their affiliation with the American nation by abandoning their blankets, beads, and braids and accepting the civilizing power of fitted bodices, cotton undergarments, and lace collars (Figure 10).[19]

Bodies also become pathways to the wider universe. Consider the Cuban Catholic Eucharistic celebration, in which devotees ingest "the

10. Sioux woman, circa 1870.

body of Christ." Or, among many other examples, consider forms of trance: spirit possession among middle-aged northern Sudanese Muslim women, who were inhabited, and made ill, by *zarain*, invisible and nocturnal beings; spirit mediumship among middle-class Victorian Protestant women, who contacted deceased husbands and mothers in the other world; or shamanism among the Bear River, who consulted ritual specialists to perform curative rites that called on spirits for aid in the healing process. In these instances bodies are channels joining this world and another world. In some traditions, however, bodies are not so much paths as emblems: they symbolize the cosmos. As I have noted, Zoroastrians imagine the body as a cosmic battleground, and in some Daoist interpretations, which combine autocentric and allocentric framing, the head corresponds to the heavens, the heart to the earth, and the lower abdomen to the underworld (Figure 11). It is in this sense that religiously formed bodies, which are simultaneously organic, domestic, communal, and cosmic spaces, function as the initial watch and compass.[20]

THE HOME

Religiously formed bodies function as watch and compass, but the religious also autocentrically and allocentrically orient themselves by constructing, adorning, and inhabiting domestic space. Religion, in this sense, is housework. It is homemaking. Yet homes vary widely in form, permanence, and scale. Home is not always a permanent dwelling, and it is not always a built structure. For some hunter-gatherers it might mean no more than a clearing in the brush. The !Kung bushmen most often do not inhabit permanent structures; rather, the family eats and sleeps around an open fire that is near other families. For them, the entire encampment is the home. This is in keeping with some of the meanings of the term *home*. The Indo-European roots of the English term indicate that it is a "dwelling place," but the term can refer to anything from a single fixed residence to a collection of dwellings in a village or town. As one theoretical geographer has noted, the English term

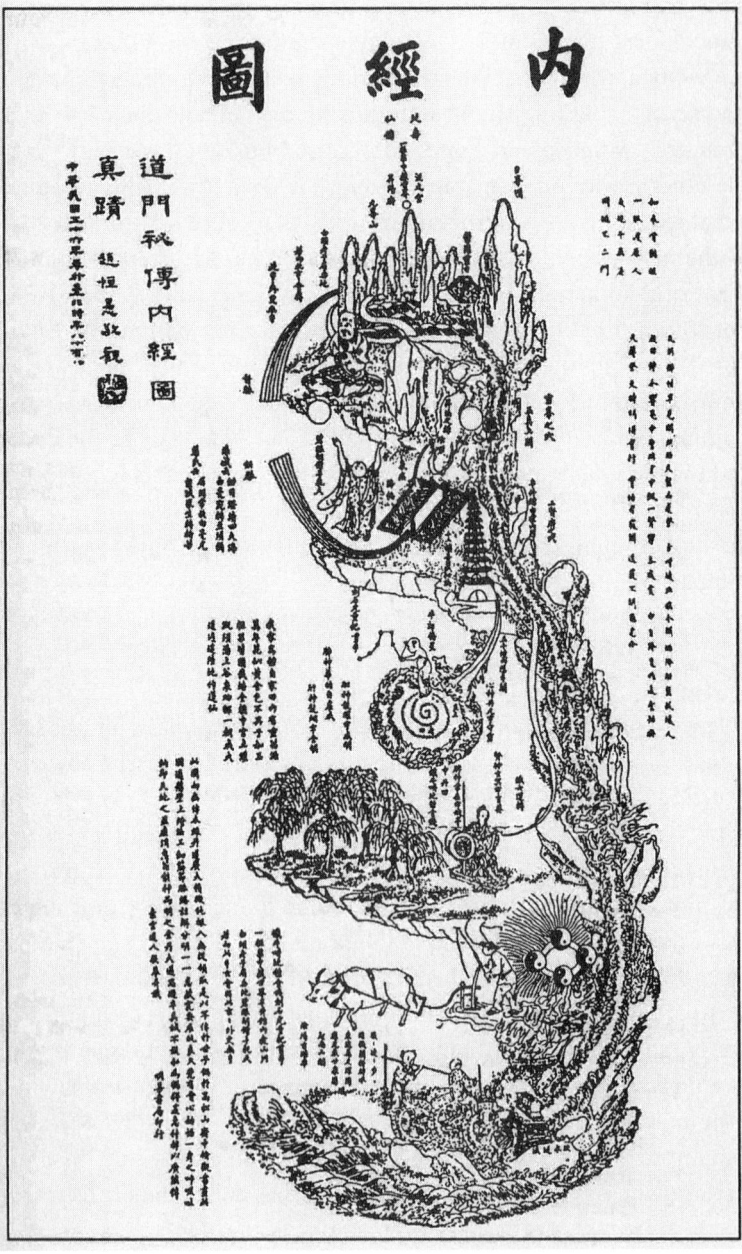

is related to the German *heimat*, "whose sense slides along the continuum from 'domicile' to 'world.'" So just as bodies are organic-cultural sites that interconnect with other spaces, the imagined boundaries of the home contract and expand across cultures and in different semantic contexts. Home, then, might refer to places of varying scale: a clearing, a hut, a nation, the earth, or the universe. In this wider sense, religious dwelling means finding a place or making a space, however small or large. However, as I am using it here in a more narrow sense, *home* refers to an intimate controlled space, whether cleared or constructed, that provides for bodily needs—shelter, sleep, sex, healing, and food—and usually, though not always, is inhabited by some members of the family.[21]

As confluences of cultural as well as organic processes, bodies are social spaces, but in some ways the human collectivity originates with the home. As the first and smallest inhabited space, its boundaries open and close to the wider society. Just as the physical body mirrors the social body in some ways, so too domestic spaces and practices reciprocally interact with culturally constructed images of the society and the cosmos. To illustrate, consider anthropologist Fredrik Barth's ethnographic representation of domestic space among the Baktaman, whom I mentioned earlier. The group occupied a tract of mountain rain forest near the center of New Guinea. The huts' arrangement in the main Baktaman hamlet reflects the male-dominated ancestor cult. At the far left, surrounded by a border of sanctified ground, sit the Yolam and Katiam temples, which enshrine the bones of deceased male ancestors and house senior men from the clan. Facing the most sacred spaces in the village are the two men's houses, which are larger, elevated, and forbidden to women and children. Off to the far right are the women's houses, where women, children, and pigs reside. Beyond the village boundaries are huts where menstruating women stay during their

11. The Cosmic Body, woodblock print, nineteenth century. Baiyun Temple, Beijing. The head corresponds to the heavens, the chest to earth, and the lower abdomen to the water and river delta areas close to the underworld.

monthly cycle. Myths and rituals encode this mapping of domestic and cultic space: for example, one Baktaman myth about the first ancestors—an elder sister and two younger brothers—explains the origin of gender-segregated housing and male-controlled worship. According to the myth, women originally inhabited the temple or cult house, but the primordial sister eventually chose to move to her younger brother's hut and leave the temple to men: "What a good house you have," she said, "will you change with me?" "And," the myth concludes, "so the men took over the cult houses." This religiously sanctioned segregation of domestic and worship space reflects and reinforces the ancestor cult, which highlights taboos and privileges men.[22]

Social hierarchy and cosmic order are not always as transparent in the arrangement of homes or the design of exteriors—the men's houses were on stilts, after all, and they faced the worship space—and the home's religious significance usually is inscribed in its internal organization and interior furnishing. Whether it is an undivided enclosure like a conical hut or a split-level multiple-room house, interior space is mapped not only by the pragmatics of use—cooking ought to happen where smoke from the fire can escape—but also by the prescriptions of piety. Artifacts on the threshold can mark the space as religious—as in the Jewish practice of affixing a *mezuzah* to the doorpost—but religions also designate interior domestic spaces for sleeping, eating, coupling, gathering, and worshipping, and, as I noted above, prescribe what happens in those spaces.

The significance of domestic interiors for religious orientation is clear, for example, in the ways that artifacts and rituals combine to create home shrines. There are many examples from multiple cultures. Hindus set up home altars for morning and evening *pūjā*, or veneration of the gods and goddesses. In similar ways, many Buddhists, Sikhs, and Jains use artifacts to create domestic spaces for religious practice. Many Muslims and Jews also sacralize domestic space, though they don't usually enshrine images of deities. Many Muslims, for instance, use a prayer rug, or even a wall plaque, to set aside a space for daily prayer and indicate the direction of Mecca. Some Christians construct domestic altars.

12. Mexican home altar in Quintana Roo.

Cuban Americans at the Virgin's shrine told me that they created small domestic altars by placing an assortment of artifacts in their bedroom, kitchen, or living room: images of Our Lady of Charity and other saints that they had received as gifts, purchased in Miami, or carried from the homeland. In a similar way, Catholic altar makers in rural Mexico have constructed sacred spaces in their one-room dwellings. Note how one Mexican home altar juxtaposes the familial network and the metaphoric kinship system established by the cult of the saints: it includes not only images of Jesus and St. Theresa but also framed photographs of relatives (Figure 12). Even Protestants, who sometimes are portrayed as iconophobic, mark the home, or spaces within it, as sacred. For example, a 1940 entry in the *Doctrines and Disciplines of the Methodist Church* prescribed a house-blessing ritual that began with a scriptural passage: "it is written that, 'Except the Lord build the house, they labor in vain that build it.'" The rest of the domestic rite includes prayers interspersed with hymns, including one song that allocentrically maps the home in terms of the cardinal directions: "Bless the Four Corners of this House." And even if many Protestants have tried to guard against the idolatrous impulses of Catholic sensibilities, some corners in Protestant homes have included artifacts—from motto cases and bible stands to mass-produced paintings and hand-made quilts—that mark off domestic space as religious.[23]

In some instances, religious artifacts extend domestic space to yards, gardens, and neighborhoods. Consider a few examples from North America. In Miami, Cuban American followers of Catholicism and the Afro-Cuban tradition Santería built modest yard shrines that venerated saints: Saint Lazarus, Saint Barbara, and Our Lady of Charity. Most often these sites were religiously inspired landscaping, but sometimes they have served as altars for family or neighborhood rituals. As I reported in my ethnography, Mauricio, a fifty-nine-year-old yard shrine owner with obvious leanings toward Santería, organized a "block party" that drew hundreds of devotees to his yard on the Virgin's feast day. Each September 8, Mauricio told me, he invites a Santería "priest" *(un cura)* to say a mass *(una misa)* in front of the eight-foot image of Our Lady of Charity on his lawn. In a different way, Howard Finster, the former bicycle repairman and Protestant preacher, sacralized the space around his home in rural Georgia by using found objects to build Paradise Garden, an extension of domestic space that he imagined as a representation of the Garden of Eden (Figure 13). "It just come to me," the millennialist Protestant explained, "that the world started with a beautiful garden, so why not let it end with a beautiful garden?" Orthodox Jews in Toronto who constructed an *eruv* around their neighborhood were less interested in rural gardens than in suburban streets. The Torah prohibits some activities on the Sabbath, including carrying objects in public space. This

13. The Bible House, with an angel on top and a sign on the lower left that says "Welcome to the Coming of Jesus Christ," at Paradise Garden, created by Howard Finster.

prohibition has been challenging for many orthodox Jews, and the Talmud prescribes ways to get around it: establishing an *eruv*, a system of poles and wires that encircles a neighborhood or town and, thereby, transforms it from public space to domestic space.[24]

THE HOMELAND

As the *eruv* extends the boundaries of the home, the religious also move beyond intimate spaces and kinship relations to imagine the homeland—and the people within and beyond its borders. In other words, religions do more than autocentrically orient individuals in terms of bodily axes and personal memory. They do more than situate embodied persons in domestic space and familial history. Dwelling practices also position the religious in longer time frames and wider social spaces. Homemaking does not end at the front door. It extends to the boundaries of the territory that group members allocentrically imagine as *their* space, but since the homeland is an imagined territory inhabited by an imagined community, a space and group continually figured and refigured in contact with others, its borders shift over time and across cultures. As with the idea of home, the boundaries of the homeland can contract and expand. The homeland's scope depends not only on the tropes used to imagine it—*motherland* or *chosen land*—but also on the form and complexity of social organization. Small groups based primarily on kin relations, such as bands of nomadic foragers or relatively sedentary horticultural clans, might view their collective space as a rather small region. An ethnic group—or to use the language that most anthropologists now avoid, a tribe—can conjoin peoples on the basis of not only kin relations but also shared language, common practices, and contiguous territory, and they might lay claim to a larger natal space. Confederations of such groups—for instance, the Iroquois' Six Nations, which shared a common language and the Eastern Woodlands cultural area—imagined a still larger area as part of the homeland. The boundaries can expand further in other intermediate forms of communal organization such as chiefdoms: for example, the Aztec, Incan, and Mayan chiefdoms, which included thousands to millions of residents and employed cultivation techniques that yielded surpluses that, in turn, allowed for the formation of towns and cities. With the emergence of the modern nation-state, the borders of communal space enlarge again, and as transnational migrants like Cubans and others make clear, even if the homeland's space remains linked with the natal territory, it also includes the new places imagined and inhabited by the displaced peoples—refugees, slaves, exiles, and immigrants. So nationalism—and diasporic nationalism—creates an imagined community that has affective bonds with the natal land, but it also extends that bond beyond the borders of the native place. Finally, colonial empires—for instance, British, French, Dutch, or Spanish—stretch natal cartographies still further by tracing the reach of the state's expansion across national borders.[25]

Religious homemaking not only maps the boundaries of the natal place, whether this is imagined as a foraging route or a transnational empire, but also charts taxonomies of the people within and beyond its borders. In other words, it maps social space. It draws boundaries around *us* and *them;* it constructs collective identity and, concomitantly, imagines degrees of social distance. Social differentiation, which is complex in most modern nation-states but clearly present in the smallest itinerant band, varies with the scale and form of the communal organization and the tropes and practices used to imagine social space. The classic example of social differentiation is the Indian caste and class systems, but most cultures have similar taxonomies, even if they are less elaborate and systematized.[26]

Religions map natal place and social space by employing tropes— symbol, metaphor, simile, and myth—and anchoring those in artifacts and transmitting them in rituals. I already have noted how Cuban exiles use the metaphor of exile and the symbol of Mary, as well as artifacts like the cornerstone and the mural, to imagine the homeland. Let me mention two more examples of this sort of homemaking. First, at the rear of the shrine, facing the water and the island, stand copper-colored busts of José Martí and Félix Varela, two of the most influential Cuban writers of the nineteenth century. Varela was a Catholic priest who migrated to the United States, and Martí was a thinker who promoted Cuban nationalism on the island. The post-1959 socialist government in Cuba has celebrated both of them as proto-Marxist symbols, but the shrine's planning committee claimed them for the exile community and the national patroness by placing their images in Miami. Some pilgrims to the shrine might miss the nationalist significance of those busts, but few could fail to catch the meaning of another symbol, a Cuban flag, which was formed using painted stones and placed in the garden that encircles the shrine.[27]

Religions have mapped the homeland, and the peoples within and outside its borders, in many other ways as well. Some traditions have proposed that the landscape itself is sacred. For example, in India some rivers, mountains, and cities have been considered holy, so bathing in the Ganges River or visiting Banaras, one of the seven sacred cities, brings the devotee directly into contact with the gods. In some times and places, the boundaries of the homeland have been drawn by the gods. In the ancient Near East, the Sumerians linked each city-state with a deity. Since the primordial creation, they believed, each city-state had been assigned a particular god, who owned it for all eternity. So the water god, Enki, owned the city-state of Eridu, and the moon god, Nannar, reigned over the territory of Ur. In a slightly different way, Jewish sacred narratives suggest that God exhorted Abraham to relocate to the land of Canaan, and God made a promise that has bound the people to the landscape for generations: "And I will give to you, and to your offspring after you, the land where you are now an alien, all the land of Canaan, for a perpetual holding; and I will be their God." He was the God of King David, who founded a dynasty that lasted hundreds of years, and, as with David, the rule of other kings has received divine sanction in one way or another. Although ancient Chinese political theory left room for overthrowing rulers who did not do their job, texts from the Han Dynasty suggest the king's role was no less than harmonizing the three realms of the universe: Heaven, Earth, and Humanity. The ruler fulfilled this threefold obligation, one Chinese text proposed, by cultivating filial piety and the other virtues among the people; venerating his own ancestors properly; and by reverentially officiating at the public ritual offerings at the altars of Heaven and Earth. In this way the emperor established his rule over the homeland and its people—and dismissed those who lived beyond the borders as "barbarians."[28]

So spiritual cartographies of the homeland negotiate power as well as meaning. Sacred geographies are contested. This is clear, for example, in the violent disputes in the Indian city of Ayodhyā, which is simultaneously (for Muslims) the site of the Babri Mosque and (for Hindus) the birthplace of the god Rāma. In a similar way, Jerusalem is a site of contestation—Jewish, Christian, and Muslim—and Jewish claims to "the land of Canaan" conflict with Palestinian claims. Sometimes the site of contestation is not a temple or a city but a nation. Those who drew the United States' national map, which expressed America's "manifest"—and divinely sanctioned—destiny, imposed a colonialist grid on another grid: the boundaries of the six nations of the Iroquois and the other Indian nations across the continent. Sometimes one homeland displaces another. Homemaking exerts power as it makes meaning.[29]

THE COSMOS

Homemaking extends beyond the homeland's borders, and the religious also negotiate power and meaning as they imagine the structure, history, and limits of the wider landscape and the entire universe. Using allocentric reference frames, they produce geographies, cosmographies, cosmogonies, and teleographies.

Religions offer *geographies,* cognitive maps of the earth that include not only the home and the homeland but also the vast regions beyond intimate space and collective space. At its most basic, geographies involve autocentric framings that survey space in terms of the binary *here* and *there,* with *here* understood as the boundaries of the body, the home, or the homeland. This sort of mapping also involves chorographies, positioned representations of a region, as in the *pinturas* drawn by Amerindians at the request of Spanish colonial officials in the sixteenth century, but in many instances sacred geographies include mental maps that imagine the widest inhabited area of the earth. Using various geometric shapes (including the circle and the square) and a wide variety of symbols, the religious have mapped terrestrial space. In Sanskrit texts called *Purāṇas,* the flat disk of the earth is represented as

seven concentric islands, each separated from the next by oceans, and in the center of the innermost island is the mythical Mount Meru, which reaches from heaven to earth. One of the earliest printed European maps, produced by Hans Rüst in Augsburg around 1480, used a circular form to offer a "map of the world and of all countries and kingdoms with their positions in the world" (Figure 14). Like medieval maps—and this one is medieval in design and content—Rüst's printed woodcut with German lettering inscribed a Christian sacred geography. For example, note that Jerusalem is at the center, and at the top, the east, Adam and Eve stand within the walled Garden of Eden, through which flow the four Rivers of Paradise.[30]

As in this European map, representations of the terrestrial landscape often employ tropes—the symbol of the Garden of Eden—and so do *cosmographies*, representations of the structure of the entire universe, including the earth. An influential Chinese account of the universe's structure turned to the metaphor of an egg, which is also a common trope in creation stories. This elliptical theory, which was championed by Zhang Heng (78–139 C.E.) but circulated much earlier, imagined the universe this way: "Heaven is like an egg, and the earth is like the yolk of the egg. Alone it dwells inside. Heaven is great and earth is small. Inside and outside of heaven there is water. Heaven wraps around the earth as the shell encloses the yolk." This Chinese cosmography proposes two cosmic realms—heaven and earth—but there is wide variety in the ways religions have imagined the universe's structure. Roman Catholics added an intermediary realm—purgatory—and Muslims multiplied the terrestrial and celestial realms: the Qur'án counts seven heavens and seven earths. The Hindu *Upaniṣads* map seven realms. Some Pali Buddhist texts propose thirty-one realms of existence, but many Buddhists have embraced a more limited, but still com-

14. Hans Rüst, "This is a map of the world and of all countries and kingdoms with their positions in the world," circa 1477–1484. Woodcut with handcut lettering. 40.0 × 28.2 cm. Augsburg, Germany.

plex, cosmography. They have imagined a hierarchy of six realms, where different types of beings reside and where karmic forces send the reborn: at the bottom are the various hells; at the top are the heavens, the abodes of the gods. In between—and in ascending order—are realms for suffering ghosts, animals, *asuras* (semidivine or semidemonic beings), and humans. As with the Hopi of the American Southwest, even if religions imagine more subdivisions, many use autocentric reference frames to map a tripartite cosmic structure: *above, here,* and *below.* Vertical autocentric mapping often is supplemented by allocentric framing that positions the individual and the community in cosmic space. Note how one Hopi ceremonial artifact, which was built as part of an initiation into one of the male religious societies *(Wuwtsim)*, employs a central symbol (maize) to fashion a six directions altar, which Armin Geertz has called an "astrosphere altar" because it "recreates the spatial dimensions of the Hopi cosmology": axes that run north-south, southeast-northwest, southwest-northeast, and an imagined perpendicular line that intersects in the center and links the zenith *(oomiq)* and nadir *(atkyamiq)* (Figure 15).[31]

Religions not only map the contours of the terrestrial, subterranean, and celestial realms; they also orient devotees temporally and spatially by creating cosmogonies and teleographies that represent the origin and destiny of the universe. A *cosmogony* is a representation of the origin of the universe, and cosmogonic myths are most often intertwined with rituals and artifacts, just as the Wuwtsim altar is constructed as part of a complex initiation ceremony that re-creates the Hopis' primordial emergence from the underworld. A Hopi cosmogonic myth suggests that in the beginning there was only the creator, Taiowa, and "all else was endless space." It continues: "There was no beginning and no end, no time, no shape, no life. Just an immeasurable void that had its beginning and end, time, shape, and life in the mind of Taiowa the Creator." Then the creator god "conceives" of the world, and he creates Sotuknang, his nephew, to make manifest what his uncle, the creator, has conceived. The nephew, doing as he is told, arranges endless space

15. The "Astrosphere Altar," or Tawvongya, *in situ* during the Hopi Wuwtsim Ceremonial at Orayvi.

into "nine universal kingdoms." From there, the rest of the universe is created, with the help of other supernatural beings, including Spider Woman and the Twins. Most important for Hopi religious life, the myth continues by recounting the origins of the Hopi, who originated beneath the earth's surface and lived there in three previous worlds. At the beginning of the current age they ascended from the underworld to the present Fourth World, the World Complete, and after that "the people divided into groups and clans to begin their migrations." In this sense, the Hopi cosmogonic myth maps natal space and social space as well as cosmic space.[32]

Many other cosmogonic myths do the same, but those narratives have varied widely across cultures and periods—even within the same religious tradition. The Hopi myth represents the origin of the universe as a creation, but there are variations among such myths, and not all traditions imagine the universe's origin this way: religions, I suggest, have either presupposed the universe as already *existing* or imagined it as eternally *enduring,* or, if they narrate an ultimate cosmic origin they imagine that as either a process of *emerging* or, as in the Hopi example, an act of *creating.*[33]

The first two cosmogonic types, which view the universe as already existing or perpetually enduring, point to narrative traditions that reject or de-emphasize the claim that the universe had an ultimate origin—or redirect attention to other concerns. Most Buddhist traditions, for example, have challenged the premises of those who ask about cosmic origins. Such questions, the Buddha suggested in a famous passage in the *Cūla-Māluṅkya Sutta,* are unhelpful. The Pali text mentions ten matters "unexplained" by the Buddha, including whether the world is eternal, and it recounts an encounter between the Buddha and an insistent monk who pressed him for answers. In response, the Buddha told him a story about a man struck by a poisoned arrow. Just as that man should not try to reconstruct a full biography of the archer before pulling out the arrow, so too, the narrative implies, devotees should avoid such questions. The Buddha's focus was on the pragmatic concerns of life: to relieve suffering. As he tells the insistent monk, "Whether one holds the view that the world is eternal, or whether one holds the view that the world is not eternal, there is still birth, ageing, death, grief, despair, pain, and unhappiness—whose destruction here and now I declare."[34]

Some myths from other traditions do not redirect inquirers' attention or deny ultimate origins; they focus instead on natal space and social space, tracing the origins of the community. An Inuit myth, for example, begins by assuming the existence of the terrestrial landscape, but one without human inhabitants: "It was in the time when there were no people on the earth plain." The myth goes on to recount the unintended and unexpected origin of humans from a peapod that Raven, the trickster god, had created: "I made that vine, but did not know that anything like you would ever come from it." It is not that a careful listener could not reconstruct a cosmography and cosmogony from the narrative, since the story assumes a three-tiered universe (heaven, earth, and the sea floor) and presupposes that Raven has played a primary role in each realm. But this is not the story's focus. Rather, the Inuit narrator seems more interested in the differences among the spirits who dwell in the sky, earth, and water and, most important, the differences between inland and coastal peoples.[35]

Other myths do not simply assume the existence of the universe, but self-consciously imagine it as *enduring:* the world is eternal and time is cyclical. In these accounts there is no ultimate origin, but only the initiation of another cycle. And as with some Hindu myths that recount the role of Brahmā as creator and Śiva as destroyer, sometimes supernatural agents participate in the ebb and flow of these endless cosmic cycles. Another Indian tradition, Jainism, reaffirms the notion that the universe is eternal. The *Mahāpurāṇa,* a Jain text from the ninth century, directly challenges narratives that tell of a creator and a creation, raising questions about those stories: for example, how can an immaterial god create that which is material? In this Jain account, as in some Hindu narratives, the uncreated world is "without beginning or end."[36]

Many myths chronicle a cosmic beginning, although they imagine it variously as an emergence or a creation. Some portray cosmic origins as an impersonal process in which the universe *emerges* from some inanimate substance—even if supernatural agents get into the act later in the story. For example, consider two cosmogonic myths that take water as the primordial stuff from which all things emerge. In an ancient Near Eastern text that recounts a Babylonian cosmogony, the *Enuma Elish* imagined the time before the gods and the universe. At the start, there was only the ocean *(Apsu)* and the primeval waters *(Tiamat)*. These two "mingled together" and "in the water the gods were created." The natural divine forces then go on to order the chaos and produce the universe, but it first emerged from the waters. In a similar way, the *Śatapatha-brāhmaṇa,* a Hindu text written in India, proposed that "in the beginning this (universe) was water, nothing but a sea of water." And the waters are granted primal creative agency: "The waters desired, 'How can we be reproduced?'" They performed devotions and heat was generated, and from that process "a golden egg was produced." After a year, in turn, that egg produced the creator, Prajāpati, who broke open the egg and began the next stage in the production of the universe.[37]

These Babylonian and Indian myths eventually got gods into the act, but many other myths narrate the universe's origin as the creative act of one or more supernatural agents. These creation myths vary widely depending on several factors: the number of gods involved, whether they had some primordial stuff to work with; and how they actually initiated the creative process. Creator gods originate the universe in multiple ways—from speaking to vomiting—but there are five basic variations: crafting, ordering, procreating, battling, or differentiating. In differentiating creation stories, which resemble emergence myths, the universe emanates from the divine body. These accounts are common among Polynesian cultures. In a Tahitian story, for example, in the beginning the creator god Ta'aroa "dwelt in his shell." "It was round like an egg," the account continues, "and revolved in space in continuous darkness." The shell cracks open, and the deity overturns his shell to form a dome for the sky, and gradually the whole universe emanates from the original divine substance, so in this account the creative process is one of differentiating the subsequent plurality of things from the original unity of the divine body. When the primordial stuff is imagined as chaos, and not as the divine body itself, creator gods order rather than differentiate. The Pelasgians, who brought narratives about the Near Eastern mother goddess with them to Greece, suggested that "in the beginning, Eurynome, the Goddess of All Things, rose naked from Chaos, but found nothing substantial for her feet to rest upon, and therefore divided the sea from the sky, dancing lonely upon its waves." Her dancing set the wind in motion, and from the North Wind she created the great serpent Ophion, who coupled with her. She then assumed the form of a dove, and laid the "Universal Egg." With the egg's hatching, the process of creation continued until everything was in place. This story involves coupling, and some other myths suggest that the world originates from an act of procreation between two divine beings, as in the myth told by the Jivaran Indians of Ecuador in which the universe is the result of the sexual union of two divine "parents"— Kumpara, the creator, and Chingaso, his spouse—who start the creative process by producing a son, Esta, the sun. In other myths that involve two co-eternal supernatural agents or forces, the interactions are less amorous. In the Manichaean creation myth, for example, the world begins with two principles that are imagined as good and evil, light and darkness. The creative process involves the continuing battle between these forces, and the attempt to release the light from the darkness in matter. Other accounts, which imagine a single benevolent divine being, narrate the origin as a process of crafting, and those from Western monotheistic traditions—as well as some myths in other traditions and cultures, including the Zuni—propose that the creation is out of nothing. According to the Priestly account in Genesis (1:1–2:4a)—one of two creation myths in the Hebrew Bible—in the beginning there was only a watery chaos, as in the Babylonian myth, and from that the divine, an autonomous eternal power, creates "the heavens and the earth."[38]

The Genesis account and other cosmogonic myths focus on beginnings, but, as I suggest in the next chapter, religions also imagine a *telos*, an "ultimate object or aim," a temporal and spatial endpoint. In other words, they offer *teleographies*. The religious, I propose, mark and cross all sorts of boundaries, including the ultimate horizon of human life.

Chapter Five

We are beings at the limit . . .

    Richard Kearney, *Strangers, Gods, and Monsters*

Indian tradition has always offered a way to "cross over" whatever the situation, be it overcoming a personal problem, passing over to a new stage of life *(āśrama)*, crossing from one life to rebirth, traversing the realms *(loka)* for a temporary visit to heaven *(svarga)* or hell *(naraka)*, or ultimately transcending the cycle of reincarnation itself.

    Katherine Y. Young, "Tīrtha and the Metaphor of Crossing Over"

CROSSING

The Kinetics of Itinerancy

I have analyzed how dwelling practices situate the religious in time and space, positioning them in four chronotopes: the body, the home, and the homeland, and the cosmos. Yet religions, I suggest, are not only about being in place but also about moving across. They employ tropes, artifacts, rituals, codes, and institutions to mark boundaries, and they prescribe and proscribe different kinds of movements across those boundaries. I argue that religions enable and constrain *terrestrial crossings,* as devotees traverse natural terrain and social space beyond the home and across the homeland; *corporeal crossings,* as the religious fix their attention on the limits of embodied existence; and *cosmic crossings,* as the pious imagine and cross the ultimate horizon of human life.

A prominent historian once noted that U.S. religious history had been characterized by three centuries during which "people in general did an incredible amount of moving around." The movement of peoples within and across the boundaries of the homeland is not new, and it is not confined to the modern West. Although the pace and form of the movements have changed, people have been on the move since the wanderings of the first humanoid species out of Africa. Population geneticists have traced the migrations of genes, just as students of culture have traced the movements of languages, artifacts, and practices across the globe. As world historian Peter N. Stearns suggested in *Cultures in Motion,* each period of human history has brought new crossings, from the development of agriculture about 9000 B.C.E. and the emergence of civilizations along river valleys in Asia and Africa about 3500 B.C.E. to the sustained exchanges along the medieval trade routes and the colonialist encounters between 1450 and 1750 C.E. Focusing on more recent movements, James Clifford proposed that "everyone is on the move, and has been for centuries: dwelling-in-travel." And from the wanderings of nomadic clans to the round-trip journey of jet-plane pilgrims, religions have prompted travel.[1]

⇢ Mediating Terrestrial Crossings

To highlight the differences between nomads wandering on foot—or by camel or horse—and contemporary pilgrims resorting to air travel is to acknowledge that terrestrial crossings vary according to the shifts in travel and communication technology. Technology mediates religious crossings. Oxen and asses drew wheeled carts in Mesopotamia as early as 3000 B.C.E., and camels were a primary means of transport in the Sahara 2,500 years later. In other parts of the world other animals, including the horse, were used to transport people, goods, and practices across the terrain. For aquatic crossings, water craft have been around for at least 5,000 years, and the form of religious travel shifted with changes in sea transport. Ocean travel was easier for the Chinese at an earlier date than for European ships, and their junks were the most advanced ships in the world at the end of the fourteenth century. A century later, when the Portuguese developed the caravel, a small three-masted ship, it opened new possibilities for transcultural contact and exchange. In 1497 Vasco da Gama rounded the Cape of Good Hope, and made it all the way to the west coast of India. Catholic priests were on that ship, and later in the sixteenth century Portuguese mariners brought missionaries to all parts of their colonial empire in Asia, Africa, and the Americas. The same happened with the widespread use of the four-masted galleon in the seventeenth century and the steamboat in the nineteenth century. Each technological change prompted increased, and transformed, contacts. For example, the steamship allowed less dangerous and more frequent oceanic crossings and mediated the transnational exchanges with America and Europe that transformed Buddhism, Shintō, and Christianity in Meiji Japan. Rail, automobile, and air travel also transformed transportation—and the transported religions. Despite ongoing segregation and occasional lynchings on trains, many ex-slaves in late-nineteenth-century America commonly symbolized spiritual journeys as railway travel, viewed the train as a means of escape northward toward liberty, and imagined conversion as the moment when "Jesus handed me a ticket." Turning to other forms of transport, many middle-class Hindu migrants to the United States in the late twentieth century used regular air travel to maintain connections between India and the diaspora, and this affected religious practice in both places. So even though there is no simple linear progression in transportation technology in any region or across the globe, since multiple technologies co-exist at the same time, and even though religious practice is not determined only by mode of transport, we can distinguish biped and quadruped religion, galleon and steamship religion, railroad and airplane religion. We can even talk about motorcycle religion, as with the Unchained Gang, a Pentecostal outreach ministry that has traveled to Indiana prisons and biker rallies to spread the Christian gospel (Figure 16).[2]

In the same way, changes in communication technology have had

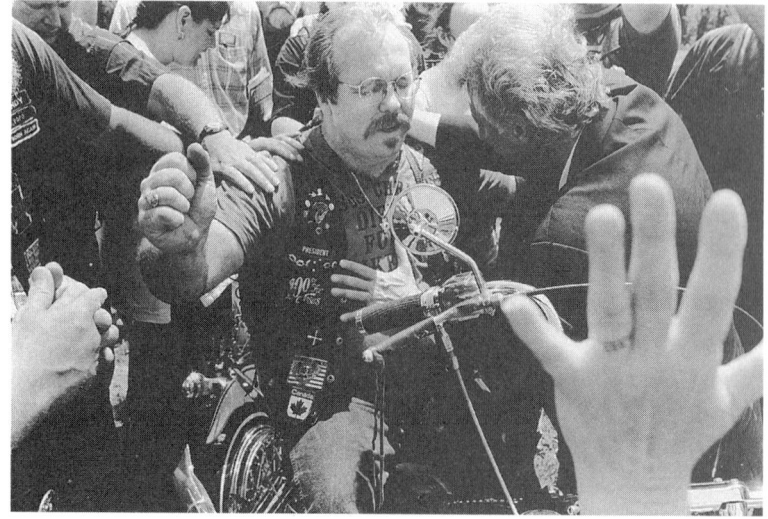

16. The blessing of the bikes. In 1996 at the House of Prayer in Ellettsville, Indiana, Irv Goldman, a traveling evangelist, lays his hand on the chest of Pastor Larry Mitchell, president of the Unchained Gang, before Mitchell and others set out on a journey to bring others to Christianity.

implications for the sorts of crossings available to the religious. To note only a few of the Western innovations since the early modern period, the introduction of movable type made texts available to many more people, just as the electric telegraph (1836), telephone (1876), radio (1899), television (1926), and computer (1949) expanded and transformed how technology mediated interpersonal contacts and virtual transits. As with travel technology, the Chinese were ahead of the Europeans: they had paper a thousand years earlier and printing as early as the late seventh century. Yet as many scholars have noted, the Western introduction of the printing press had enormous implications in Europe and around the world. The Protestant Reformation, for instance, was the first self-conscious attempt to use that recently invented media to channel a mass religious movement. As historian Mark U. Edwards has noted, "The printing press allowed Evangelical publicists to do what had been previously impossible, quickly and effectively reach a large audience with a message intended to change Christianity. For several crucial years, these Evangelical publicists issued thousands of pamphlets discrediting the old faith and advocating the new." In the twentieth century, radio, television, and film also opened new possibilities for religious communication, including appeals for conversion during Charles E. Fuller's "Old Fashioned Revival Hour" radio program in the United States, representations of the sacred and the demonic in Ghanaian popular cinema, and dramatization of Hindu classics in the televised *Mahābhārata* in India. With the widespread use of the computer in the late twentieth century came other changes, as Internet technology and electronic mail mediated traditional and new forms of religious practice: devotees could hear the Muslim call to prayer online, email "cybermonk" to ask about Buddhist meditation practice, or attend a virtual Roman Catholic mass on their home computer. As with travel technology, multiple media forms have co-existed at the same time, and none fully determines religious practice, but it can be illuminating to consider the differences among print religion, telegraph religion, radio religion, television religion, and computer religion.[3]

→ Round-Trip Travel: Pilgrimage and Missions

Terrestrial crossings are mediated by divergent transport and communication technologies, and they also vary according to the nature of the journey and the motive for the transit. That travel can be one-way, as when persecuted Puritans sought permanent shelter in the British colonies or when Hindu devotees have journeyed to the holy city of Banaras to die—and begin a different kind of journey. Yet much religiously motivated travel is a round-trip passage for one purpose or another. The Hindu *sadhu* Ludkan Baba, the Rolling Saint, made an unconventional terrestrial crossing in 2004 when, as part of his ascetic practice and moral strategy, he vowed to roll the eight hundred miles from his home in central India's Madhya Pradesh state to the Pakistani city of Lahore,

17. Mohan Singh, whom some followers and reporters have called Ludkan Baba or the Rolling Saint, makes his way through Hodal on his way north toward Pakistan in 2004.

where he hoped to urge the Pakistani president to reach a lasting peace with his homeland (Figure 17).[4]

More conventional round-trip religious travel includes pilgrimage to sacred sites and missions to spread the faith. From a family's circumambulation of the small holy well at Glendalough in pre-Famine Ireland to a contemporary bus ride around the eighty-eight sacred places of Shikoku, where Japanese devotees venerate Kūkai, founder of Shingon Buddhism, pilgrimage has been an important ritual practice in a number of cultures and religions. Pilgrims travel to sites they consider sacred for a variety of reasons. As one anthropologist has suggested, devotees embark on instrumental, devotional, normative, wandering, initiatory, and obligatory journeys. For example, some pilgrims go for instrumental purposes such as healing, as they do at the Grotto in Lourdes, the transnational Roman Catholic shrine in southwestern France. Soon after Bernadette had her visions of the Immaculate Conception on the site in 1858, water from the nearby spring began to be celebrated for its curative powers. Since then the injured and the ill have drunk from the Grotto's fountains and bathed in its pools as they have sought miraculous intervention. Although some Muslim pilgrims to the Ka'ba, the flat-roofed shrine in Mecca, have drunk water from the *Zamzam*, a well that is known to grant blessings to those on *ḥajj*, most have traveled to the Arabian Peninsula not only for instrumental reasons but also to fulfill a fundamental religious obligation (Figure 18).[5]

Like pilgrims to Mecca and Lourdes, most missionaries also go on round-trip journeys beyond the homeland's borders. The term *missionary* is of Latin and French origin, and it refers to a person sent on a mission. It has referred more narrowly to a Christian charged with spreading the faith, though by extension scholars have used it to label emissaries of other traditions as well. Not all religious traditions have dispatched representatives to convert others, and even those that have a history of such activity—especially Christianity—have not supported religious emissaries as vigorously in all times and places. However, trying to follow Jesus' scriptural injunction to "make disciples of all nations" and emulate Paul, who proclaimed the gospel in Rome "with all boldness and without hindrance," some Christians have done their best to "make disciples" beyond the homeland's boundaries. Some have evangelized with little ecclesiastical or governmental support and by attempting to entice converts by appeals to reason, as with Ramón Lull (ca. 1232–1316), the Franciscan tertiary and lay missionary who preached to Muslims in the Iberian Peninsula and northern Africa. At other times missionaries were representatives of the state and used coercion, even violence, to win converts. Charlemagne, whom Pope Leo III crowned Holy Roman Emperor in 800, turned to coercion to bring the Saxons to the faith, even laying out penalties in the *Capitulatio de partibus Saxoniae* that included death for any Saxon who refused bap-

18. Muslim pilgrims circumambulating the *Ka'ba*.

tism. Missionaries have been less prominent during most of Islamic history, yet there are some instances of systematic attempts to seek converts. For example, the Ismāʿīlī Shīʿī caliph-imāms of the Fāṭimid Dynasty, especially al-Muʿizz (r. 953–975), the Fāṭimid ruler who transformed the caliphate from a regional power to an expansive empire, did draw on a network of *dāʿīs* or "religio-political missionaries" within and outside the boundaries of the Islamic state. Before and after al-Muʿizz's rule, those missionaries managed to gain Ismāʿīlī converts from northern Africa to the Indian subcontinent. As with Islam and Christianity, at some moments in its history, Buddhism also has been spread by state-sponsored representatives of the faith. Buddhists, for example, have trumpeted Aśoka's role in the tradition's early expansion. They have suggested that Aśoka (ca. 300–232 B.C.E.), who was the third ruler of the Indian Mauryan Empire, sent missionary-monks, including his own son Mahinda, to regions within and beyond his empire, including Sri Lanka.[6]

The fact that some missionaries have been directly or indirectly linked with a sponsoring state—such as Aśoka's Mauryan Empire, al-Mu'izz's Ismāʿīlī empire, or Charlemagne's Holy Roman Empire—indicates how the concern to spread the faith often has intertwined with political, cultural, and economic motives. These sorts of religious crossings have negotiated power as well as meaning.

⤳ Religious and Other Crossings

In turn, other itinerant practices—colonization, war, trade, tourism, and migration—sometimes have been linked with religiously inspired travel in complex ways. Sometimes the gods consecrate the soldiers' march to foreign soil; sometimes tourism overlaps with pilgrimage as consumers of aesthetic pleasures and leisure diversions invest their travel with spiritual significance. Migrants sometimes have been propelled by visions of religious utopias, traders have carried their faith along with their bartered goods, and colonizers have venerated the flag as well as the cross or the crescent. In some cases, they have been lured by coins as well as by converts. As I suggested in Chapter 3, religion, economy, society, and politics are transfluvial currents, transverse flows that cross and, thereby, impel new cultural streams. And multiple motives converge in some terrestrial crossings. Cubans' migration to South Florida after 1959 had political and economic causes—as they boarded planes, ships, or rafts to flee Castro's socialism—but many imagined that crossing (and their dwelling in the new land) using religious tropes: the symbol of the patroness and the metaphor of exile, as with the *balsero* who holds an image of the Virgin aloft as rescuers approach his raft after the dangerous passage by sea to South Florida (Figure 19). Florida and Cuba were once part of New Spain, and early Spanish Catholic colonization in Mesoamerica also was propelled and sustained by multiple overlapping motives, even if Aztec narratives of the conquest emphasized that the Spaniards' "bodies swelled with greed" for Moctezuma's gold. The colonizers were driven by nationalist competition for territory, Catholic obligation to the "heathen," and the male quest for adventure—as well as the potent allure of minerals, gold at first and silver later.[7]

Silver was discovered in Mexico in the mid-sixteenth century, but other trade goods were more important in the economic exchanges along the Silk Road, the ancient and medieval trans-Asian network of roads where commercial, military, diplomatic, cultural, and religious interests crossed. That complex overland route, mostly east and west, lasted from the second century B.C.E. to the fifteenth century C.E. and stretched from the Mediterranean to China. Biped and quadruped religions traversed that path, as merchants transported multiple religious practices—Buddhist, Christian, Muslim, Jewish, Manichaean, and Zoroastrian. Sogdian and Iranian merchants had brought Nestorian Christianity to China by the seventh century. Missionaries also used the opportunity the route afforded, and at least as early as the tenth century, Sufi masters traveled with Silk Road caravans to spread their practices to Central Asia. Buddhist merchants and monks also took the overland route, and, as one interpreter has noted, sometimes religion and trade became mutually reinforcing: "the expansion of Buddhism brought an increased demand for silk, which was used in Buddhist ceremonies, thereby further stimulating the long-distance trading activity that had facilitated the spread of Buddhism in the first place." The transregional pathway, which had been cleared by the desire for economic exchange and the concern for military security, also allowed other forms of religious travel, including pilgrimage: Christian Turks from Mongolia made their way to the holy sites in Palestine by the fif-

19. A Cuban *balsero* holds an image of Our Lady of Charity aloft as rescuers approach his raft in 1994. © Walt Michot/The Miami Herald.

teenth century, and as early as the fifth century Chinese Buddhist pilgrims like Faxian had followed the Silk Road west and south to seek the origins of their faith in India.[8]

↦ Crossing Social Space and Constituting Social Roles

The Indian society those medieval travelers encountered classified residents according to a more or less fluid hierarchy of social distinctions—the four primary *varnas* or classes and the hundreds, even thousands, of *jātis* or castes. And religions not only mark those shifting economic and social boundaries, but prompt crossings that traverse social space, just as some leaders in India—for instance, Mohandās Gāndhi and Bhimrao Ramji Ambedkar—have appealed to religion to challenge the class and caste systems. Sometimes religions propel devotees across lines of social stratification and transport them to altered social status. Although women remained subservient to men in most ways and class lines sometimes proved intransgressable—as when Hildegard of Bingen defended the exclusion of non-nobles from the noble convents by arguing that "the lower class should not elevate itself above the higher"—some marginalized women in the twelfth century who joined religious communities found that Catholicism allowed nuns temporary and incomplete passage over some social obstacles. Even if the color line remained in place back home, Malcolm X reported that the pilgrimage to Mecca allowed him to cross racial boundaries: "Never have I witnessed such sincere hospitality and the overwhelming spirit of true brotherhood as is practiced by people of all colors and races here in this Ancient Holy Land." In a similar way, the religious sometimes have claimed that their faith has prompted economic mobility as well. In a lecture that he delivered more than six thousand times across the United States and around the world, Russell Conwell, founder of Philadelphia's Baptist Temple, claimed that even the poorest of his listeners had "acres of diamonds" within their reach, and it was their "Christian godly duty" to get them.[9]

After a career as a lawyer, in 1879 Conwell had been ordained as a

Baptist minister, an example of the way in which religions also mediate devotees' transitions to new social roles. Religious rituals authenticate some religious specialists—including ministers, priests, nuns, monks, rabbis, imāms, healers, diviners, and shamans. In some cultures where politics and religion intertwine, spiritual rites consecrate rulers too, and not only the pope's establishing of Charlemagne as Holy Roman Emperor. In ancient Mesoamerica, for example, rituals marked the transition to the new social roles of priest and warrior, and the Mayan kings ascended to the throne through an elaborate religious rite that included bloodletting, whereby the gods passed into the world to be reborn and the royal person achieved new spiritual and political status. Rituals also mark the shift of status among the Yorùbá in contemporary western Africa—including the *oba* or chief, who serves as political and religious authority for the town, the *oloogun* or medicine specialist, who prescribes cures for physical and spiritual maladies, and the *babalawo* or diviner, who communicates with the gods to discern future events.[10]

⇥ Compelled Passages and Constrained Crossings

In earlier centuries, the ancestors of the Yorùbá were sold into slavery and forced to make the harsh transatlantic passage chained in slave ships, and it is important to note that religions do not only enable crossings of the natural landscape or social space. They also *compel* passages and *constrain* movements. They justify the forced or coerced migration of peoples, as with slavery to the United States and Latin America, where slavery's Christian advocates in the Atlantic World appealed to sacred narratives to defend their practices. For example, citing scriptural passages (such as Timothy 6:1–5) for support, the Reformed minister Samuel B. How published a volume in 1856 entitled *Slaveholding Not Sinful,* and, as Frederick Douglass noted, some masters "found religious sanction for [their] cruelty": one of his own masters even recited a scriptural passage—"He that knoweth his master's will, and doeth it not, shall be beaten with many stripes"—as he whipped a lame young woman until she bled. We do not know if that young woman ever made the passage out of slavery, as Douglass did, but religions also slow or block terrestrial crossings of other kinds as well. In most Orthodox Jewish synagogues, custom has prescribed that women cannot cross the line that divides them from the male worshipers, and men were discouraged from visiting some sacred sites in Okinawa. Dutch Calvinist sermons buttressed racial apartheid in South Africa, where blacks could not cross into whites-only neighborhoods. In India, even though religiously sanctioned social taboos have eased in urban areas, Hindu marriages across caste lines are still proscribed in some rural villages, and religious institutions have restricted or discouraged interreligious marriages—and lineage crossings—in many other cultures and periods.[11]

CORPOREAL CROSSINGS

As the betrothed, with their garments tied together, circumambulate a sacred fire at the climax of the traditional Hindu wedding *(vivāha),* they make a crossing of a different kind. In a literal sense, as the man and woman walk around the fire, they make a terrestrial crossing, but they are doing more than that. They are performing a rite of passage *(saṃskāra),* and the religious also cross the limits of embodied life and traverse the transitions through the life cycle.[12]

→→ Confronting Embodied Limits

We are "beings at the limit," as Richard Kearney suggested in the passage I quoted at the start of this chapter, and religions confront limit situations of various kinds. One limit is the boundary between the embodied self and the natural world, and encountering that limit can evoke joy or sadness, or a range of other emotions. It is the line where the individual encounters, to use Max Weber's language again, the world's perfections and imperfections (Figure 20). It's where the individual meets corporeal limitations (illness and death) and suffers natural disasters (floods and earthquakes). It's where questions mount and answers fail. At the same time, the limit is the bridge to sexual intimacy,

20. Sitting in front of a skull and bones in 1989, a Theravadin Buddhist monk meditates on the inevitability of death. Dondanduwa, Sri Lanka.

where embodied selves meet, and the path to natural wonders, where the self moves outside itself—the meaning of *ecstatic*—and encounters the world's perfections. It is the line that, when crossed, allows religiously mediated encounters with the natural world that generate delight. So as I am using the term here, limit situations are culturally mediated moments—or time-spaces—when selves approach the threshold of the humanly possible and face the limitations of embodied existence. The limit is the zone where theodicies are born and nature mystics exhalt.[13]

To say that religions *confront* limit situations and that encounters at the limit of the embodied self are *mediated* is to suggest that religions provide tropes, narratives, codes, artifacts, and rituals that mark those boundaries and clear paths across them. Religions interpret limits and promote crossings. As long as we don't go too far toward an epistemology that denies any stubborn reality beyond the self, we could even say that religions constitute or create the limits they seek to cross. A life-threatening fever could be confirmation of the sufferer's sinfulness, for example, or the welcome passage to a better world. A comet's trail across the winter sky could be a sign of divine wonder or a millennial warning of the world's impending doom. There are no culturally unmediated experiences, and religions mediate encounters with corporeal and natural limits.[14]

Some of those encounters are painful, and, as I noted in Chapter 3, religions confront suffering, including natural evil. Religions make sense of life-threatening fevers, and other natural evils like floods and tsunamis, famines and hurricanes, plagues and tumors. To put it differently, natural evils pose questions that religions formulate and answer. Why did the flood wash away my village? Why did my daughter die from that fever? The formulation of the problem of evil varies across and within religious traditions: For example, should we ask which deeds in my daughter's past life led to the karmic retribution that brought on the fever or should we ask why a good, omnipotent God would allow it? And the answers also vary among and within traditions. Weber offered a typology of theodicies, explanations for evil. He pointed to (1) "messianic eschatologies," which promise it will all work out in the end; (2) deterministic views, which suggest that humans cannot do much about the course of events; (3) "dualism," which posits two co-eternal forces, Good and Evil or Light and Darkness, that struggle for control in the universe; and (4) "the doctrine of karma," which suggests that humans get what they deserve since "guilt and merit within this world are unfailingly compensated by fate in the successive lives of the soul." We could add a few other types to Weber's list, including approaches that suggest natural evil tests, improves, or punishes the sufferer or those that appeal to mystery and note the distance between the human and the divine. Consider, for example, God's "thundering" answer to the lament of Job, a righteous man who had lost his children and his flocks and had contracted leprosy: "Where were you when I laid the foundation of the earth?"[15]

Job, who is eventually silenced by God's counterinterrogation, had begun by asking a simple question that expressed his frustration: "Why did I not die at birth, come forth from the womb and expire?" Although religious elites in systematized traditions sometimes have framed the questions—and answers—about natural evil abstractly, often disease and disaster have prompted pragmatic questions: How can we avoid another flood in the village? Didn't we perform the rite properly? Have we transgressed the will of the gods? And since religions offer healing, as well as relief from other natural evil, the devout also have asked not only why the child got the fever but what they can do about it. As when a Yorùbá *oloogun* serves as a conduit for the healing power of the *òrìṣàs* or a Pentecostal minister enacts the transforming power of Christ's atonement on the cross, religions diagnose maladies and prescribe cures. Religions sometimes try to propel devotees across natural barriers, such as injury and disease.[16]

It's difficult to say where the natural world ends and the human community begins, and the religious, drawing on figurative language, moral codes, and ritual practices, also identify and transform moral evil, suffering that arises not from impersonal forces in the natural world but from the free actions of persons in human communities. The Confucian thinker Mengzi, who lived in China in the fourth century B.C.E., turned to horticultural images to explain moral evil and seek a solution. Humans are born with inclinations to do the good—as our spontaneous reactions to suffering, for instance the sight of a child falling into a well, show us. However, Mengzi proposed, these inclinations are "sprouts" that must be "cultivated" by proper moral education, just as farmers must tend to seeds for them to grow. Turning to a very different metaphor—and offering an alternate diagnosis and cure for moral evil—the North African Christian theologian Augustine pointed to the ways that the inherited constraints of original sin couple with the added constraints of habit to restrain humans as they try to do the good. Augustine was "held fast" by the "fetters" of habit, which "had the strength of iron chains," he told readers of the autobiography he wrote at the end of the fourth century. Moral education is not enough, in other words, and the only way to escape moral evil, to be "set free from a nature thus doomed to death," is to find your will transformed by "the grace of God, through Jesus Christ, our Lord."[17]

Augustine and Mengzi both recognized the challenge of accounting for evil, and religious responses to the world's imperfections are not always satisfying and not always simple. Sometimes the religious complain that moral and natural evil seems too horrific to be contained by the usual explanations. Sometimes situations bring answers to a limit, as when some Jews shook an angry fist at the God of Abraham, Isaac, and Jacob, who seemed to abandon the six million during the Holocaust. Many—though not all—post-Holocaust Jews made their way back to the synagogue, if only to continue the argument with their god. However, especially after the late 1960s, some Jews suggested that the usual explanations fail to make sense of that event. In *After Auschwitz*, Richard Rubenstein claimed that God is dead after the concentration camps, and even those who have offered more moderate responses have remained troubled by that instance of moral evil. For example, Conservative rabbi and Jewish historian Arthur Hertzburg acknowledged that "I have never found a way to absolve God." In a similar way, natural evil sometimes has brought answers to a limit, as with the great Lisbon earthquake, which shook the earth on All Saints Day in 1755 and killed approximately 60,000 people in southern Iberia and northwest Morocco. Many Christians at the time might have sided with John Wesley, Methodism's founder, when he discerned "the hand of the Almighty" at work in that earthquake. Like other natural interventions of the divine, Wesley proposed, it was designed to convey a message: "Love not the world." Yet other contemporaries, including Voltaire, found the traditional theological explanations wanting. In his "Poem on the Lisbon

Disaster" Voltaire lamented "the scattered limbs beneath the marble shafts" and the tens of thousands who had been "entombed beneath their hospitable roofs." He also challenged the certainty of contemporary interpreters of the "hellish gulf in Portugal" who could discern meaning or absolve God:

> Are ye so sure the great eternal cause,
> That knows all things, and for itself creates,
> Could not have placed us in this dreary clime
> Without volcanoes seething 'neath our feet?[18]

The religious in many traditions also have acknowledged, and sometimes celebrated, the moral ambivalence and emotional complexity of human life, with its mix of perfections and imperfections, delight and grief. The twentieth-century Catholic writer Flannery O'Connor explored that ambivalence in her work, suggesting that even the immoral and the grotesque can be revelatory. In one short story she presented a vain and hypocritical woman as a vehicle of grace, and in another she portrayed "freaks"—midgets and hermaphrodites—as "temples of the Holy Ghost," sites where "God's spirit has a dwelling." Some Buddhists, despite their acute awareness of the inevitability of suffering, have pointed to a similar complexity. Mahāyāna Buddhist philosophers have turned to abstract language to signal the presence of goodness and beauty amid the suffering of *saṃsāra,* the cycles of birth, death, and rebirth—for example, by affirming the ultimate identity of *saṃsāra* and *nirvāṇa.* Yet Bashō, the Japanese Buddhist itinerant with whom we began this theoretical journey, put it more vividly in one of his poems:

> Come, see real
> flowers,
> of this painful world.

In this Zen-inspired haiku, Bashō expresses delight—and perhaps surprise—at coming upon beauty. He invites the reader to discover joy in "this painful world." There's no denying the pain, the Japanese poet suggests, but the flowers are real enough.[19]

With some notable exceptions—for instance Manichaeism—most religions join Bashō in inviting devotees to notice the flowers, to recognize perfections and enhance delight. Religions, as I argued in Chapter 3, are about intensifying joy as well as overcoming sadness. They are about celebrating wonders as much as wondering about evil. Of course, it is not only religions that celebrate wonders. Sometimes artists and scientists—whether shaped by religious worldviews or not—have imagined a world teeming with wonders. Giambattista della Porta, the sixteenth-century Italian natural philosopher and researcher in optics who founded the first European scientific society, reflected on "the Causes of Wonderful Things" in the introduction to his major work, and Michael Faraday, the nineteenth-century British chemist and physicist known for his experiments in electricity and magnetism, remarked that "nothing is too wonderful to be true." From Tang Dynasty Chinese landscape painters to nineteenth-century Romantic poets, artists also have found—or imagined—wonders in the natural world. Daoism, which imagined mountains as the dwelling place of the immortals, inspired many of those Chinese painters, just as Christian themes informed the verse of Romantic poets like Samuel Taylor Coleridge and Ralph Waldo Emerson, who proposed that "Nature is ever an ally of Religion." In his famous 1836 essay "Nature," Emerson also exhorted readers to take a closer look at the stars in particular, since they "awaken a certain reverence." Yet many natural forms have awakened reverence among the religious—not only Bashō's flowers and Emerson's stars but other celestial, terrestrial, and maritime wonders. Some traditions, collapsing the distance between the sacred and the secular, have venerated the divine in nature or the nature as divine. There are sun gods and moon goddesses, holy rivers and sacred mountains. The sites of veneration also vary according to the topography of the homeland—so the tides, the desert, the forest, or the mountains become holy. For example, long-standing traditions in Japan affirm that *kami*, deities or sacred powers, reside temporarily or permanently in mountains, and across the landscape. The rice *kami,* one of many that inhabit the landscape, dwells in the rice fields during the growing season, ascends to the mountains in the autumn, and descends again to the fields every spring.[20]

In a similar way, religions in many cultures mark transitions in the seasonal cycle, including rituals celebrating the solstices, and sometimes devotees offer requests and gratitude to the gods for the harvest or the hunt. For example, the Green Corn Ceremony, performed by precontact tribes throughout the southeastern woodlands of the United States when the late corn crop ripened, was a rite of renewal and thanksgiving dedicated to the Corn Mother. The Bladder Feast, a midwinter ceremony celebrated among Alaskan Inuit hunters, returned the bladders of all the seals caught during the year to the sea, so that their souls might find new bodies and be caught again in the coming year.[21]

So religions confront the limitations of embodied human life, including disease and disaster, as the religious wonder about suffering, and spiritual flows transport the individual beyond the confines of the self to celebrate—and constitute—the wonders of the natural world, the blossoms near Bashō's hut in Edo and the stars above Emerson's home in Concord, from the bounty of the midwinter seal hunt to the abundance of the corn harvest in the summer field.

Traversing the Life Cycle

Although the death of an infant or mother during childbirth can bring suffering, religious traditions have celebrated the arrival of a child as one of the world's wonders. Religions mark not only the cycle of the seasons but also the transitions in the life cycle, conveying the individual from birth to death. The anthropologist Arnold van Gennep called the rituals that mark those transitions *les rites de passage,* drawing on analogies between societies and houses. Just as dwellers pass through rooms, corridors, and doorways in their home, members of a society cross thresholds *(limen)* that lead from one social status to another. Through rites of passage the individual leaves one status, passes through

21. Birth of the Hindu god Kṛṣṇa. Nineteenth-century miniature painting, North India.

a liminal, or transitional, state, and arrives at a new developmental stage and social role. Religions imagine those transitions differently—just as the design and structure of homes vary across cultures—and traditions mark them by drawing on narratives, tropes, and artifacts as well as rituals. Whatever the variations—for example, the Inuit ritually celebrate a boy's killing of his first seal as an important developmental stage—most religions have erected thresholds at birth, puberty, marriage, and death.[22]

Birth is the first of those thresholds (Figure 21). In childbirth, a woman—although the Wana in Indonesia claim men get pregnant and carry the fetus for seven days before it enters the womb—brings a new life into the home and the homeland. Like other rites of passage, childbirth actually involves several moments, each marked ritually in some religious traditions: conception, pregnancy, birth, naming, and initiation. Initiation might mean, for example, Christian infant baptism or Jewish male circumcision, or some other postpartum ritual. The Bukidnon people of the northern mountains on Mindanao in the Philippines have several postpartum rituals designed to exorcise evil spirits and encourage benevolent ones. Those spirits have been involved in the process since conception, according to Bukidnon beliefs. When a woman becomes pregnant, the spirit *(magbabaya)* at the "navel" of heaven sends one of his subordinate spirits as the human soul, *gimukod*. After the birth of that child with the heaven-sent soul, the father buries the placenta beneath the home's floor or hangs it from a tree. Then *magbabaya* transports the placenta to heaven and infuses it with a guardian spirit, which becomes a sibling of the newborn. Sometimes after birth the midwife detects evil omens in the umbilical cord, and in those cases the *datu,* or ritual specialist, performs another ceremony that includes animal sacrifice to petition the spirits and safeguard the infant.[23]

Muslims safeguard the infant in other ways. Islamic postpartum rites include circumcision for boys, from a week to thirteen years after birth, and Islamic custom prescribes other practices at the birth of a child. As soon as possible after that birth, comes the first rite: the father or an imām recites the *shahādah*—the first pillar of faith—in the child's right ear and then the left. Usually the whispering in the right ear takes the more elaborate form of the *adhān,* or the call to prayer that Muslims hear five times a day. It begins with the *takbīr,* "God is Great" *(Allāhu Akbar),* repeated three times, then the *shahādah* itself: "There is no God but God, and Muhammad is his messenger." In this way, the name of God is the first word the child hears, and then a chewed date is placed in the child's mouth, signaling the beginning of life outside the womb. Seven days later, many Muslims perform another ritual, *'aqīqah,* which gathers family and friends to welcome the new family member. At that ceremony, the parents usually name the child, who now has identity as a full member of the family and the community.[24]

Islam does not have an elaborate initiation rite at puberty, but many other religions do. In many of those ritualized transitions to adulthood, the young woman or young man has special power at the threshold moment, and moral codes and ritual prescriptions exhort community members to either approach or avoid the person—and objects associated with him or her. Among North American tribes, for example, pubescent Apache girls wear a copy of the beaded buckskin dress of White Painted Woman, the goddess of life who originally received the gift of menstruation, and the community aims to touch objects she has handled and eat foods she has blessed. In a slightly different Chinook rite, the menstruating daughter of the chief is hidden from the community and attended only by a postmenopausal woman. She engages in prolonged fasting and ritualized bathing, in a creek far from the village, and she is encouraged to keep her distance during this long transitional period: "She must never look at people. She must not look at the sky, she must not pick berries. It is forbidden. When she looks at the sky it becomes bad weather. When she picks berries it will rain." Other religious traditions include fewer prohibitions, but still mark the passage to adulthood, as with the Bar Mitzvah ceremony for thirteen-year-old Jewish boys. In the months before that ceremony, the boy masters the skills—including chanting the *Haftarah,* or selection from the Book of the Prophets—that prepares him to be an adult member of the community with the responsibility to observe the *Mitzvat,* or religious acts.[25]

The next major transition in that young man's life is marriage, and religions mark this transition too, by publicly sealing the union, establishing new kin relations, and constituting the new family. The Shintō wedding ceremony does all those things. That ceremony, which has long roots in indigenous and Chinese traditions but was not standardized until the twentieth century in Japan, invokes the *kami* as witnesses to the public ritual. As one recent version of the rite prescribes, the participants offer the *kami* food and sake, and the bride and groom take vows that bind them together: "Growing old together, until our hair is long and white, we have been caused to be tied." It also links them with the wider world: "So does our bond exist in the universe, just as the sun and moon exist in the heavens, just as the mountains and rivers exist on earth." Those natural bonds form social ones as well, reaffirming a lineage of ancestors and descendants:

> The connection to the ancestors is to be continued and not neglected. The family name should flourish, be highly respected and widely known. Our grandchildren and grandchildren should continue forever.

The Latter Day Saints (LDS), who dedicated a temple in Tokyo in 1980 and have built more than sixty others outside the United States, affirm the eternity of marriage in another way. According to LDS doctrine, Adam and Eve were given to each other in the Garden of Eden, at the culmination of God's creative process, and in a "celestial marriage" in the temple Mormon couples also make an eternal covenant with God, each other, and future generations, who will form a family in the celestial kingdom after the resurrection. The eternity of the couple's bonds is vividly symbolized by the mirrors on the opposite sides of the temple's celestial room: as they kneel to face each other across an altar in the middle of the room, the mirrors reflect an endless series of images of the couple, who will remain together after death.[26]

Even if the LDS couple will reunite in the celestial kingdom for all eternity, at some point they will die, and Mormonism, like other traditions, also propels adherents across that final threshold of the life cycle. The Latter Day Saint funeral serves several functions, as one church leader noted: "It helps console the bereaved and establishes a transition from mourning to the reality that we must move forward with life. Whether death is expected or a sudden shock, an inspirational funeral, where the doctrines of resurrection, the mediation of Christ, and certainty of life after death are taught strengthens those who must now move on with life." In turn, as ethnologist Louis-Vincent Thomas has proposed, most other funeral rites serve these same functions: (1) they preside over the future of the departed; (2) attend to the surviving close kin; and (3) revitalize the group, which has been disturbed by the death of one of its own. The community moves from disintegration to integration, the family moves from grief to acceptance, and the deceased moves from death to the afterlife.[27]

Even if they have served similar functions, rituals that mark the passing of the dead have varied widely across cultures, from a tenth-century Viking's conflagration in which the deceased, accompanied by a female slave, was burned along with his ship, to a contemporary American Catholic burial, which usually involves solitary interment in a coffin. As with the Scandinavian and American rites, funerals usually include multiple practices, from rites of separation to rites of integration. The community prepares, displays, and disposes of the corpse and then reintegrates the mourners as it replenishes the community and conveys the dead to another state or place. For example, separation from the dead and restoration of the community began for early-nineteenth-century Moravians, a Christian sect organized in 1457, when the *posaunenchor,* or trombone choir, played a hymn from the church's tower or entrance to announce the death. The hymn even identified the age, status, and gender of the deceased: "Hayn" meant it was a little boy, for example, and "Nassau" told the community a widow had passed on. The funeral service, which helped the family mourn and the community heal, provided more particulars about the departed, as it also reassured them about her ultimate fate. During that service, which included responsive reading and hymn singing, the minister read a memoir, the traditional Moravian biographical or autobiographical account of the deceased's life. Consider the memoir read aloud at the funeral of Susanna Zeisberger in 1824. The account, most of it in Zeisberger's German script and the rest finished after her death by an anonymous community member, recounted her birth in Lancaster, Pennsylvania, in 1744 and her marriage in 1781. Like other missionary-minded Moravians, soon after that "she embarked on a journey with her dear husband to Indian land," where they endured capture by "terrible savages" and enjoyed the kindness of her "faithful Indian Sisters" who slipped her food.

The anonymous narrator picks up the tale of terrestrial and corporeal crossings with her later years and last weeks, when she suffered from "a consumptive cough." Finally, at eighty years of age, she "blessedly went home." The next step in her "homeward journey"—and the community's reintegration—was the burial itself, when they interred Susanna's corpse in "God's Acre," the unadorned graveyard whose entrance bore an inscription attesting to the risen Christ's power over death and whose uniform marble gravestones signaled the deceased's spiritual equality before God.[28]

Moravian missionaries like Zeisberger have preached the gospel on the Indian subcontinent too, and the religious traditions that have flourished there have very different funeral rites. Sikh death rituals, for example, involve cremation—and a more elaborate series of separation and integration practices. The Sikhs, who predominate in the Punjab, imagine death using several different tropes: they say the deceased has finished her life span *(purā ho giyā)* or, employing metaphors about dwelling and crossing, they say the departed has taken abode in heaven *(surgwās ho giyā)* or completed the pilgrimage of this world *(sansār yātrā poori kar giyā)*. The pilgrimage to the next world begins with the ritual of *dharti te paunā,* lifting the corpse from the bed to the ground, which reconnects the deceased with *dharti-matā,* mother earth, and secures a more auspicious death. Then in a series of practices that constitute the funeral *(atam-sanskār)* they give the corpse a ritual bath, which purifies the body, thereby making it ready to be carried on the bier by the sons and brothers of the deceased. When the procession approaches the cremation ground, the chief mourner, the eldest son, makes a circle around the bier with water from an earthen pot, which he shatters on the ground to symbolize the release of the corpse's soul. Then the procession continues to the cremation ground, where they perform the ritual burning of the corpse *(agni-bhaint).* All that is left then is to restore the community and secure the fate of the deceased. If it was a father who died, the son receives the turban, symbol of household authority, at the ritual feast after the funeral, and, if it is in India, three days later the ashes are scattered in the sacred Ganges River, from where the deceased crosses beyond death's threshold.[29]

⤳ Compelled Passages and Constrained Crossings (Again)

Yet religions also compel and constrain corporeal crossings at transitions in the life cycle. The menstruating Chinook daughter must leave the village and cannot return until after a series of purification rites, and—as with a widow burning on her husband's funeral pyre in the Hindu practice of *satī*—though the surviving tenth-century account of the Viking funeral recounts that they asked for volunteers among the dead master's slaves, the slave's passing hardly seems voluntary. Usually the Muslim father—not the mother—whispers the *shahādah* in the newborn's ear, and the girl preparing for her Bat Mitzvah is exempted from some of the commandments required of her male counterpart after the Jewish puberty rite. Caste restrictions have prohibited lineage crossings in Hindu—and Sikh—marriages, and other prescribed codes and rituals enforce limits on sexuality as well as on marriage. Although temporary homosexuality occurs in some male and female puberty rites and gender inversion accompanies some communal festivals, religions often have prohibited sexual relations—and marital bonds—between those of the same gender or the same family. Other codes constrain and compel crossings at funeral rites. In the Sikh ritual, for example, women cannot carry the bier or enter the cremation ground.[30]

COSMIC CROSSINGS

Some Sikhs within and outside the cremation ground have imagined death as the completion of an earthly pilgrimage, and all religions propose that death is not a barrier but a transition. Not only do religions enable and constrain terrestrial and corporeal crossings, but they also permit and restrict other sorts of crossings. As I suggested in the last chapter, religions produce teleographies, representations of the end, the temporal and spatial limit of human life, the ultimate horizon. Those teleographies are cartographies of desire. They map what the religious want. What do they want? One Hindu account detailed the four "ends" of humans: they want to fulfill moral obligations *(dharma)*, secure material well-being *(artha)*, find sensual pleasure *(kāma)*, and achieve final liberation *(mokṣa)*. Yet there are many more ends, and even when traditions seem to agree—on liberation as a goal, for instance, among Indian religions—the religious differ about what that might entail. So no single or simple answer is possible. Religious women and men have wanted lots of things. The ends vary across cultures, among religions, within sects, and across the lifespan—and even from hour to hour. But a theory of religion—if it is to explain not just how religions function but why they manage their hold on people—must offer some account of what the religious want and what religions offer. The previous chapter offered a partial answer to that question: they want to find their own place. Like the displaced Cubans in Miami, humans don't have their bearings, and they want to be oriented in the body, the home, the homeland, and the cosmos. But we can say more, and here is where religion as *dwelling* meets religion as *crossing*. As I have suggested, the religious want to negotiate the limits of embodied existence, confronting suffering and intensifying joy—and traversing the stages of life. And the religious seek ways to imagine and realize the zenith of human flourishing, however that is conceived. They draw on tropes, artifacts, and rituals to produce teleographies, representations of the ultimate horizon and the means of crossing it.[31]

⤛ Transporting and Transforming Teleographies

There are two prominent types of religious teleographies, even if there is enormous variation within each type, most traditions include both, some individuals alternate between the two, and this typology fails to include some ways of imagining religious means and ends. These two

Table 5.1 A typology of religious teleographies.

	Transporting	Transforming
Horizon	Horizon as *boundary* between this world and another world.	Horizon as a personal or social limit or *limitation*.
Space	Focused more on the *home* and the *cosmos,* on domestic and cosmic space.	Focused more on the *body* and the *homeland,* on corporeal and social space.
Crossing	Crossing as change in *location:* ascent, descent, rebirth, encounter, communication.	Crossing as change in *condition:* insight, purification, healing, reform, revolution.

types—transporting teleographies and transforming teleographies—can be analyzed according to the horizon they imagine, the space they highlight, and the crossing they propose (see table).

As I noted in the last chapter, spiritual homemaking maps the farthest horizon of human existence, and *transporting* traditions imagine that horizon as a boundary between this world and another world. For the Hopi it is the boundary that separates them from the underworld, from which they emerged and where they will return. The Aztecs imagined an earthly realm separated from thirteen celestial and nine subterranean realms. For ancestor cults, like the Baktaman of New Guinea, it is the border between the realm of the living beings and the realm of absent spirits, as it is in different ways for traditions that highlight shamanism, spirit possession, or spirit mediumship, such as nineteenth-century American Spiritualism, which marked a line between this world and the "other world." For dualist traditions like Manichaeism, the horizon separates two eternal realms, matter and spirit, or the realm of light and the realm of darkness. For many monotheists—most Muslims and Christians, including Cuban Catholics at the shrine—it is the boundary between earth and heaven, however that celestial realm is imagined. Indian teleographies—Hindu, Jain, and Buddhist—often have imagined a boundary between the "near shore" and the "farther shore": the ultimate horizon is the division between the round of rebirths *(saṃsāra)* and the realm where those cosmic transmigrations—and all they bring—come to an end *(mokṣa).*[32]

Focused more on the body and the homeland than on the cosmos—and, so, more "this-worldly" in Weber's language—*transforming* teleographies imagine the ultimate horizon as a personal or social limit. Both teleographies can imagine the horizon as an individual or a collective end, and for transforming traditions that focus on the individual, the horizon is represented as an ideal personal condition: for example, insight, purity, or health. In Sōtō Zen, the horizon is a transforming insight into the true nature of things, just as it is in forms of Advaita Vedānta, and sometimes that insight concerns the past or the future, as in traditions, like the Yorùbá, that use divination practices. Humans in the Manichaean worldview are a mixture of light and darkness, and the first step to full flourishing, the liberation of the eternal soul, is an awakening of the *psuché* to its true divine origin in the realm of light. In healing cults, including some forms of religious Daoism, the horizon is health or longevity. In twelve-step programs, which can be quasi-religious, the horizon is some other form of mental or physical well-being: sobriety, for example. In clan traditions where spiritual or material pollution is a central concern, purity is the imagined personal horizon. Where the religious propose a collective end, the horizon can be imagined in a variety of ways. It can be the borders of the chosen land, as in some forms of Judaism; and, as with Cuban Catholics in Miami and other diasporic groups, it can be the boundaries of the homeland. With more or less abstract ends in mind, transforming teleographies can imagine the horizon as a collective condition—from shared prosperity to social justice—as with millennialist cargo cults and the Protestant Social Gospel—and a range of quasi-religious practices, including civil religion, environmental activism, and Marxist utopianism.[33]

Readers will have noticed that Cuban Catholics appeared in my discussion of both types of teleographies, and this signals that these ideal types do not mirror any particular tradition perfectly. Both modes often are found within the same religion. Most Cubans I interviewed at the shrine seemed more focused on the horizon as the shoreline of their island nation, but I encountered them at the shrine of their national patroness, and it seems natural that a collective transformative end predominated in our conversations. Yet when I talked long enough I also found—often when they mentioned illness or death—that they embraced a traditional Christian cosmography and eventually hoped to cross the boundary that separated them from a future life in heaven, which was usually, though not always, imagined as another cosmic realm.

So among Cuban Catholics—and many others—these two teleographies imagine different kinds of crossing, different paths to the religious end. All traditions seem to share—to use theorist Kenneth Surin's phrase—a "desire for the new." In one way or another, they presuppose that things as they are—or as they appear—are not all they could be. Seeking to heighten joy or ease suffering, they presuppose that some change is necessary. Transforming teleographies imagine religious crossing as a change in *condition:* it is personal insight, healing, or purification. *The Platform Sutra,* for example, champions wisdom or insight—"seeing into your own nature"—as the necessary transformation. Using meteorological tropes, the eighth-century Chan text attributed to Huineng compares the human condition to a cloudy day: "sun and moon are always bright, yet if they are covered by clouds" we cannot see the light. In a similar way, humans have "inherent enlightenment," and they must penetrate the clouds of delusion and awaken to their true nature as enlightened beings, or buddhas. Or, in other times and places, the cosmic crossing is a collective transformation that brings reform, uplift, revolution, and, in the end, more just and satisfying social relations, as with the Kingdom of God that some American Social Gospel Protestants and Latin American Catholic liberation theologians have hoped Jesus will inaugurate. For example, in his 1917 volume *A Theology for the Social Gospel,* the American Baptist theologian Walter Rauschenbusch imagined salvation as "the regeneration of the social order." It is "the necessity and the possibility of redeeming the historical life of humanity from the social wrongs which now pervade it."[34]

On the other hand, for transporting traditions cosmic crossing is imagined as a change in *location:* it is ascent or descent—or transversal movement across some border. It is rebirth in another realm, up or down, or it is an encounter or communication with supernatural agents or suprapersonal forces that inhabit some other celestial, terrestrial, or subterranean world. For the Inuit in Alaska it is passage to the land of the dead in the sky or in the sea; for Pure Land Buddhists in Japan it is rebirth in Amida's Western Paradise; and for the Yorùbá in western Africa it is transport to the good heaven *(orun rere)* to dwell among the ancestors. The Qur'án promises Muslims who traverse the "straight road" that they will be transported after death to 'Illiyyín, where they will enjoy a royal banquet and "laugh on couches," while at the day of reckoning *(yawm ad-dīn)* those who went astray will be transported to Jahím, where they will burn in its fire. Sister Susanna, the Moravian missionary remembered at the 1824 funeral, made "her homeward journey" to heaven, where "her redeemed soul went over into Jesus' arms and lap." And other Christians have used the journey metaphor to imagine the cosmic crossing, as with Bonaventure of Bagnoregio's thirteenth-century work, *The Mind's Road to God,* which charted the path to a mystical vision of the divine, and John Bunyan's seventeenth-century allegory, *The Pilgrim's Progress,* which traced the itinerary of Christian on his travel from the earthly realm to the celestial city.[35]

Relying on the journey metaphor but figuring it as aquatic passage rather than terrestrial travel, religions in India have emphasized the importance of *tīrthas,* a term that originally referred to a ford, or a place to cross a river. Extending the metaphor, some Hindus, Buddhists, and Jains have talked about crossing the river of existence, and those fords can be places, persons, or practices. So Hindus have imagined pilgrimage sites as *tīrthas,* places where a crossing occurs, just as gurus and devotional practices ferry the devotee across to the other shore. In Buddhism, the Buddha's *dharma,* or teaching, is the vehicle that carries the

22. Statues of the Twenty-Four Tīrthaṅkaras at Śatruñjaya, a Jain pilgrimage site above the town of Palitana in Gujarat, India, that includes 863 temples.

follower across, and even the body can function as a means of transport: for example, Śāntideva exhorted readers of his poetic reflection on the bodhisattva path, *Bodhicaryāvatāra,* to "take advantage of this human boat / free yourself from sorrow's stream," and the eighth-century Indian Buddhist hoped that "for those who want to go across the water" he could "be a boat, a raft, a bridge." Jains venerate twenty-four beings—the most recent is Nataputta Vardhamāna, known as Mahāvīra, who lived a little over 2,500 years ago in northern India—who have made the passage themselves and ferried others across, and the Jain tradition explicitly appeals to aquatic tropes by calling the venerated *tīrthaṅkaras,* because they establish *(kara)* the ford *(tīrtha)* to cross the river of rebirth and reach the other shore of liberation (Figure 22).[36]

→► Concealed Crossings

In this chapter I have analyzed terrestrial, corporeal, and cosmic crossings, and I hope the usefulness of the crossing metaphor seems clear in the interpretation of Muslim pilgrims, Shintō marriages, Sikh funerals, and Jain liberation. Those examples, and the others I have offered, seem to be about movement, about crossing of some sort. However, using one theorist—Bruno Latour—and two case studies—one Christian and one Buddhist—I want to suggest that the trope of crossing has even wider application in the study of religion, even with narratives, rituals, codes, and artifacts that are less obviously about movement.

Playing with the twin themes of *close* and *distant,* Bruno Latour's Templeton Lecture, "Another Take on the Science and Religion Debate," opens ways of talking about religion that, with some revision, can interpret these more subtle dynamics. Religions don't transfer information, Latour suggests; they transport persons. So the "conditions of felicity" for religious language, the grounds on which one might say it is "true," require that religious speech-acts produce new states that make the distant close. Drawing on analogies with lovers' talk and emphasizing the Roman Catholic doctrine of transubstantiation, the notion that the consecrated host embodies the "real presence" of Christ, Latour suggests that religions do not deal with *the beyond,* as most interpreters suggest. *The near* is religion's domain. "Religion does not even attempt to race to know the beyond, but attempts at breaking all habits of thoughts that direct our attention to the far away, to the absent, to the overworld, in order to bring attention back to the incarnate, the renewed presence of what was before misunderstood." Religious speech-acts initiate movement "which aims at jumping, dancing towards the present and the close, to redirect attention away from indifference and habituation, to prepare oneself to be seized again by this presence that breaks the usual, habituated passage of time." And *truth* in this context means the ability to mediate between the distant and the near, the past and the present. Emphasizing the "flowing character" of religious language, action, and artifact, Latour suggests that "freeze framing, isolating a mediator out of its chains, out of its series, instantly forbids the meaning to be carried in truth." "Truth," he continues, "is not to be found in correspondence—either between the word and the world in the case of science or between the original and the copy in the case of religion—but in taking up again the task of continuing the flow of prolongating the cascade of mediations one step further." So religions, analogized as rivers or waterfalls, generate and sustain a "cascade" of mediators that transform persons as they bring close what was imagined as distant.[37]

Latour gets religion moving, but we can accelerate and multiply the movements even more. His account needs one more nudge, since religions don't only dwell in presence and bring the distant near. He commits one of the sins he chiseled onto his own tablet of prohibitions: Latour "freeze frames" religious movements. Religions bring the distant close, as he suggests, but they are flows that also propel adherents back and forth between the close and the distant. Religions move between what is imagined as the most distant horizon and what is imagined as the most intimate domain. To use traditional Christian language, they travel vertically back and forth between transcendence and immanence. They bring the gods to earth and transport the faithful to the heavens. And they move horizontally, back and forth in social space. The religious also are propelled through time, allowing travel among imagined pasts, presents, and futures. As itinerants, the religious never remain anywhere or anytime for long. It is in this sense, I suggest, that religions are flows, translocative and transtemporal crossings.

Let me illustrate those crossings, and extend the usefulness of this trope for the study of religion, by interpreting a Christian artifact and a Buddhist narrative that don't seem to have much to do with crossing. First, consider an artifact that Latour interprets in his Templeton Lecture: Fra Angelico's "The Resurrection of Christ and the Women at the Tomb," a fifteenth-century fresco he painted, with the assistance of an apprentice, in the convent of San Marco, Florence (Figure 23). The image does not approximate multiple-exposure photography's capturing

23. Fra Angelico, "The Resurrection of Christ and the Women at the Tomb," 1440–41. Fresco, 189 × 164 cm, on the wall of cell 8 at the Convento di San Marco, Florence.

of movement, or even Marcel Duchamp's *Nude Descending a Staircase,* which puts Cubist cartography in motion. There are few overt signs of movement in the Dominican friar's painting of Christ's empty tomb: the heavenly messenger points, and the four women gathered at the tomb gesture in ways that indicate surprise or disappointment or awe. Yet as Latour suggests, there is redirection going on in this representation of a scene from the Gospel of Mark. Note that "the angel's finger points to an apparition of the resurrected Christ which is not directly visible to the women because it shines in their back." As the passage from Mark's Gospel suggests, the fresco nudges viewers to find presence amid absence:

> As they entered the tomb, they saw a young man [a heavenly messenger], dressed in a white robe, sitting on the right side; and they were alarmed. But he said to them, "Do not be alarmed; you are looking for Jesus of Nazareth, who was crucified. He has been raised; he is not here. Look, there is the place they laid him. But go, tell his disciples and Peter that he is going ahead of you to Galilee; there you will see him, just as he told you."[38]

In an indirect way, the image, which would have been in conversation with the scriptural passage for many fifteenth-century Christian viewers, transports the women (and the viewers) to Galilee, where Jesus awaits them all. Yet even more prominent in the fresco, the large and central image of the risen Christ is the elephant in the room. It is the presence misread as absence. This hovering image brings the divine close, and transports pious viewers—since there seems little immediate hope for the women, who persist in their inattention—to the here and now. As Latour proposes, the visual redirects viewers: "there is nothing to see *there*, but you should look *here* through the inward eye of piety to what this fresco is supposed to mean: elsewhere, not in a tomb, not among the dead but among the living."[39]

And I would suggest that the painting can move viewers in other ways, and not only by stirring affect. The image directs viewers out from the empty tomb to find the sacred among the living, in Galilee and everywhere else, but viewers also cross back and forth, as their attention shifts—to the hovering Christ, to the alarmed women below, to the angel's finger pointing upward, back to the Christ again, and then to the apparent absence that surrounds the viewers themselves. There in the cavernous emptiness, the image invites them to ask: where can I find the risen Christ? It transports them across social space to seek him among others outside the tomb, and—with Christ's apparition chastising them for their inattention—the fresco brings viewers back to the here and now to seek presence in absence.

Consider another religious trace that illumines concealed crossings, even if at first it also might seem to have little to say about movement of any kind. It is a narrative from the *Mumonkan,* a thirteenth-century collection of forty-eight cases (Chinese: *gong'an;* Japanese: *kōan*) edited by a Chinese Chan master in the Song Dynasty and used for generations in ritual settings, the private interviews with teachers, as a tool for understanding reality as it is. This *kōan* recounts an encounter between the Tang Dynasty Chan master Zhaozhou Congshen, or Joshu in Japanese, and a monk who came to him one day for advice about how to attain enlightenment:

> Once a monk made a request of Joshu. "I have entered the monastery," he said. "Please give me instructions, Master." Joshu said, "Have you had your breakfast?" "Yes, I have," replied the monk. "Then," said Joshu, "wash your bowls." The monk had an insight.[40]

There has been a great deal of commentary on this enigmatic story, but most interpretations point to the ways that the *kōan,* as Latour might say, redirects the monk's attention from absence to presence, from the distant to the near. It transports the earnest monk to where he already is. Seeking a distant state, he gazes upward and outward. Yet the Chan teacher's response propels him back toward the here and now. As one Japanese interpreter, Zenkei Shibayama, suggested in a lecture *(teisho),* the conclusion of the narrative—"the monk had an insight"—documents the monk's transformative redirection. "His spiritual eye was opened to the fact that it is as it is—that he, as he is, is 'it'; that 'it' cannot be outside himself. Once having awakened, he has always been 'it.' Essentially he has always been 'it,' the Truth. His walking, standing, or sitting are nothing but 'it.' "[41]

As I have noted, there is a long tradition in Chan Buddhism of emphasizing that all beings have Buddha-nature, original enlightenment, so to look outside the self is silly, even if you are seeking human or suprahuman exemplars of wisdom and compassion, buddhas and bodhisattvas. Explaining the source of most spiritual confusion, the Chinese Chan teacher Linji, who founded the lineage that came to emphasize *kōan* practice, put it this way in one lecture attributed to him: "When students today fail to make progress, where's the fault? The fault lies in the fact that they don't have faith in themselves! . . . But if you can just stop this mind that goes rushing around looking for something, then you'll be no different from the patriarchs and buddhas. Do you want to get to know the patriarchs and buddhas? They're none other than you, the people standing in front of me listening to this lecture on the Dharma!" Just as Linji tried to redirect and transport his monastic students, so the *kōan* of Joshu's Bowl enacts a movement. It shifts devotees from there to here. It says: what you seek is not distant or outside yourself. It is close. It is *here*. However—and here Latour's theoretical vision reaches its interpretive limits—the monk requires the redirecting response from the master, and subsequent adherents need to hear the narrative again and again, because they don't spend much time *here*. If they ever manage it temporarily and partially, they always slip back to *there*. If not, why would subsequent generations need to ponder this *kōan,* and others, again and again? The religious not only need to be propelled to imagined pasts and desired futures, they need to be called back, summoned to the present. Narratives, rituals, codes, and artifacts do that. In the Linji Chan tradition, that is also what *kōan* practices do. But to remain where the story of Joshu positions hearers, fixed in the here and now of enlightened *presence,* is to "freeze frame" the dynamics of religion in practice, which always shifts back and forth in time and space. The sweet torture that some mystics have reported—that the transforming and transporting presence never lasts—is a shared fate. Immanence is no less fleeting than transcendence. Like the shimmering divine presence barely noticed and then forgotten in Fra Angelico's fresco, the "insight" pursued in Chan stories doesn't bring rest for long. Religions' translocative and transtemporal work is never done. The religious, even in these and other less obvious ways, are on the move. Whether lamenting at Christ's empty tomb or carrying the monk's breakfast bowl, in pilgrimage and in marriage, and as they traverse the ultimate horizon of human life, the devout are crossing.[42]

CONCLUSION

An Itinerary

As with other travelers on other roads, all that's left of this theoretical itinerancy is to return where I started and ask what all this moving around has meant. As I noted in Chapter 1, the Greek term *theōria* originally signified travel. In turn, theory, I suggested, is an *itinerary* in all three senses of that term: a proposal for a journey, a representation of a journey, and the journey itself. With this itinerancy planned and completed, like Bashō who left accounts of his travels, I want to conclude by offering a representation, a positioned sighting of where I've been. First, before I can offer some suggestions about the meaning and value of this theoretical wandering, I return to a fundamental issue I addressed in Chapter 1: how do we assess the adequacy of this theory, or any theory, for the interpretation of religion in varied cultural contexts? Second, I return to the scene at the annual festival in Miami that prompted my journey—to see what this theory illumines and what it obscures. Finally, I consider the implications of the theory for the study and teaching of religion. In a sense, then, I conclude by proposing other routes in the study and the classroom.

ASSESSING THEORY'S INTERPRETIVE POWER

This theory does not try to formulate universally applicable laws or trace religion's historical origin. Unlike some other understandings of theory, it does not aim at explanation or prediction. It does not claim to offer an omnispective mirroring—a god's-eye view—of the fixed religious landscape. Instead, it offers an interpretation, a positioned sighting of the shifting terrain, a situated account of the complex ways that women and men have negotiated meaning and power through religions. The locative approach I have advocated suggests that even if all theories have blind spots, there are more or less acceptable interpretations, where acceptable means internally coherent and contextually useful. In other words, claims made in one place should not conflict with claims made elsewhere, and we can appeal to professional obligations and pragmatic criteria to assess this theory of religion.[1]

Although I hope that by including a wide range of examples in Chapters 4 and 5 I have persuaded readers of the theory's potential interpretive reach, a final pragmatic assessment of this theory as a tool for the analysis of religion in other times and places cannot be made in advance. Time will tell. Readers will decide. From my point of view, this theory, like others, will prove to be adequate if it meets important professional obligations and relevant pragmatic standards. Among the kinds of questions we might ask of the theory are the following: Does it mark the boundaries of religion, distinguishing it from other cultural trajectories and, thereby, helping scholars to meet their role-specific obligation to reflect on their field's constitutive term? Does it nudge scholars to be more self-conscious about their own position and more modest about the claims they make on the basis of their positioned sightings? Does it encourage scholars to ask generative questions about the people and practices they study? Does it redirect scholars' attention to themes and issues that had been obscured by other theories and, so, promote richer and more complicated accounts? In particular, does it encourage greater attention to the relational dynamics of religion in this era of transnational flows? Are those on the move—including migrants, pilgrims, and missionaries—easier to notice? Religious women have been crossing and dwelling, and we can ask if this theory proves to be helpful in recognizing and interpreting the religious practices of women, who have been marginalized or ignored in some other theories. Does my analysis of the ways that religions orient individuals and groups in four chronotopes allow scholars to attend more fully to sites such as the body and the home, and does the focus on the homeland lead interpreters to reaffirm the importance of the links between religion and collective identity? Does my discussion of forced and constrained crossings help to analyze some of the complex ways that power is at work in the practice of religion? Does my typology of religious teleographies offer insights, and point to unexpected continuities and discontinuities, as scholars consider the multiple ways the religious have imagined the ultimate horizon of human life? Does this theory avoid essentialist notions of what religious traditions are and provide a lexicon that allows interpreters to talk meaningfully about the hybrid products of transcultural contacts and exchanges? Finally, in my view, this theory will be useful if it sparks more conversations and generates other accounts—even, or especially, accounts that challenge this one.

You might already be provisionally persuaded that the theory seems internally coherent and contextually useful, but if you are not yet convinced, no final assessment of the theory's interpretive reach seems possible in advance of scholars' attempts to employ it in the study of the religious practices of women and men in varied cultural contexts. This does not mean, however, that we can say nothing at this point about the meaning and value of this theoretical itinerancy. By returning to the annual festival in Miami that prompted the journey, we can ask what interpretive work the theory can do in the analysis of those particular religious practices. We can ask what it illumines and what it obscures. That, in turn, might offer some hints about its potential uses—and limits—in other cultural contexts.

DWELLING AND CROSSING AT THE ANNUAL FESTIVAL

In Chapter 3 I defined religions as "confluences of organic-cultural flows that intensify joy and confront suffering by drawing on human and suprahuman forces to make homes and cross boundaries." I think this definition—and the tropes it draws on and the theory inscribed in it—can provide a coherent and useful interpretation of the feast-day celebration. Along the way, I have referred to examples of Cuban Catholic piety in Miami, and I won't repeat all that here. It might be helpful, however, to give evidence of the definition's usefulness by briefly applying it—phrase by phrase—to interpret the annual festival, highlighting the two primary tropes of my theory—dwelling and crossing (see Figure 1).

→→ Positioned Sightings
Confluences of organic-cultural flows. In the broadest sense, the metaphor of flow—and the concomitant talk about confluence and transfluence—captures the movement, and movements, that I first noticed that night in Miami: not only the exiles' migration to America and the Virgin's boat ride to the mass but also the devotees waving handkerchiefs, lifting children, and carrying Mary. The metaphor also captures the bonds across the generations and the links between Miami and Havana. And there were other sorts of relations. The confluence of tropes, artifacts, narratives, and institutions that produced the practices at the annual rite also led to the spiritual hybridity there, as devotion to Ọṣun mixed with veneration of Mary and the centuries-old exchange between Afro-Cuban Santería and Spanish Roman Catholicism continued, even if the clerical officials and the sponsoring institution, the Archdiocese of

Miami, tried to map the boundaries of orthodoxy and orthopraxy. But religions were not the only cultural currents crossing: the aquatic metaphors also point to the ways that religion mixed with politics and economy, other transfluvial currents, at the annual festival and at the Miami shrine, as devotees petitioned Mary to restore democracy and capitalism on the island.

Intensify joy and confront suffering. As the weeping of devotees around me signaled—including the woman who sobbed in Spanish "We need her to save Cuba"—when devotees prayed to Our Lady of Charity to restore democracy and capitalism in Cuba they also confronted the suffering of dislocation and longed for the joy of restoration. Less focused on the limits of embodied existence like disease and death—at least at the feast-day rite and at the shrine rituals—the displaced community turned to religion to make sense of what they understood as moral evil: the exile from the island and the separation from family members who remained. The trope of exile provided the idiom for expressing their longing as well as their sadness, as the "Libre '94" in yellow flowers signaled their hope that the island would be liberated in the coming year. And this part of my definition acknowledges the role of emotion, which was so important in the diasporic religion of Cuban migrants in South Florida.

Human and suprahuman forces. The feast-day rosary and mass included the usual references to the Christian Trinity—including Christ's embodied presence in the Eucharist—but most of those I spoke with in the crowd that night, and other nights, turned to another suprahuman force, Mary, for intervention. That appeal to Our Lady of Charity—and the imagining of an ultimate horizon—distinguished the practices at the festival from those at a political rally or an economic summit, even if politics and economy intertwined at the celebration that September night. So this theory provides a theoretical lexicon that acknowledges many of the interests at work in the Cuban diaspora's piety while still drawing some boundaries, however fluid, around the religious.

To make homes. Religions, I proposed, are about dwelling, and that trope not only makes sense of the shrine's consecration, as I argued in Chapter 4, but it helps to interpret the feast-day ritual. As watch and compass, Cubans' transtemporal and translocative practices provide orientation. They mark the ritual calendar—not only setting aside times to celebrate Jesus' birth, death, and resurrection but also marking September 8 as the time to gather each year to venerate Our Lady of Charity. That veneration at the feast-day rite also includes retrospective and prospective practices that imagine a distant past and a desired future: they sang a hymn, "La Virgen Mambisa," that recalled Our Lady of Charity's role in the nineteenth-century wars for independence, and, as I have noted, the "Libre '94" inscribed in yellow flowers, the Virgin's color, called on the national patroness to protect the exiles and transform the homeland. As compass, Cuban Catholicism not only marked bodies—for example, the traditional white *guayabera* shirts of the men in the confraternity and the yellow blouses of many women in the crowd—but also positioned devotees in another chronotope, the homeland. Using autocentric and allocentric reference frames, embodied practices at the rite, including the waving of the Cuban flag and the singing of the Cuban national anthem, positioned them near the patroness and north of the island.

Cross boundaries. Religion at the shrine was not only about being in place; it was about moving across, and Cuban American piety prescribed and proscribed different kinds of crossing—terrestrial, corporeal, and cosmic. Even if religious flows crossed with other transfluvial currents in the migration from the island, biblical tropes like *exile* named their terrestrial crossings by plane, ship, and even raft. From the nuns of the Apostolate of the Sacred Heart of Jesus who arrived on a

Pan Am flight from Havana to Miami in 1961 to the *balseros* who made the perilous passage by sea in later years, many of the Miami exiles claimed that the Virgin safeguarded them on their journey (see Figure 19). Even if the usual rites of passage—baptisms, marriages, and funerals—are prohibited at the shrine, the Virgin also prompted some corporeal crossings, as when mothers prayed to Our Lady of Charity, or *Ọṣun*, the patroness of childbirth, for help in conceiving or aid in giving birth, and some of the younger devotees in the crowd were initiated into the community when parents formally presented them to the Virgin as an infant. Although there are no funerals at the shrine, the names of many of the older devotees at the festival also would be read aloud from the shrine's altar when they died. Finally, the Cubans' piety envisioned an ultimate horizon and a way to cross it, and both types of cosmic crossing were imagined by those at the feast-day ritual. When they prayed to "Our Father, who art in heaven"—and at other points during the mass that night—Cuban migrants reaffirmed a traditional Christian cosmography and teleography, as they imagined salvation as transport to another realm. They also imagined salvation as a transformation, a change in their collective condition: again referring to biblical narrative, they compared themselves to the Jews who yearned to be delivered from bondage and conveyed to the Promised Land. At the annual festival, the thousands of devotees in the crowd responded to the priest's chant of "¡Viva la Virgen de Caridad!" by shouting in unison "Salva a Cuba." It was Cuba too that needed saving, and for that saving they appealed to the national patroness, a *tīrthaṅkara* or ford-maker who had traveled the seas and established a crossing place. Sometimes, however, terrestrial and corporeal crossings at the festival and the shrine were constrained. The clergy on the altar during the feast-day mass were men, while Catholic women were prohibited from crossing those social boundaries and pursuing ordination to the priesthood. And because of U.S. travel and trade restrictions and Cuban economic hardships and political practices, Cubans on both sides of the Straights of Florida felt constrained in their movements. So did some Afro-Cuban followers of

Santería, who sensed some easing of the constraints at the feast-day celebration, where clergy on the altar could not enforce orthodoxy or orthopraxis as effectively, but they still did not feel completely at home at the shrine's public rituals.[2]

✦ Blind Spots: Two or Three Things I Don't Know

In calling attention to these constrained and enabled crossings—and all the rest—this account of religion seems more useful than I might have hoped for at that festival in 1993 when I began searching for alternative theories. Yet this theory, like other theories, obscures some things as it illumines others. Purposeful wandering is not omninavigation, and positioned sightings aren't omnispection. This theoretical itinerancy has taken me only so far, and I can see only so much. There are blind spots. Interpreters who use this theory to make sense of religious practices I have not analyzed in this book—and some that I have—will discover for themselves its uses and its limits. But it even obscures some things at the festival and the shrine. The distinguished anthropologist Marshall Sahlins once published a piece called "Two or Three Things I Know about Culture." Playing with that title and focusing on just one phrase in my definition—"confluences of organic-cultural flows"—let me briefly consider two or three things I *don't* know about religion: two or three places where sightings come to end, where a cloud of wind and sand blows up along the path.[3]

First, what kind of flows do we mean, and if we take this metaphor seriously what are the methodological implications for the study of religion? In Chapter 3, I proposed that scholars use aquatic metaphors and imagine their work as analogous to those who study fluid mechanics, applying what Gilles Deleuze and Félix Guattari called a "hydraulic model" from the "itinerant, ambulant sciences." As with scientists who study hydrodynamics, interpreters of religion should "follow a flow in a vectorial field." But what sort of "flows" are religions, and what does it mean to "follow" those flows? If we choose aquatic tropes over others, and lean on the analogies with categories and methods from fluid mechanics and geophysics, what are the limits and benefits of moving toward a hydrodynamics of religion? Are religious flows, imagined as streams of water, uniform in velocity, volume, and direction? Depending on the trajectory of religious streams and the converging force of transfluvial currents—politics, economy, and so on—are they alternately like the curl of an oceanic wave, the drift of a bending river, and the ripples in a rocky creek? Are religious flows sometimes like surface turbulence or faucet drippings, to mention two examples that physicists and mathematicians have pondered a great deal, and so are they chaotic systems that are "sensitive to initial conditions," including their initial geographical location and historical context? And if religious flows are nonlinear systems, like heart rhythms or faucet drippings, does that mean that the only appropriate aim is interpretation, not prediction or control, as some scholars who have pondered the implications of chaos theory for the humanities and social sciences have argued? If so, exactly what would that interpretation entail, for example, in historical analysis? David Ruelle, the mathematical physicist, has argued that it means historians need to note that "some historically unpredictable events or choices have important long-term consequences." Yet as another scholar has suggested, tracing those events and choices might leave interpreters in a "morass of causes." To put it in my terms, if we try to trace the complex flows that emerge from "initial conditions," will interpreters be washed away while trying to chart the transfluence of innumerable causal currents?[4]

To illustrate some of the challenges of enacting this sort of interpretive hydraulics, how might we analyze the 1973 consecration of the Miami shrine to Our Lady of Charity? What were the initial conditions that exerted disproportionate influence, and how would we follow the flow of those forces? Would that tracing of flows lead us back to the interplay of psychological forces in Fidel Castro's childhood home on a sugar plantation near Biran, the political interests that shaped nineteenth-century Spanish (and American) struggles in the Cuban battle for independence, or economic forces at work in the seventeenth century among the royal slaves who worked in the copper mines of El Cobre, where Afro-Cubans first venerated Our Lady of Charity on the island? Or further back still: to the western coast of Africa, where slaves first boarded ships bound for Cuba in the early sixteenth century, or to the medieval Mediterranean world as Marian devotion took shape? Which flows should the interpreter follow, and if the answer is all of them, and more, then would that ever allow analysis of more than a single event, and even then only with the sense that surely we have missed some of the transverse currents that have propelled religious history? It's hard to know where such an interpretation would begin and end.[5]

It's also hard to know where nature ends and culture begins. I have talked about "organic-cultural" flows, but sightings seem to come to an end, and other questions arise, there on the hyphen. In Chapter 3, I addressed this issue. I suggested that religions emerge from the interaction of constraining organic channels and shifting cultural currents. I proposed that religions are processes in which social institutions (the shrine's confraternity) bridge organic constraints (hippocampal neural pathways and episodic memory processes) and cultural mediations (the symbol of Mary and the metaphor of exile) to produce reference frames (the Cuban American community as diaspora and the shrine as diasporic center) that orient devotees in time and space. Those reference frames yield a wide range of verbal and nonverbal representations that, in turn, are institutionally, ritually, and materially transmitted— and enfolded back into the complex biocultural process. In the next chapter, on the kinetics of dwelling, I considered some of the neurophysiological processes involved in human perception and representation of time and space, as I discussed religion's function as watch and compass. And I earlier endorsed Clifford Geertz's suggestion that the most we can say is that mind and culture are "reciprocally constructive."[6]

Maybe that's as far as our sightings can go. We may just have to get used to those blind spots and adjust our vision accordingly, but I would not dismiss the possibility that we might come to see and say more about the interplay of organic and cultural processes in religion—and not just about temporal and spatial representation. How do the dynamics there on the hyphen of nature-culture affect the kinetics of dwelling and crossing? Can further study teach us more about the neurophysiological processes at work as religions confront suffering and enhance joy and as devotees attempt to overcome illness and traverse the other limits of embodied existence? How do biological developmental processes across the lifespan converge with mediating cultural forces in religious affect, cognition, and practice among children, adolescents, and the aged? How are organic processes at work in the ways humans have imagined the ultimate horizon and the ways of crossing it? As some have suggested, are human brains inclined to posit minimally counterintuitive suprahuman agents who inhabit other domains? There has been research that bears on these and other questions at the hyphen, but my theory does not go much farther than gesturing toward those answers, even if it does reserve a place for more questions and answers about the transfluence of nature-culture.

Even if we attend to those organic-cultural flows, the agency of individuals seems to be lost amid the flow of impersonal biological and social forces—to mention a third theoretical blind spot. Consider one example. We can remain sensitive to the ways that clerical roles have been overemphasized in Catholic historiography and still argue that Bishop Agustín Román, the exiled Cuban priest who founded the shrine and directed it for three decades, had more to do with the diasporic piety practiced there than anyone else, and maybe as much influence as those biological, political, economic, and religious flows I keep talking about (Figure 24). Soon after his appointment as shrine director in 1967, Román labored to get a provisional chapel erected. With that small worship space secured, the next year he organized the Confraternity of Our Lady of Charity, the lay organization that would support the work of the shrine. He spent hours and hours calling Cubans on the phone, adding names to the shrine's directory, until it had tens of thousands of

24. Auxiliary Bishop Agustín Román, who enters behind the Cuban flag and six young women representing the six Cuban provinces, blesses the crowd at the feast-day mass in Miami in 2003.

names. At his invitation, those devotees came to the shrine for weekday masses and Sunday romerías, and it was Román who made the choice to organize devotions at the shrine according to the geography of the homeland, so that all former residents of the same town in Cuba returned to the shrine on the same weekday evening for a mass and all those from the same province returned for a Sunday rosary and procession. He also oversaw the fund-raising, design, and construction of the shrine. He worked with the muralist who painted the history of Cuba on the interior wall and consulted with the architect who placed the six-sided cornerstone, which mapped the provincial landscape of the homeland, beneath the altar. Yet in all my talk about the confluence and transfluence of flows, Bishop Román's decisive role might be obscured.[7]

There are ways to correct for this sort of impaired interpretive vision, even if blind spots always remain, and this theory, with its aquatic and spatial metaphors, still illumines much more than it obscures. We can try to say more about what the hydraulics of religion might look like, remain open to new ways of imagining the interplay of nature and culture, and seek to reaffirm the role of personal agency in the kinetics of religious dwelling and crossing. On the last issue, for example, we might try to expand the theoretical lexicon in ways that highlight individual agency and collective action in dwelling and crossing by talking about religious homemakers and ford-makers. So, to use U.S. examples, the Puritan John Winthrop was a homemaker as he led the band of seventeenth-century Protestant migrants to settle the Massachusetts Bay Colony, imagined as a "city on a hill," and Martin Luther King was a ford-maker, or *tīrthaṅkara*, when he turned to religious tropes, institutions, and practices to peacefully agitate for passage across social boundaries during the civil rights movement of the mid-twentieth century. Like these leaders, religious founders such as the originator of Christian Science, Mary Baker Eddy, not only discovered crossing places but also generated new streams to cross. To take the metaphor further, they were eddies—pun intended—or divergent currents that, in turn, were swirled by transfluvial forces. In that sense, Eddy, King, Winthrop—and Román too—functioned as headwaters, the source and upper end of a religious stream. They propelled and redirected devotees through the crisscrossing fissures in the cultural terrain, creating new beds and streams as they went. And to shift the aquatic image again, like aquifers, long after the spiritual flows they propelled had seeped down into subterranean cultural basins, so deep no one seemed to notice anymore, the residue of their efforts conducted groundwater that would surface again in new springs, some of which would emerge as new headwaters.[8]

If you squirm a bit at this extended play with aquatic tropes—and I might have been carried away by the flow of metaphors—I hope you concur with my main points here: that theories always obscure some things as they illumine others; that there are ways of trying to adapt to the blind spots that come with any theoretical sighting; and that my own theory illumines more than it obscures. My definition—and the tropes that inform it and the theory embedded in it—illumines much of what I encountered at the feast-day celebration and the shrine, as I have suggested in this conclusion and throughout this book. This definition provides language to talk about displacement and emplacement, the central themes in the lives of Cuban Americans at the shrine. It acknowledges the prominent role of emotions in diasporic piety, and it highlights the functions of tropes—the metaphor of exile and the symbol of the Virgin—that have been so important in how devotees in Miami have constructed their collective identity. It allows the interpreter to consider negotiations for power as well as meaning as religion constrains as well as enables crossings of all sorts. It provides an idiom to notice the complicated interreligious exchanges on the island and in exile, and it illumines the place of politics in piety, while still marking religion's boundaries.

If you are persuaded that all of this is true, it should not surprise you that this theory of religion as crossing and dwelling makes sense of Cuban American devotion to Our Lady of Charity, since it is a positioned sighting from the festival and the shrine—just as all theories of religion have been positioned sightings, whether or not scholars have acknowledged that. Yet as I tried to suggest by appealing to examples from many other times and places, I think the theory does not only illumine what I encountered at the Miami shrine and the feast-day rite. Even if blind spots remain, and a final pragmatic assessment will have to await attempts to apply the theory more widely, I think it might prove to be useful in the interpretation of religion elsewhere. From the arrangement of domestic spaces in the Baktaman ancestor cult in New Guinea to the Jain veneration of the *tīrthaṅkaras* at a pilgrimage temple above the town of Palitana in Gujarat, I have proposed, religions are about the kinetics of homemaking and itinerancy. They are about dwelling and crossing.

DWELLING AND CROSSING IN THE STUDY AND THE CLASSROOM

The tropes of dwelling and crossing, also have even wider application. They are useful for imagining the study and teaching of religion, and other fields in the humanities and social sciences. In the classroom and the study, scholars are dwelling-in-crossing and crossing-in-dwelling. Returning to my analysis of theorizing in Chapter 1 and extending my analysis of religion in Chapters 4 and 5, I suggest that interpretation and pedagogy are about being in place and moving across.

⤞ Pedagogy as Turning Back and Moving Across

In teaching, as in research, the first step is reflexive positioning. The word *reflexive* means "turning back"; it is a turning back to the self and, I would add, to the community. When instructors are at their best, they acknowledge where they are. In the classroom—when teaching an introductory course, for example—this means relating the categories, issues, and approaches of the field to those of other fields in the university. It means saying something about the place of religious studies in the mission of the university, the aims of general education, and the goals of the liberal arts. This entails more than meeting the role-specific obligation to be clear about the meaning of the field's constitutive term—though it means that too. It means self-consciously acknowledging how different approaches from the humanities and social sciences—and, in some instances, the natural sciences—might lead to different accounts of what we're studying. For example, a class session on Malcolm X's autobiographical narrative of his conversion to the Nation of Islam and pilgrimage to Mecca, which I mentioned in the last chapter, might focus on literary tropes, psychological development, historical context, gender relations, urban geography, neurological processes, economic forces, and racial codes. Not all approaches will get equal time, of course, but students need to have some sense of how the instructor's approach compares with those that other scholars might take on the same topic. To revise a famous line from Max Müller, who said that he who knows only one religion knows none: the student who knows only one approach knows none.[9]

Pedagogical positioning also involves being clear about the local terrain, the students' backgrounds, and the teacher's location. If teaching, like research, offers a positioned sighting, local history and institutional ethos matter. Teaching about Cuban Catholics at a private university in Miami, a multilingual city where Cubans predominate, is not the same as teaching about it in Chapel Hill, and teaching southern undergraduates about slave religion in a public university building named after a KKK supporter changes the context of the conversation in some ways. The instructor's own social location—gender, class, race, faith, and family—also shapes what happens in the classroom, and this should be acknowledged where and when it is institutionally appropriate and pedagogically useful. However, selective and strategic bracketing of the instructor's own position sometimes can be very effective in encouraging students to arrive at their own conclusions about the subject at hand. For example, if I reveal that my mother was in a convent for a year before she married—that's true—it shapes how students interpret my in-class comments about Cuban Catholicism, and it influences how they understand my comments about those Cuban nuns getting off the plane in Miami. Making decisions about how much to say about local history, institutional context, and personal location can be difficult, and those decisions turn, in part, on judgments about the students. And pedagogy as dwelling means doing all that is possible—and it's a challenge in a large lecture hall—to know the students. Some relevant information is available from the admissions office—the demographic profile, regional distribution, and test scores of the entering class. Teachers gain some of it in before-class banter and office-hour conversations. Some of it remains inaccessible, no matter how hard instructors work at it.[10]

Yet teaching at its best means finding students where they are, and in that sense, and other senses, pedagogy is also about moving across. Although instructors never have final or complete success, they try to imaginatively transport themselves to the chairs around the seminar table and the inclined rows of seats in the lecture hall. And teaching involves other sorts of crossings: it means—to appeal to an overused phrase—"active learning," students engaged in the making and sharing of knowledge, thereby crossing the line between learner and teacher. It also means traversing other boundaries, since teaching and learning in the humanities and social sciences involve transtemporal and translocative movements. In a process that is as intellectually challenging as it is morally urgent, undergraduates imaginatively move across the classroom's threshold to understand other ways of being human. They travel to other cultures and periods. To appeal to an aphorism by the eighteenth-century German writer Novalis, humanities and social science education—and the study of religion in particular—makes the familiar strange and the strange familiar. It exoticizes the near and familiarizes the distant. That means, for example, making Cuban Catholic piety strange for the descendants of Cuban migrants in a Miami classroom and making it familiar for African American Baptist undergraduates in Chapel Hill. It means making Islam strange for Iranian American students in Los Angeles and making it familiar for white Protestant evangelicals in Dallas. When it's effective, teaching—and learning—means moving back and forth between the familiar and the strange, and the familiarization of the other generates a limited but transformative empathy, which is one mark of the educated person, the humane neighbor, and the effective citizen. Teaching—and learning—is transport that transforms.[11]

➤➤ Interpretation as Turning Back and Moving Across
Religious studies scholars' role-specific obligations include commitments to research as well as to teaching, and in doing research they also are always in place and always in transit. They are dwelling and crossing.

As I have stressed throughout, theories are positioned sightings, and so are other forms of interpretation—literary, historical, psychological, sociological, archeological, and ethnographic. Interpreters are situated as they chronicle historical shifts, translate sacred texts, conduct psychological experiments, analyze survey data, excavate archeological remains, or observe ritual practices. In each instance, scholars function within a network of social exchange and in a particular geographical location, and in their work they use collectively constructed professional standards. They stand in a built environment, a social network, and a professional community.[12]

At the same time, interpreters are never fully or finally in one place. So where are interpreters when they do their work? Although I didn't realize it at the time, I began to formulate an answer to this question that night at the annual festival—and on another day when I stood before an image of Our Lady of Charity. Even though I was no longer a practicing Catholic and my politics were to the left of most devotees, I spontaneously and inexplicably whispered a prayer in Spanish for the liberation of Cuba, a prayer I had heard hundreds of times, including on that warm September night in 1993 at the annual feast-day celebration: "Virgen Santísima, salva a Cuba." I wasn't sure why I did that—and I'm still not. Had I temporarily and partially "gone native," prompting me to identify with a religious and political worldview I did not share? Had my childhood piety temporarily resurfaced? Was it simply an act of respect for those who had been so kind and told me so many sad stories? Whatever prompted that prayer, I decided, it offered some insights about the interpreter's position. Interpreters are not in one place or between places, but always crossing boundaries, always moving across. The diasporic religion of Cuban Catholics at the Miami shrine is translocative and transtemporal, propelling devotees back and forth in time and space. And interpretation is translocative and transtemporal too. The scholar moves back and forth from the desk to the archives, from home to the field, from here to there and now to then. Of course, scholarly travels are less forced and less dangerous than the coerced crossing of the nuns who arrived at the Miami airport in 1961 and the perilous passage of *balseros* who clung to home-made rafts and sometimes never landed on the Florida shore. The crossing of many migrants—and the failed attempts at crossing—has meant economic hardship for their families, physical injury for themselves, and even arrest, deportation, or death. So I cannot stress too strongly the extraordinary difference in social power. Yet scholars of religion are more like those Cuban migrants—and Malcolm X heading to Mecca, Faxian traversing the Silk Road, and Bashō hiking toward Kisagata—than most accounts of the interpretative task have acknowledged.[13]

So at the feast-day ritual, and while whispering that prayer to the Virgin, I was already in motion. Those were moments of transit in the longer process of interpretation. At the annual festival in 1993 I was neither hovering above it all nor planted in any fixed space. My professional position and personal location constrained what I could see from where I stood in the crowd that night—and determined what remained in shadow—but I was on my way across. In that zone of contact I was moving back and forth between fact and value, inside and outside, the familiar and the strange, between the home and the field, the past and the present, Miami and Havana, between clear sightings and blind spots, between old theories and new questions. The notions of religion I carried with me to the festival that night offered angles of vision, just as they obscured a great deal of the flux around me: the Virgin winding her way through the overflow crowd, the weeping and waving, the translocative and transtemporal crossings as devotees transported themselves to the Cuba of memory and desire. Those blind spots prompted questions, which, in turn, initiated more crossings—this theoretical itinerary, which has arrived at an account of religion that emphasizes movement, relation, and position. These crossings have led to a theory that challenges the usual notions of religion as static and bounded and the prevailing assumptions, enacted in the authorial voice of most scholarly studies, that the interpreter is everywhere at once or nowhere in particular. And even if sand and rain blow up at times to obstruct the view, I've tried to suggest, this theory can offer aid in other purposeful wanderings. It can allow positioned sightings of religion in other times and places, since, as I began to sense that warm September night in Miami, the religious are always in place and moving across. The religious—and scholars too—are dwelling and crossing.[14]

NOTES

ILLUSTRATION CREDITS

ACKNOWLEDGMENTS

INDEX

NOTES

1. Itineraries

Epigraphs: James Clifford, "Notes on Travel and Theory," in James Clifford and Vivek Dhareshwar, eds., *Traveling Theories, Traveling Theorists* (Santa Cruz: University of California at Santa Cruz Center for Cultural Studies, 1989), 177. Georges Bataille, *Theory of Religion* (New York: Zone Books, 1992), 11.

1. Interview no. 109, 11 February 1992, female, age fifty-seven, born Guanajay, Cuba, arrived 1966. Quoted in Thomas A. Tweed, *Our Lady of the Exile: Diasporic Religion at a Cuban Catholic Shrine in Miami* (New York and Oxford: Oxford University Press, 1997), 126. This account of the opening of the feast-day mass is taken from Tweed, *Our Lady of the Exile,* 116.

2. E. B. Tylor, *Primitive Culture,* vol. 1 (1871; London: John Murray, 1920), 424. Rudolf Otto, *The Idea of the Holy* (1917; London and Oxford: Oxford University Press, 1958), 5. Paul Tillich, *Theology of Culture* (New York: Oxford University Press, 1959), 7–8. Melford E. Spiro, "Religion: Problems of Definition and Explana-

tion," in Michael Banton, ed., *Anthropological Approaches to the Study of Religion* (London: Tavistock, 1966), 96. Clifford Geertz, *The Interpretation of Cultures* (New York: Basic Books, 1973), 90.

3. On Afro-Cuban Santería and Roman Catholicism, see Tweed, *Our Lady of the Exile*, 43–55. On Ọṣun, who is much more complex than just the goddess of the river, see Joseph M. Murphy and Mei-Mei Sanford, eds., Ọ̀ṣun, *across the Waters: A Yoruba Goddess in Africa and the Americas* (Bloomington: Indiana University Press, 2001).

4. Acknowledgment of the theorist's position is more common in some disciplines and subfields than others. For example, feminist theorists and cultural anthropologists are more inclined to consider positionality. Among the works on theories of religion that consider positionality—framed as reflexivity—see Pierre Gisel and Jean-Marc Tétaz, eds., *Théories de la religion: Diversité des practiques de recherche, changement des contexts socio-culturels, requêktes réflexives* (Geneva: Labor et Fides, 2002).

5. L. Mjøset, "Theory: Conceptions in the Social Sciences," in Neil J. Smelser and Paul B. Baltes, eds., *International Encyclopedia of the Social and Behavioral Sciences*, vol. 23 (Amsterdam: Elsevier, 2001), 15641–15647.

6. Hilary Putnam, *Realism with a Human Face* (Cambridge, Mass.: Harvard University Press, 1990), 3–29. On the understanding of theory and "laws" in the natural sciences, there seems to be some evidence that even the "laws of nature" can change over time, even if only minutely, as suggested for example by astrophysicists' observations of the absorption of quasar light by gas clouds floating in deep space. See J. K. Webb, M. T. Murphy, V. V. Flambaum, V. A. Dzuba, J. D. Barrow, C. W. Churchill, J. X. Prochaska, and A. M. Wolfe, "Further Cosmological Evolution of the Fine Structure Content," *Physical Review Letters*, 87.9, August 27, 2001, 091301-1–091301-4. I refer in this paragraph to the idea of culturally constructed categories, and I talk about "construction" in various senses throughout the book. I do so, however, with the philosopher Ian Hacking's caution in mind about the uses and limits of the metaphor of "social construction." Ian Hacking, *The Social Construction of What?* (Cambridge, Mass.: Harvard University Press, 1999).

7. James Clifford, *Routes: Travel and Translation in the Late Twentieth Century* (Cambridge, Mass.: Harvard University Press, 1997), 2–3. Before Clifford's highlighting of travel, Michel de Certeau offered a provocative analysis of *walking* and *walking rhetorics*, though he did not reimagine theory in these terms. See Michel de Certeau, *The Practice of Everyday Life* (Berkeley: University of California, 1984), 91–110. The three meanings of the term *itinerary* are taken from "Itiner-

ary," *Oxford English Dictionary Online* (2001). For a theoretically engaging analysis of travel and travel writing, see Patrick Holland and Graham Huggan, *Tourists with Typewriters: Critical Reflections on Contemporary Travel Writing* (Ann Arbor: University of Michigan Press, 1998).

8. In suggesting that theory involves tropes as well as concepts, I am disagreeing with Gilles Deleuze and Félix Guattari, who suggest that the former is the province of religion and the latter the domain of philosophy. Gilles Deleuze and Félix Guattari, *What Is Philosophy?* (1991; New York: Columbia University Press, 1994), 2, 89–93.

9. On the "spatial turn" in theory, see Mike Crang and Nigel Thrift, eds., *Thinking Space* (London and New York: Routledge, 2000), xi; and R. Andrew Sayer, "Space and Social Theory," in Sayer, *Realism and Social Science* (London: Sage, 2000), 108. See also Edward W. Soja, *Postmodern Geographies: The Reassertion of Space in Critical Social Theory* (London: Verso, 1989). Michel Foucault, "Of Other Spaces," *Diacritics* 19 (Spring 1986): 22. The observation from Bruno Bosteels is taken from Bosteels, "From Text to Territory: Félix Guattari's Cartographies of the Unconscious," in Eleanor Kaufman and Kevin Jon Heller, eds., *Deleuze and Guattari: New Mappings in Politics, Philosophy, and Culture* (Minneapolis: University of Minnesota Press, 1998), 146. See also Bruno Bosteels, "A Misreading of Maps: The Politics of Cartography in Marxism and Poststructuralism," in Stephen Barker, ed., *Signs of Change* (Albany: State University of New York Press, 1996), 109–136. Iain Chambers, *Migrancy, Culture, Identity* (London and New York: Routledge, 1994), 92. Sam Gill, "Territory," in Mark C. Taylor, ed., *Critical Terms for Religious Studies* (Chicago: University of Chicago Press, 1998), 310. In a similar way, Ronald L. Grimes has criticized Jonathan Z. Smith's spatial theory of ritual and suggested that a more helpful theory might privilege action, not space. Jonathan Z. Smith, *To Take Place: Toward Theory in Ritual* (Chicago: University of Chicago Press, 1987). Ronald L. Grimes, "Jonathan Z. Smith's Theory of Ritual Space," *Religion* 29.3 (July 1999): 261–273.

10. For an introduction to the life and work of Matsuo Kinsaku (1644–1694), who came to be called Bashō in 1681 after a disciple planted a *bashō* (banana) tree at the poet's hut, see Makato Ueda, *Matsuo Bashō* (New York: Twayne, 1970). Bashō, *The Narrow Road to the Deep North and Other Travel Sketches* (New York: Penguin, 1977). For another translation and analysis of Bashō's prose works, see David Landis Barnhill, trans., *Bashō's Journey: The Literary Prose of Matsuo Bashō* (Albany: State University of New York Press, 2005). Strabo, *Geography,* vol. 1 (Cambridge, Mass.: Harvard University Press, 1917), 455. On the Amerindian *pinturas,* see Barbara E. Mundy, *The Mapping of New Spain: Indigenous Cartogra-*

phy and the Maps of the Relaciones Geográficas (Chicago and London: University of Chicago Press, 1996). On native cartography, see also Louis De Vorsey, Jr., "Silent Witnesses: Native American Maps," *Georgia Review* 45.4 (Winter 1992): 709–726. On the differences between geography and chorography, and Strabo and Ptolemy, see Derek Gregory, "Chorology (Chorography)," in R. J. Johnston et al., eds., *The Dictionary of Human Geography,* 4th ed. (Oxford: Blackwell, 2000), 79–80. For two scholarly articles that use the term *dynography,* see G. Furst et al., "Diagnostic Imaging Following Reconstructive Surgery of the Arteries of the Legs" [translated from the German], *ROFO—Fortschritte auf dem Gebiet der Rontgenstrahlen und der Bildgebenden V.* 151 (December 1989): 666–673; A. M. K. Wong et al., "Motor Control Assessment for Rhizotomy in Cerebral Palsy," *American Journal of Physical Medicine and Rehabilitation* 79.9–10 (September–October 2000): 441–450.

11. The passage from *The Records of a Weather-Exposed Skeleton* is included and analyzed in David Barnhill, "Bashō as Bat: Wayfaring and Antistructure in the Journals of Matsuo Bashō," *Journal of Asian Studies* 49.2 (May 1990): 279–280. It is Barnhill who notes "the predominance of wayfaring images" in Bashō's work.

12. Bashō, *Narrow Road to the Deep North,* 128, 129. I have taken the translation of the Kisagata poem here from David Barnhill, trans., *Bashō's Haiku: Selected Poems* (Albany: State University of New York Press, 2004), 96. On Bashō's poetry, see also Makoto Ueda, *Bashō and His Interpreters: Selected Hokku with Commentary* (Stanford, Calif.: Stanford University Press, 1991), and Haruo Shirane, *Traces of Dreams: Landscape, Cultural Memory, and the Poetry of Bashō* (Stanford, Calif.: Stanford University Press, 1998).

13. On *theory,* see *The Oxford English Dictionary Online,* 2001. Ian Rutherford, "*Theoria* and *Darśan:* Pilgrimage and Vision in Greece and India," *Classical Quarterly* 50.1 (2000): 133–146. The nine meanings of *theōria,* according to Rutherford, are: (1) a festival; (2) a spectator at a festival; (3) a sacred delegation to a sanctuary; (4) the action of a sacred delegation, roughly "pilgrimage" in the modern English sense; (5) consultation of an oracle; (6) an official sent from a sanctuary to announce a festival; (7) sightseeing, or "religious sightseeing"; (8) exploration; and (9) a state official or "overseer." James Clifford, "Notes on Travel and Theory," in James Clifford and Vivek Dhareshwar, eds., *Traveling Theories, Traveling Theorists* (Santa Cruz: University of California at Santa Cruz Center for Cultural Studies, 1989), 177. For a visual representation of Theoria, see the Calendar Frieze, Pyanopsion to Gamelion, Athens, Little Metropolis. According to Luwdwig Deubner, the crowned woman beside the table is Theoria, the personification of beholding: Ludwig Deubner, *Attische Feste* (Berlin: Akademie-Verlag, 1956), 248–254. Another scholar, Erika Simon, is less sure and thinks the female figure could

be Pompe, the personification of the procession at Panathenaia. Erika Simon, *Festivals of Attica: An Archaeological Commentary* (Madison: University of Wisconsin Press, 2002), 6, 101–102. On theory and praxis, see Bruno Snell, *Die Entdeckung des Geistes: Studien zur Entstehung des europäischen Denkens bei den Griechen* (Göttingen: Vandenhoeck and Ruprecht, 1975), 275–282.

14. William James, "On a Certain Blindness in Human Beings," in James, *Essays on Faith and Morals* (Cleveland and New York: Meridian, 1962), 259, 263–267. Bashō, *Narrow Road to the Deep North*, 128. Emphasis mine. Friedrich Nietzsche, *The Will to Power* (New York: Vintage, 1968), 325. As I discovered after I drafted this chapter, Ann Burlein also has used the phrase "blind spots," but she uses it to talk about the ways that multidisciplinary work can "illuminate blind spots." I focus here more on the ways that blind spots always remain. Ann Burlein, *Lift High the Cross: Where White Supremacy and the Christian Right Converge* (Durham, N.C., and London: Duke University Press, 2002), xvii.

15. Richard Rorty, *Philosophy and the Mirror of Nature* (Princeton: Princeton University Press, 1979), 38–41, 371. Donna Haraway, "Situated Knowledges: The Science Question in Feminism and the Privilege of Partial Perspective," *Feminist Studies* 14.3 (Fall 1988), 581. Donna Haraway, *Simians, Cyborgs, and Women: The Reinvention of Nature* (New York: Routledge, 1991), 191. Bashō, *Narrow Road to the Deep North*, 105, 120, 124. In discussing the sound of the cuckoo Bashō slightly misquotes a poem by Saigyō. Barnhill's translation of the poem about fleas manages to evoke three senses—touch, sound, and smell: "fleas, lice / a horse peeing / by my pillow." Barnhill, trans., *Bashō's Haiku*, 94. If we keep in mind the parallels between the Greek *theōria* and the Hindi *darśan*, it is relevant to note that, as anthropologist John Stanley points out, there are three kinds of darśan. From weakest to strongest, they are seeing the temple's spire *(sikar)*, seeing the image of the deity, and, the most powerful darśan, not only seeing but touching the image. In this sense, it means embodied contact. Rutherford, "*Theoria* and *Darśan*," 144. J. M. Stanley, "The Great Maharashtrian Pilgrimage: Pandharpur and Alandi," in Alan Morinis, ed., *Sacred Journeys: The Anthropology of Pilgrimage* (Westport, Conn.: Greenwood, 1992), 65–87.

16. Hilary Putnam, *Reason, Truth, and History* (Cambridge: Cambridge University Press, 1981), 49–74.

17. Putnam also appeals to Dewey's notion of "warranted assertability": see Putnam, *Realism with a Human Face*, 21, 41. The quote is from Putnam, *Reason, Truth, and History,* 49–50. I should note that elements of this "locative" epistemology have a longer lineage; in some form it extends at least to Friedrich Nietzsche's "perspectivist" analysis of truth. See Nietzsche, *The Will to Power*, 304–307, 322–

323, 326, 330. By suggesting that scholars should not focus on "experiences" I am endorsing Robert H. Sharf's argument: "it is ill conceived to construe the object of the study of religion to be the inner experiences of religious practitioners. Scholars of religion are not presented with experiences that stand in need of interpretation but rather with texts, narratives, performances, and so forth." Robert H. Sharf, "Experience," in Taylor, *Critical Terms for Religious Studies*, 94–116. For Max Weber's view of "understanding" (*verstehen*), see Max Weber, *Economy and Society*, vol. 1, ed. Guenther Roth and Claus Wittich (Berkeley: University of California Press, 1978), 8–11. By citing Hilary Putnam and alluding to pragmatism, I am gesturing toward philosophical lineages. Many readers will not care about such things. Those readers can abandon this note now and return to the text—while there is still time to save themselves from boredom. For those who do care, it might help to say a bit more. I am not a card-carrying member of any philosophical club. No one would have me, and I am not inclined to join. However, on questions about truth, meaning, and interpretation I have been influenced by pragmatism. Cornell West, a proponent of "prophetic pragmatism," has suggested that if we highlight questions of epistemology we can discern three main types of pragmatists. All affirm "epistemic antifoundationalism," the view that there are no unmediated facts or neutral observations and that meaning can be understood in terms of effects. Yet, West suggests, they disagree on other matters: (1) "conservative pragmatists," like Hilary Putnam and Charles Sanders Pierce, worry about relativism and affirm some form of realism; (2) "moderate pragmatists" such as John Dewey and William James do not worry about relativism and affirm a sort of "minimalist realism"; and (3) "avant-garde pragmatists," like Richard Rorty, share the moderates' lack of concern about relativism but move fully toward an "antirealist" epistemological position. In terms of West's typology, my position is closest to the conservative and moderate views, since I affirm a modified nonrepresentational form of realism. On some issues I would put not only Putnam in the conservative camp, as West does, but also James. I agree with much of David C. Lamberth's—and not Rorty's—interpretation of James. James, Lamberth argues, affirms a radical empiricism that avoids both cognitive relativism and naïve realism. To further clarify my position, it might help to mention David Depew and Robert Hollinger's periodization of the stages of American pragmatism. They identify three stages or phases: (1) classical pragmatism, which emerged in the late nineteenth and early twentieth century in the writings of James and Dewey; (2) positivized pragmatism, which predominated in the middle decades of the twentieth century as some positivists and analytical philosophers like Rudolf Carnap and W. V. O. Quine took a pragmatic turn; and (3) postmodern pragmatism, a third phase that can be dated from the publication of Richard Rorty's *Philosophy and the Mirror of Nature* in 1979. My approach to questions about interpretation has been influenced by the first and third phases in pragmatism's history. Cornell West, "Theory, Pragmatisms, and Politics," in Robert Hollinger and David Depew, eds., *Pragmatism: From Progressivism to Postmodernism* (Westport, Conn.: Praeger, 1995), 314–325. David Depew and Robert Hollinger, "General Introduction," in Hollinger and Depew, eds., *Pragmatism*, xv–xvii. David C. Lamberth, *William James and the Metaphysics of Experience* (Cambridge: Cambridge University Press, 1999), 203–241.

18. Putnam, *Reason, Truth, and History*, 74. Here I am reaffirming Hilary Putnam's view of interpretation in other ways too. In a later essay, the philosopher rejected what he called an "adolescent error" that "haunts the subject of interpretation": "That everything we say is false because everything we say falls short of everything that could be said is an adolescent sort of error . . ." He suggested that John Austin's comment about justification—"enough is enough, enough isn't everything"—applies to interpretation as well as to justification. "Still, *enough is enough, enough isn't everything*. We have practices of interpretation. Those practices may be content-sensitive and interest-relative, but there is, given enough context—given, as Wittgenstein says, the language is in place—such a thing as *getting it right* or *getting it wrong*. There may be some indeterminacy of translation, but it isn't a case of 'anything goes.'" Putnam, *Realism with a Human Face*, 120, 122. For an overview of modern Western thinking about "interpretation," as well as a proposal for a theory of interpretation in religious studies that goes in a slightly different direction, see Hans H. Penner, "Interpretation," in Willi Braun and Russell T. McCutcheon, eds., *Guide to the Study of Religion* (London and New York: Cassell, 2000), 57–71.

19. Haraway, *Simians*, 183–201. Haraway, "Situated Knowledges," 583–585, 589. Thomas A. Tweed, ed., *Retelling U.S. Religious History* (Berkeley: University of California Press, 1997), 6–10. My view has some parallels with the "emplacement perspective" advocated by anthropologist Harri Englund, who wants to attend to "subjects whose embodied presence is situated in history": see "Ethnography after Globalism," *American Ethnologist* 104 (May 2002): 277. By emphasizing the constructed character of scholars' categories and the social context of scholarship, I am siding with others who make a similar point about the field of religion, even if I would not follow them on all matters. See Bruce Lincoln, *Theorizing Myth: Narrative, Ideology, and Scholarship* (Chicago: University of Chicago Press, 1999), and Russell T. McCutcheon, *Manufacturing Religion: The Discourse of Sui Generis Religion and the Politics of Nostalgia* (New York: Oxford University Press, 1997). I

would not follow McCutcheon, for example, in his championing of an "unapologetically reductionist" naturalist approach to the study of religion (17); nor do I agree with the strongest version of his political critique of the profession or the strongest version of the epistemology that grounds his critique of the study of religion. Categories are socially constructed and categorizers construct reality-for-them, as McCutcheon suggests, but after we have talked about categories and categorizers, we still have not said all we need to say about religion and its study. There is something more to say, and in saying it we need to avoid un-nuanced idealist, materialist, and essentialist views. For a further expression of his views, see Russell T. McCutcheon, *The Discipline of Religion: Structure, Meaning, Rhetoric* (London and New York: Routledge, 2003).

20. Some scholars have noted that their theories have emerged from the study of a particular group in a particular time and place. For example, anthropologist Stewart Guthrie acknowledged that his theory of religion as anthropomorphism "grew out of an earlier effort to describe and interpret a particular Japanese religious movement." He found that "the movement resembled other religions primarily in its anthropomorphism—in viewing the world as humanlike." Stewart Guthrie, *Faces in the Clouds: A New Theory of Religion* (1993; New York: Oxford University Press, 1995), ix, vii. The "earlier effort" was Stewart Guthrie, *A Japanese New Religion: Risshō Kōsei-kai in a Mountain Hamlet* (Ann Arbor: University of Michigan Center for Japanese Studies, 1988). In a similar way, Harvey Whitehouse was clear that his theory of two "divergent modes of religiosity" (imagistic and doctrinal) emerged from his ethnographic case study of the Pomio Kivung movement in Papua New Guinea, where he found "two contrasting politico-religious regimes." The case study was Harvey Whitehouse, *Inside the Cult: Religious Innovation and Transmission in Papua New Guinea* (Oxford: Clarendon, 1995). His theory followed five years later: Whitehouse, *Arguments and Icons: Divergent Modes of Religiosity* (Oxford: Oxford University Press, 2000). See also his later summary: Whitehouse, *Modes of Religiosity: A Cognitive Theory of Religious Transmission* (Walnut Creek, Calif.: Alta Mira, 2004).

21. Joseph M. Kitagawa and John S. Strong, "Friedrich Max Müller and the Comparative Study of Religion," in Ninian Smart et al. eds., *Nineteenth Century Religious Thought in the West,* vol. 3 (Cambridge.: Cambridge University Press, 1985), 197–199. Nirad C. Chaudhuri, *Scholar Extraordinary: The Life of the Rt. Hon. Friedrich Max Müller* (London: Chatoo and Windus, 1974). David McLellan, *Karl Marx: His Life and Thought* (London: Papermac, 1987), 1–16, 262–280. Lynn Gamwell and Richard Wells, eds., *Sigmund Freud and Art: His Personal Collection of Antiquities* (Binghamton: State University of New York Press; and London:

Freud Museum, 1989), 15–29. Although Marx himself experienced "grinding poverty" in London and noticed it elsewhere in that city, where he emigrated in 1849, he had observed poverty earlier from the relative comfort of his middle-class childhood home in Trier. There was little industry in that Rhineland city, Germany's oldest, and it suffered from unemployment and inflation. As Marx's biographer notes, one-fourth of the town's population lived on charity (McLellan, 262–280). The worst year seems to have been in London in 1852, when Marx had to pawn his coat to buy paper and borrow money to bury his daughter. Marx certainly addressed religion in his works composed after he arrived in London, but he wrote some of his most important religious critiques earlier—including *Contribution to the Critique of Hegel's Philosophy of Right* (1844) and *Theses on Feuerbach* (1845). In that sense, his earlier observations of economic inequality in Trier were important for the theoretical reflections that have been influential in the field of religious studies. Finally, I talk here about theory "illuminating" regions of the religious world, but it is more complicated than that. It is important to acknowledge that our scholarly categories and theoretical framework help to create the world they interpret.

22. Michel de Certeau, *Culture in the Plural* (1974; Minneapolis: University of Minnesota Press, 1997), 123. Morris Jastrow, Jr., *The Study of Religion* (1901; Chico, Calif.: Scholars Press, 1981), 1. Gerardus Van der Leeuw describes the phenomenological approach to the study of religion and its "intellectual suspense" *(epoché)*. See G. Van der Leeuw, *Religion in Essence and Manifestation*, vol. 2 (1933; New York: Harper and Row, 1963), 683–689.

23. For a brief but lucid account of the "reflexive turn," see James L. Peacock, *The Anthropological Lens: Harsh Light, Soft Focus,* 2nd ed. (Cambridge: Cambridge University Press, 2001), 74–85. Ludwig Wittgenstein, *Philosophical Investigations,* 3rd ed. (New York: Macmillan, 1953), section no. 217, p. 85. Hilary Putnam, *The Many Faces of Realism* (LaSalle, Ill.: Open Court, 1987), 85. Putnam gave a series of lectures, which became a book, on pragmatism, and there he suggested that pragmatism "as a way of thinking" was "of lasting importance, and an option (or at least an 'open question') that should figure in present-day philosophical thought." He went to suggest that there are thematic parallels between pragmatism and the philosophy of the later Wittgenstein. Hilary Putnam, *Pragmatism: An Open Question* (Oxford: Blackwell, 1995), xi, 27–55.

24. Tweed, *Our Lady of the Exile,* 10. Gillian Rose, "Situated Knowledges: Positionality, Reflexivities, and Other Tactics," *Progress in Human Geography* 21 (1997): 305–320.

25. Mộng-Lan, "Trail," *Jubilat* 2 (Fall/Winter 2000): 5–15. The poem is also re-

printed in Robert Creeley, ed., *The Best American Poetry 2002* (New York: Scribner Poetry, 2002), 108–117. Arjun Appadurai, ed., *Globalization* (Durham, N.C., and London: Duke University Press, 2001), 5. For a discussion of the constraints on crossing, see Chapter 5 below. See also John Allen and Chris Hamnett, eds., *A Shrinking World?: Global Unevenness and Inequality* (New York: Oxford University Press, 1995).

26. Here and throughout the book, when I refer to "power" I usually mean, following Anthony Giddens's definition, the ability to enact decisions by controlling individuals or mobilizing institutions. Anthony Giddens, *The Constitution of Society* (Berkeley: University of California Press, 1984), 29, 256–257. My understanding of power, which acknowledges the complex interplay of personal agency and social forces as it also considers the multiple and overlapping social arenas where individuals and groups contest for control, has been enriched by many other theorists, including Michael Mann, Manuel Castells, and Michel Foucault. Michael Mann, *The Sources of Social Power*, 2 vols. (Cambridge: Cambridge University Press, 1986, 1993). Manuel Castells, *The Information Age: Economy, Society, and Culture*, 2 vols. (Oxford: Blackwell, 1996, 1997). Michel Foucault, *Remarks on Marx: Conversations with Duccio Trombadori* (New York: Semiotext(e), 1991). Michel Foucault, *Power/Knowledge: Selected Interviews and Other Writings, 1972–1977* (New York: Pantheon, 1980).

27. "William Laurence Saunders," in William S. Powell, ed., *Dictionary of North Carolina Biography*, vol. 5 (Chapel Hill: University of North Carolina Press, 1994), 286–287. Marguerite Schumnn, *The First State University: A Walking Guide* (Chapel Hill: University of North Carolina Press, 1985), 64. United States Congress, *Report of the Joint Select Committee to Inquire into the Condition of Affairs in the Late Insurrectionary States . . .* , vol. 2, Report no. 6, December 1871 (Washington, D.C.: Government Printing Office, 1872). "Under the Dome," *News and Observer* [Raleigh], April 30, 1938, 54. J. G. Hamilton, *Reconstruction in North Carolina*, Studies in History, Economics, and Public Law, 58/141 (New York: Columbia University Press; and London: Longmans, Green, 1914), 461. The Southern Historical Collection at the University of North Carolina at Chapel Hill contains letters and clippings that provide leads about Saunders's involvement with the KKK, including an anonymous death threat apparently written by an angry African American who begins the missive "you murderer you" and goes on to accuse Saunders of being present at the lynching of "four Negroes": Anonymous to William Laurence Saunders, William Laurence Saunders Papers, November 27, 1871, Southern Historical Collection, no. 2638, folder 14, 1870–1876. Among the many sympathetic (and evasive) interpreters of Saunders's activities, see Alfred Waddell,

The Life and Character of William L. Saunders, L.L.D. (Wilmington, N.C.: Jackson, Bell, and Steam Power Presses, 1892). Waddell defended Saunders by suggesting that the congressmen had encountered "*a man,* who knew how to guard his rights and protect his honor; and . . . he was discharged with his secrets (if he had any) locked in his own bosom, and carrying with him the respect and admiration of all who witnessed the ordeal through which he had passed" (6). Of course the built environment of many other southern and northern universities also inscribes links with slavery. See, for example, this account of a debate at Yale: Kate Zernike, "Slave Traders in Yale's Past Fuel Debate on Restitution," *New York Times on the Web,* August 13, 2001, *www.nytimes.com.*

28. Natalie P. McNeal, "Students Protest KKK Image UNC's Edifice's Name Evokes," *News and Observer* [Raleigh], 15 October 1999, 1B, 7B. Keith H. Basso, *Wisdom Sits in Places: Landscape and Language among the Western Apache* (Albuquerque: University of New Mexico Press, 1996).

29. Hilary Putnam, among others, has challenged the fact-value binary. He argues that it is sometimes useful to distinguish between factual claims and value judgments, but that this distinction is not helpful when it is rendered as the difference between the "objective" and the "subjective." In a helpful phrase, he has talked about the "entanglement of fact and value." See Hilary Putnam, *The Collapse of the Fact/Value Dichotomy and Other Essays* (Cambridge, Mass.: Harvard University Press, 2002), 28–45. Power and meaning were negotiated in some public controversies in the study of religion during the 1980s and 1990s. For an analysis of those controversies, and their implications for the study of religion, see Laurie L. Patton, *The Scholar and the Fool: Scandal and the Cultural Work of the Secular Study of Religion* (Chicago: University of Chicago Press, forthcoming). I am grateful to Nancy Ammerman and Ray Hart for encouraging me to clarify my understanding of the relation between theory and "normative" claims.

30. I return to the question about how to assess theories in the Conclusion.

2. Boundaries

Epigraphs: Timothy Fitzgerald, *The Ideology of Religious Studies* (New York: Oxford University Press, 2000), 4. Michel Serres with Bruno Latour, *Conversations on Science, Culture, and Time* (Ann Arbor: University of Michigan Press, 1995), 121.

1. Of course, other scholars besides Fitzgerald, who is quoted in the first epigraph in this chapter, also have suggested that we drop the term *religion,* and stop

trying to define it, including Wilfred Cantwell Smith in his compelling and influential 1962 volume: "Neither religion in general nor any one of the religions, I will contend, is in itself an intelligible entity, a valid object of inquiry, or of concern wither for the scholar or the man of faith . . . My own suggestion is that the word, and the concepts, should be dropped." Wilfred Cantwell Smith, *The Meaning and End of Religion: A Revolutionary Approach to the Great Religious Traditions* (1962; San Francisco: Harper and Row, 1978), 12, 50. Other scholars also have advocated for the abandonment of the term *religion*. See Daniel Dubuisson, *L'Occident et la religion: Mythes, science, et idéolgie* (Brussels: Éditions Complexe, 1998); and Dario Sabbatucci, *La Propspettiva storico-religiosa* (Formello: Edizioni SEAM, 2000). An English translation of Dubuisson's volume is available: Daniel Dubuisson, *The Western Construction of Religion: Myths, Knowledge, and Ideology* (Baltimore: Johns Hopkins University Press, 2003). I cite that version below.

2. J. H. Leuba, "Introduction to a Psychological Study of Religion," *The Monist* 9 (January 1901): 201.

3. Although it has not happened in religious studies, a discipline's constitutive term can change over time. Geography provides a good example. From the founding of the Association of American Geographers through the 1920s, scholars in that field focused on "human ecology" or the interaction between humans and land. Under the influence of Richard Hartshorne's methodological statement of 1939, *The Nature of Geography, region* was widely accepted as geography's central term from the 1930s through the 1950s. While some professional geographers endorse *place* or *location,* most today would suggest that since the 1960s *space* now functions as the discipline's constitutive term. This disciplinary history is traced in Edward J. Taaffe, "The Spatial View in Context," *Annals of the Association of American Geographers* 64.1 (March 1974): 1–16. Richard Hartshorne, "The Nature of Geography," *Annals of the Association of American Geographers,* 29.3 and 29.4 (September and December 1939): 173–658. Hartshorne's influential work was reprinted and revised in 1946 and 1959, when its vision of the field still enjoyed widespread acceptance. See Richard Hartshorne, *Perspective on the Nature of Geography* (Chicago: Rand McNally for The Association of American Geographers, 1959).

4. John Hollander, *The Night Mirror: Poems* (New York: Atheneum, 1971). John Hollander, *Rhyme's Reason: A Guide to English Verse* (New Haven, Conn.: Yale University Press, 1981), 1. John Blacking, *How Musical Is Man?* (London: Faber and Faber, 1976), 32, 42–43. See also John Blacking, *Music, Culture, and Experience: Selected Papers of John Blacking,* ed. Reginald Byron (Chicago: University of Chicago Press, 1995).

5. Stanley Sadie, ed., *The New Grove Dictionary of Music and Musicians* (Lon-

don: Macmillan, 1980). William Harmon, ed., *A Handbook to Literature*, 8th ed. (Saddle River, N.J.: Prentice Hall, 2000). Ian Chilvers and Harold Osborne, eds., *The Oxford Dictionary of Art* (New York: Oxford University Press, 1997).

6. "Religion, definition of" in *The Harper Collins Dictionary of Religion* (San Francisco: HarperSanFrancisco, 1995), 893.

7. Philip Alperson, "Introduction," in *What Is Music?: An Introduction to the Philosophy of Music*, ed. Philip Alperson (University Park: Pennsylvania State University Press, 1994), 9–10. "Music" in Stanley Sadie, editor, and John Tyrrell, executive editor, *The New Grove Dictionary of Music and Musicians*, 29 vols. (New York: Grove Dictionaries, 2000). "Art" in *The Dictionary of Art*, ed. Jane Turner, 34 vols. (New York: Grove's Dictionaries, 1996), the online version, November 1998 edition *(http://www.groveart.com)*.

8. David N. Livingstone, *The Geographical Tradition: Episodes in the History of a Contested Enterprise* (Oxford: Blackwell, 1992), 304. Emphasis mine. Jonathan Z. Smith, "Religion, Religions, Religious," in *Critical Terms for Religious Studies*, ed. Mark C. Taylor (Chicago: University of Chicago Press, 1998), 281–282.

9. "Definition," *The Oxford English Dictionary Online*, 2002. As philosopher Alexander Matthews notes in *A Diagram of Definition*, scholars have enumerated many types of definitions. One philosopher distinguishes circular, coordinative, eliminative, explicative, and contextual definitions; another talks about prescriptive, ostensive, verbal, implicit, recursive, nominal, and real definitions. If nonspecialists—and more than a few specialists—find themselves disoriented by definitions, it seems almost impossible to avoid getting completely lost as they machete their way through the thicket of *definitions of definition*. But gaining some clarity on this fundamental point can help in the long run, since readers need to know precisely what scholars are claiming for their definitions. How else can they be in a position to offer informed and judicious assessments? Alexander Matthews, *A Diagram of Definition: The Defining of Definition* (Assen, The Netherlands: Van Gorcum, 1998), 45. The first list of types of definitions Matthews cites is from Arthur Pap's *Semantics and Necessary Truth;* the second is from Anthony Flew, "Definition," in *Dictionary of Philosophy*, 2nd ed. (New York: St. Martin's Press, 1984), 86–87. For a helpful anthology of philosophers' reflections on definition that ranges from Plato to Rickert, see Juan C. Sager, ed., *Essays on Definition* (Amsterdam and Philadelphia: John Benjamins, 2000). See also James H. Fetzer, David Shatz, and George N. Schlesinger, eds., *Definitions and Definability: Philosophical Perspectives* (Dordrecht, Boston, and London: Kluwer, 1991). Robert D. Baird, *Category Formation and the History of Religions*, 2nd ed. (Berlin and New York: Mouton de Gruyter, 1991), 6. Mapping the boundaries of religion has meant distin-

guishing it from other areas of human life, including science and magic. On the ways that science and magic have functioned as "foils" for those trying to distinguish the religious, see Randall Styers, *Making Magic: Religion, Magic, and Science in the Modern World* (New York: Oxford University Press, 2004).

10. Rodney Stark and Roger Finke, *Acts of Faith: Explaining the Human Side of Religion* (Berkeley: University of California Press, 2000), 85. The propositions and definitions are all listed in the "Appendix," 277–286.

11. William James, *The Varieties of Religious Experience* (1902; New York: Penguin Books, 1982), 28.

12. Ibid., 31.

13. Robert Borofsky, Fredrik Barth, Richard A. Shweder, Lars Rodseth, and Nomi Maya Stolzenberg, "When: A Conversation about Culture," *American Anthropologist* 103.2 (June 2001): 434, 443, 444.

14. James H. Leuba, "Appendix: Definitions of Religion and Critical Comments," in Leuba, *A Psychological Study of Religion: Its Origin, Function, and Future* (1912; New York: AMS Press, 1969), 339–363. There have been a number of recent attempts to consider the task of defining religion. For example, see Smith, "Religion, Religions, Religious," in Taylor, *Critical Terms in the Study of Religion;* Thomas A. Idinopulos and Brian C. Wilson, eds., *What Is Religion?: Origins, Definitions, and Explanations* (Leiden: E. J. Brill, 1998); Armin W. Geertz, "Definition as Analytical Strategy in the Study of Religion," *Historical Reflections/ Réflexions Historiques* 25.3 (Fall 1999): 445–475; and William E. Arnal, "Definition," in Willi Braun and Russell T. McCutcheon, eds., *Guide to the Study of Religion* (London and New York: Cassell, 2000), 21–34; Kathleen M. Sands, "Tracking Religion: Religion through the Lens of Critical and Cultural Studies," *Council of Societies for the Study of Religion Bulletin* 31 (September 2002): 70. On *visual culture* Chris Jenks argues, "Within the academy, 'visual culture' is a term used conventionally to signify painting, sculpture, design, and architecture; it indicates a late-modern broadening of that previously contained within the definition of 'fine art.'" And he and his colleagues broaden the term still further to include advertising, photography, film, television, and propaganda. Chris Jenks, ed., *Visual Culture* (London and New York: Routledge, 1995), 16. See also David Morgan and Sally Promey, eds., *The Visual Culture of American Religions* (Berkeley: University of California Press, 2001), xiii. On the history and uses of the term *religion,* see also Peter Harrison, *"Religion" and the Religions in the English Enlightenment* (Cambridge: Cambridge University Press, 1990), and Attila K. Molnár, "The Construction of the Notion of Religion in Early Modern Europe," *Method and Theory in the Study of Religion* 14.1 (2002): 47–60. As I note in the next paragraph, Fitzgerald

proposed *politics, ritual,* and *soteriology* as alternatives. Timothy Fitzgerald, *The Ideology of Religious Studies* (New York: Oxford University Press, 2000). William Cantwell Smith proposed *faiths* and *tradition,* and I have no objection to using those two terms as synonyms, but I am not convinced they solve the problems raised by the term *religion.* Smith, *Meaning and End of Religion.* Daniel Dubuisson recommended we use *"formations cosmographiques"* (cosmographic formations): Dubuisson, *The Western Construction of Religion,* 17–22, 69–76, 198–213. This interesting suggestion, however, does not seem to avoid the second and fourth objections to definitions. It is certainly a term that emerged in the West, and it seems to have few obvious linguistic equivalents in non-Western languages. It also is not immediately clear that it has much more cross-cultural reach than the term it replaces. Further, as with Paul Tillich's notion of religion as "ultimate concern," one advantage of Dubuisson's term—its ability to include atheist, agnostic, and materialist conceptions of the world—is also a source of its limitation, for now the question of boundaries emerges again. What is *not* a cosmographic formation? All this is not to mention a final objection—that, for good or ill, the new phrase has not been the constitutive term for a field of study for the past century and a half.

15. A. L. Kroeber and Clyde Kluckhohn, *Culture: A Critical Review of Concepts and Definitions,* Papers of the Peabody Museum of American Archeology and Ethnology, Harvard University, vol. 47 (Cambridge, Mass.: Peabody Museum, 1952). For a discussion of some of the problems with *culture,* see Robert Brightman, "Forget Culture: Replacement, Transcendence, and Relexification," *Cultural Anthropology* 10 (1995): 509–546. In another important piece, anthropologist Lila Abu-Lughod tries to "disturb the culture concept" since it has "problematic connotations," including "homogeneity, coherence, and timelessness." Lila Abu-Lughod, "Writing against Culture," in Richard G. Fox, ed., *Recapturing Anthropology: Working in the Present* (Sante Fe: School of American Research Press, 1991), 143, 154, 157. For a critique in cultural geography, see Don Mitchell, "There's No Such Thing as Culture: Towards a Reconceptualization of the Idea of Culture in Geography," *Transactions of the Institute of British Geography,* n.s., 20 (1995): 102–116. Fitzgerald, *Ideology,* 4, xi. For a cross-cultural study of *religion,* and allegedly analogous concepts, see Hans-Michael Haußig, *Der Religionsbegriff in den religionen: Studien zum selbst-und religionsverständnis in Hinduismus, Buddhismus, Judentum und Islam* (Berlin and Bodenheim bei Mainz: Philo, 1999).

16. "Politics," in *The Oxford English Dictionary,* 2nd ed. (Oxford: Clarendon, 1989), from the online edition: *Oxford English Dictionary Online* (2001).

17. "Ritual" in *Oxford English Dictionary.* Roy A. Rappaport, *Ritual and Reli-*

gion in the Making of Humanity (Cambridge: Cambridge University Press, 1999), 3, 1, 24.

18. "Soteriology," in *The Concise Oxford Dictionary of the Christian Church,* ed. Elizabeth A. Livingstone (Oxford: Oxford University Press, 1977). Fredrik Barth, *Ritual and Knowledge among the Baktaman of New Guinea* (Oslo: Universitetsforlaget; New Haven, Conn.: Yale University Press, 1975), 124–127.

19. Melford E. Spiro, "Religion: Problems of Definition and Explanation," in Michael Banton, ed., *Anthropological Approaches to the Study of Religion* (London: Tavistock, 1966), 88. Max Weber used "ideal types" in a variety of ways in his works. For a helpful theoretical discussion, see Max Weber, "'Objectivity' in the Social Sciences and Social Policy," in Weber, *Methodology in the Social Sciences* (New York: Free Press, 1949), 49–112. See also Max Weber, *Economy and Society,* vol. 1, ed. Guenther Roth and Claus Wittich (Berkeley: University of California Press, 1978), 4–7, 20–22. Of course, if a category illumines nothing that interests an interpreter, the term will be judged of little use. But this is a matter of degree, and a term will rarely offer no interpretive benefits at all.

20. Smith, "Religion, Religions, Religious," 281. Smith, *Dictionary of Religion,* 893. Emphasis mine.

21. Talal Asad, *Genealogies of Religion: Discipline and Reasons of Power in Christianity and Islam* (Baltimore: Johns Hopkins University Press, 1993). David Chidester, *Savage Systems: Colonialism and Comparative Religions in Southern Africa* (Charlottesville: University Press of Virginia, 1996). Donald Lopez, *Prisoners of Shangri-La: Tibetan Buddhism and the West* (Chicago: University of Chicago Press, 1998). Richard King, *Orientalism and Religion: Postcolonial Theory, India, and the Mystic East* (New York: Routledge, 1999). The British Christian theologian Graham Ward, who also acknowledges the colonialist and capitalist origins of "religion," and its recent commodification, offers a genealogy of the social production of "religion." Yet he resists definition (and use) of the term and—unlike Asad, Chidester, Lopez, and King—predicts and champions a theological turn. "The turn to theology offers the only possible future for faith traditions," Ward has suggested, although those traditions will need to avoid fetishizing their faith as they do battle in the ever more widespread and ferocious "culture wars" that will follow. Graham Ward, *True Religion* (Oxford: Blackwell, 2003), vii–5.

22. Smith, ed., "Religion, definition of," *Dictionary,* 893.

23. Peter Gay, "Introduction," in *The Freud Reader* (New York: W. W. Norton, 1989), xiii. Sigmund Freud, *The Future of an Illusion* (1927; New York: W. W. Norton, 1989), 62, 55, 56.

24. Freud, *Illusion,* 55, 42.

25. This is not to say that tropic analysis is not useful in the sciences too. Consider the work of Gerald Holton, the scholar of physics and historian of science, who wrote the influential *Thematic Origins of Scientific Thought: Kepler to Einstein* (Cambridge, Mass.: Harvard University Press, 1973). In a more recent piece, Holton proposed that "in studying major scientists, I have repeatedly found the same courageous tendency to place one's bets early on a few nontestable but highly motivating presuppositions, which I refer to as themata." Holton goes on to note how certain tropes (or "themata")—including *symmetry* and *unity*—functioned in the work of Albert Einstein. Gerald Holton, "Einstein and the Cultural Roots of Modern Science," in Peter Galison, Stephen R. Graubard, and Everett Mendelsohn, eds., *Science in Culture* (New Brunswick, N.J.: Transaction, 2001), 24.

26. James W. Fernandez, "Introduction: Confluents of Inquiry," in James W. Fernandez, ed., *Beyond Metaphor: The Theory of Tropes in Anthropology* (Stanford: Stanford University Press, 1991), 6, 7. See also Dorothy Holland and Naomi Quinn's earlier interdisciplinary volume, which explored the role of metaphor and metonymy in constructing "cultural models" that organize cultural knowledge: Dorothy Holland and Naomi Quinn, eds., *Cultural Models in Language and Thought* (Cambridge: Cambridge University Press, 1987). A very helpful account of the major approaches to the theory of metaphor, especially in the humanities, chronicles four stages from the publication of I. A. Richards's *Philosophy of Rhetoric* in 1936 to the appearance of John Searle's *Expression and Meaning* in 1979: "Metaphor," in Wendell V. Harris, ed., *Dictionary of Concepts in Literary Criticism and Theory* (Westport, Conn.: Greenwood, 1992), 222–231. See Donald Davidson, *Inquiries into Truth and Interpretation,* 2nd ed. (Oxford: Clarendon Press, 2001), 245–264. Richard Rorty, "Unfamiliar Noises: Hesse and Davidson on Metaphor," in Rorty, *Philosophical Papers,* vol. 1 (Cambridge: Cambridge University Press, 1991), 162–172; and Nancy K. Frankenberry, "Religion as a 'Mobile Army of Metaphors,'" in Nancy K. Frankenberry, ed., *Radical Interpretation in Religion* (Cambridge: Cambridge University Press, 2002), 171–187.

27. Paul Friedrich, "Polytropy," in Fernandez, *Beyond Metaphor,* 17–55.

28. Nelson Goodman quoted in Friedrich, "Polytropy," 39. Edward Quinn, "Metaphor," in *A Dictionary of Literary and Thematic Terms* (New York: Facts on File, 1999), 192–193. Quinn gives the useful example of the indirect metaphor from Eliot's poem. T. S. Eliot, *The Complete Poems and Plays, 1909–1950* (New York: Harcourt, Brace, and World, 1971), 6, 4. Freud, *Illusion,* 55.

29. G. W. F. Hegel, *The Christian Religion: The Lectures on the Philosophy of Religion, Part III, The Revelatory, Consummate, Absolute Religion,* ed. and trans. Peter C. Hodgson (Missoula, Mont.: Scholars Press, 1979), 2. F. Max Müller, *Lectures*

on the Origin and Growth of Religion, as Illustrated by the Religions of India (New York: Charles Scribner's Sons, 1879), 1. Rudolf Otto, *The Idea of the Holy* (London: Oxford University Press, 1976), 11. Peter A. Angeles, "Definition," in *Dictionary of Philosophy* (New York: Barnes and Noble Books, 1981), 56–59.

30. Davidson, "What Metaphors Mean," 261. Harris, "Metaphor," *Dictionary,* 224. Max Black, "Metaphor," *Proceedings of the Aristotelian Society,* n.s., 55 (1954–55): 288. Thomas A. Tweed, *Our Lady of the Exile: Diasporic Religion at a Cuban Catholic Shrine in Miami* (New York and Oxford: Oxford University Press, 1997), 67. My own view of tropes, and of metaphor in particular, has been shaped to some extent by the Davidsonian tradition's emphasis on metaphor's uses. However, I also have profited from the "interactionist" theory of I. A. Richards, Max Black, Nelson Goodman, and others, as well as Robert J. Fogelin's reflections on figures, and especially his defense of metaphor as "elliptical similes," and Eva Feder Kittay's refinement of the interactionist theory and proposal of a "perspectival" theory of metaphor. Robert J. Fogelin, *Figuratively Speaking* (New Haven, Conn.: Yale University Press, 1988). Eva Feder Kittay, *Metaphor: Its Cognitive Force and Linguistic Structure* (Oxford: Clarendon Press, 1987). Empirical and theoretical studies in cognitive science also offer interesting angles of vision on metaphor. On metaphors as "class-inclusion assertions," see Sam Gluckberg and Boaz Keysar, "Understanding Metaphorical Comparisons: Beyond Similarity," *Psychological Review* 97.1 (1990): 3–18. For an introduction and overview, see Matthew S. McGlone, "Metaphor" in Lynn Nadel, ed., *Encyclopedia of Cognitive Science,* vol. 3 (New York and Tokyo: Nature Publishing Group, 2003), 15–18; and Dedre Gentner and Brian Bowdle, "Metaphor Processing, Psychology of," in *Encyclopedia of Cognitive Science,* vol. 3, 18–21. For a summary of research and theory on analogy more broadly, including metaphor, see Dedre Gentner, Keith J. Holyoak, and Boicho N. Kokinov, eds., *The Analogical Mind: Perspectives from Cognitive Science* (Cambridge and London: MIT Press, 2001). The view of metaphor I outline here informs what I say in Chapters 3 and 4, and throughout, about the functions of religious tropes.

31. Harris, "Metaphor," *Dictionary,* 224. Nelson Goodman, *Languages of Art: An Approach to a Theory of Symbols* (Indianapolis: Hackett, 1976), 71–73. Victor Turner, *Dramas, Fields, and Metaphors: Symbolic Action in Human Society* (Ithaca, N.Y.: Cornell University Press, 1974), 29. Turner endorses the "interaction view" of I. A. Richards and Max Black (29–33). Black, "Metaphor." I. A. Richards, *The Philosophy of Rhetoric* (New York: Oxford University Press, 1936). I have reservations about Black's talk about "filters" and Goodman's talk about "schemes" for a variety of reasons, especially because I am persuaded by Donald Davidson's critique of the usual notions about divergent "conceptual schemes" and Terry Godlove's chal-

lenge to the strong version of the "framework model" of religious belief. See Donald Davidson, "On the Very Idea of a Conceptual Scheme," in Davidson, *Inquiries,* 183–198; and Terry F. Godlove, Jr., *Religion, Interpretation, and Diversity of Belief: The Framework Model from Kant to Durkheim to Davidson* (Cambridge: Cambridge University Press, 1989).

32. Fernandez, "Introduction," 5. Sherry Ortner, "On Key Symbols," *American Anthropologist* 75.5 (October 1973): 1338–46. James W. Fernandez, "The Mission of Metaphor in Expressive Culture," *Current Anthropology* 15.2 (June 1974): 119–145. Turner, *Dramas,* 25–26. As Turner notes, he borrowed the term *root metaphor* from Stephen Pepper: Stephen C. Pepper, *World Hypotheses* (Berkeley: University of California Press, 1942), 91–92.

33. E. B. Tylor, *Primitive Culture,* vol. 1 (1871; London: John Murray, 1920), 424. James Martineau, *A Study of Religion: Its Sources and Contents,* 2 vols., revised American edition (Oxford: Clarendon Press; New York: Macmillan, 1888), 1. Cornelis Petrus Tiele, *Elements of a Science of Religion: Morphological and Ontological,* vol. 1 (Edinburgh and London: W. Blackwood, 1897), 4–6. Robert Crawford, *What Is Religion?* (London and New York: Routledge, 2002), 201. Stewart Guthrie, *Faces in the Clouds: A New Theory of Religion* (New York: Oxford University Press, 1993), 178. Scott Atran, *In Gods We Trust: The Evolutionary Landscape of Religion* (New York: Oxford University Press, 2002), 4. Atran actually uses the term "commitment," not belief: "Roughly, religion is (1) a community's costly and hard-to-fake commitment (2) to a counterfactual and counterintuitive world of supernatural agents (3) who master people's existential anxieties, such as death and deception." For examples of cognitive approaches, see E. Thomas Lawson and Robert N. McCauley, *Rethinking Religion: Connecting Cognition and Culture* (Cambridge: Cambridge University Press, 1990); Pascal Boyer, *Religion Explained: The Evolutionary Origins of Religious Thought* (New York: Basic Books, 2001); Harvey Whitehouse, *Arguments and Icons: Divergent Modes of Religiosity* (Oxford: Oxford University Press, 2000); and Ilkka Pyysiäinen, *How Religion Works: Towards a New Cognitive Science of Religion* (Leiden: Brill, 2001). Immanuel Kant, *Religion within the Limits of Reason Alone* (1793; New York: Harper and Brothers, 1960), 142. Rappaport, *Ritual,* 3. Christian Smith, *Moral, Believing Animals: Human Personhood and Culture* (Oxford and New York: Oxford University Press, 2003), 98, 104. Friedrich Schleiermacher, *The Christian Faith,* vol. 1 (1821–22; New York: Harper and Row, 1963), 12–18. Rudolf Otto, *The Idea of the Holy* (1917; London and Oxford: Oxford University Press, 1958), 12. David Hume, *Dialogues and Natural History of Religion* (New York: Oxford University Press, 1993), 140.

34. Friedrich Schleiermacher, *On Religion: Speeches to Its Cultured Despisers*

(New York: Harper and Row, 1958), 44–46 (*gefühl* and *anschauung*), 241 (*emfingunsweise*). John Oman translates the latter as "type of feeling" but the term might be better rendered as "type of experience," to distinguish it from the other two words that Schleiermacher uses most often to mark the nature of religion: feeling and intuition. Friedrich Schleiermacher, *Über die Religion*, Kritische Gesamtausgabe, band 12 (1831; Berlin: Walter de Gruyter, 1995), 61–64, 285. Otto, *Idea of the Holy*, 5. Mircea Eliade, *The Sacred and the Profane: The Nature of Religion* (New York: Harcourt Brace Jovanovich, 1959), 8–18. F. Max Müller, *Lectures on the Origin and Growth of Religion, as Illustrated by the Religions of India* (New York: Charles Scribners, 1879), 20–21. Frank Byron Jevons, *An Introduction to the History of Religion* (London: Methuen; New York: Macmillan, 1896), 9–10.

35. Hume, *Dialogues and Natural History of Religion*, 159. Paul Tillich, *Theology of Culture* (New York: Oxford University Press, 1959), 7–8. George M. Stratten, *The Psychology of the Religious Life* (London: G. Allen, 1911), 343. H. Bosanquet, quoted in Leuba, *Psychological Study*, 353. Smith, "Religion, Religions, Religious," 280.

36. Morris Jastrow, Jr., *The Study of Religion* (1901; Chico, Calif.: Scholars Press, 1981), 171. James, *Varieties*, 31. Tiele, *Elements of a Science of Religion*, vol. 2 (Edinburgh and London: William Blackwood, 1899), 14. Emile Durkheim, *The Elementary Forms of Religious Life* (1912; New York: Free Press, 1995), 44.

37. Edward O. Wilson, *Consilience: The Unity of Knowledge* (New York: Vintage, 1998), 280. Tylor, *Primitive Culture*. Müller, *Origin and Growth*. Freud, *Illusion*, 55–56. Durkheim, *Elementary Forms*, 44. Clifford Geertz, *The Interpretation of Cultures* (New York: Basic Books, 1973), 90. Gerald James Larson, "Prolegomenon to a Theory of Religion," *Journal of the American Academy of Religion* 46.4 (December 1978): 443.

38. Peter Berger, *The Sacred Canopy: Elements of a Sociological Theory of Religion* (Garden City, N.Y.: Doubleday, 1969), 3–25. Ninian Smart, *The World's Religions* (Englewood Cliffs, N.J.: Prentice Hall, 1989), 9. Ludwig Wittgenstein, *Philosophical Investigations* (New York: Macmillan, 1968), 11. Larson, "Prolegomenon to a Theory of Religion," 443. Wittgenstein did not employ "form of life" to describe religion in *Philosophical Investigations*, but others have applied that phrase in their accounts of religion, including Larson. Wittgenstein did talk a good deal about religion in terms of *pictures*, however: Ludwig Wittgenstein, *Lectures and Conversations on Aesthetics, Psychology, and Religious Belief* (Berkeley: University of California Press, 1972), 55, 59, 63, 66–68, 71–72. See also Hilary Putnam's insightful analysis of Wittgenstein's use of "picture" as an orienting metaphor for understanding religion: Hilary Putnam, "Wittgenstein on Religious Belief," in Leroy S. Rouner, ed., *On Community* (Notre Dame, Ind.: Notre Dame University Press, 1991), 56–75. Hegel, *The Christian Religion*, 33, 35–36. As the translator, Peter C. Hodgson, notes, *vorstellung* "produces synthetic images based on sense perception" (xxv). It is in

this sense that it can be understood as "pictorial thinking" or "representation." Van A. Harvey, *Feuerbach and the Interpretation of Religion* (Cambridge: Cambridge University Press, 1995), 229–280. In an extremely useful typology, Harvey distinguishes "beam" projection theories and "grid" projection theories. I have borrowed the first term but not the second, but not because I don't think both provide insights. Many interpreters whom Harvey classifies as grid theorists I have classified in other ways, although I see his point. Although some of his grid theorists (for example, Berger, Clifford Geertz, or Marx) do appeal to the *indirect* metaphor of a grid, I classify them here by noting what I take to be the *direct* metaphor that orients their definition: for instance, *worldview, system,* or *narcotic.* Of course, as I have noted, multiple tropes are usually at work in the most complex and satisfying definitions. Other anthropologists beside Spiro have defined religion as an "institution," for example Armin Geertz, who suggested that "religion is a cultural system and a social institution that governs and promotes ideal interpretations of existence and ideal praxis with reference to postulated transempirical powers or beings." Geertz, "Definition as Analytical Strategy in the Study of Religion," 471. Charles H. Long, *Significations: Signs, Symbols, and Images in the Interpretation of Religion* (1986; Aurora, Colo.: Davies Group, 1995), 7. Gordon D. Kaufman, *In Face of Mystery: A Constructive Theology* (Cambridge, Mass.: Harvard University Press, 1993), 36–37, 70, 432. Durkheim, *Elementary Forms,* 44. Spiro, "Religion: Problems of Definition and Explanation," 96. G. Van der Leeuw, *Religion in Essence and Manifestation,* 2 vols. (1933; New York: Harper and Row, 1963), 2:393–402. Eliade, *Sacred and Profane,* 20–65.

39. Alfred North Whitehead, *Religion in the Making* (Meridian: Cleveland, 1960), 16. Turner, *Dramas,* 25. For a helpful volume that explores issues in the representation of indigenous religions—including the moral issues—see Jacob K. Olupona, ed., *Beyond Primitivism: Indigenous Religious Traditions and Modernity* (New York and London: Routledge, 2004).

3. Confluences

Epigraphs: Gilles Deleuze and Félix Guattari, *A Thousand Plateaus: Capitalism and Schizophrenia* (Minneapolis: University of Minnesota Press, 1987), 372. Michel Serres with Bruno Latour, *Conversations on Science, Culture, and Time* (Ann Arbor: University of Michigan Press, 1995), 127.

1. J. J. Jones, trans., *The Mahāvastu,* vol. 3 (London: The Pali Text Society, 1949–56), 328–331. Francis H. Cook, *Hua-yen Buddhism: The Jewel Net of Indra* (University Park: Pennsylvania State University Press, 1977), 2.

2. G. S. Kirk, ed. and trans., *Heraclitus: The Cosmic Fragments* (Cambridge: Cambridge University Press, 1954), 381, 14. Kirk suggests that this famous saying about the river is probably not authentic, and Heraclitus' understanding is probably more accurately represented in fragment 12: "Upon those who step into the same rivers different and again different waters flow" (367). And in that passage that draws on the water analogy, and in the multiple attributions about the "flux" of things, Kirk suggests that Plato and other commentators misinterpreted Heraclitus. The Greek philosopher did not believe "that everything was changing all the time, though *many* things are so changing and everything must *eventually* change" (366). Friedrich Nietzsche, *The Will to Power* (New York: Vintage, 1968), 330, 312. James H. Leuba, *A Psychological Study of Religion: Its Origin, Function, and Future* (1912; New York: AMS Press, 1969), 42.

3. Alfred North Whitehead, *Process and Reality: An Essay in Cosmology*, corrected edition (1929; New York: Free Press, 1978), 208, 7. For an overview of the three Whiteheadean terms I cite, see Whitehead, *Process*, 18–20. Henri Bergson, *Creative Evolution* (1907; Mineola, N.Y.: Dover, 1998), 302. Brian Massumi, *Parables for the Virtual: Movement, Affect, and Sensation* (Durham, N.C.: Duke University Press, 2002), 7–9. Some interpreters who have drawn on Whitehead or Bergson also have noted the intellectual resources in Buddhism for talking about movement and relation. For example, see Minoru Yamaguchi, *The Intuition of Zen and Bergson* ("Japan" [no city listed]: published for the author by the Herder Agency, 1969); and John B. Cobb, Jr., *Beyond Dialogue: Toward Mutual Transformation of Christianity and Buddhism* (Philadelphia: Fortress Press, 1982).

4. Massumi, *Parables*, 7. Arjun Appadurai, *Modernity at Large: Cultural Dimensions of Globalization* (Minneapolis: University of Minnesota Press, 1996), 33. Marcus A. Doel, "Un-glunking Geography: Spatial Science after Dr. Seuss and Gilles Deleuze," in Mike Crang and Nigel Thrift, eds., *Thinking Space* (London and New York: Routledge, 2000), 124. Anna Tsing, "The Global Situation," in Jonathan Xavier Inda and Renato Rosaldo, eds., *The Anthropology of Globalization: A Reader* (London: Blackwell, 2002), 475. In his review of that edited volume, David Graeber rejects Appadurai's language of "flows" and endorses Tsing's suggestion: David Greaber, "The Anthropology of Globalization (with Notes on Neomedievalism, and the End of the Chinese Model of the Nation-State)," *American Anthropologist* 104.6 (December 2002): 1222–27. James Clifford, *Routes: Travel and Translation in the Late Twentieth Century* (Cambridge, Mass.: Harvard University Press, 1997), 7. Paul Carter, *Living in a New Country: History, Traveling, and Language* (London: Faber and Faber, 1992), 101. Iain Chambers, *Migrancy, Culture, Identity* (London and New York: Routledge, 1994), 5. Some theorists anticipated the emphasis on

movement and relation in some ways, for example sociologist Norbert Elias, who advocated a *process sociology* that accounted for the changing and interdependent networks that link individuals, cultures, and societies. Norbert Elias, *The Civilizing Process*, 2 vols. (1939; Oxford: Basil Blackwell, 1978, 1982). For a brief overview of Elias, see Philip Smith, *Cultural Theory: An Introduction* (Oxford: Blackwell, 2001), 146–148.

5. Sally Engle Merry, *Colonizing Hawai'i: The Cultural Power of Law* (Princeton, N.J.: Princeton University Press, 1999), 28. Bruno Latour, *We Have Never Been Modern* (Cambridge, Mass.: Harvard University Press, 1993), 3. Mark C. Taylor, *The Moment of Complexity: Emerging Network Culture* (Chicago: University of Chicago Press, 2001), 5. See also Manuel Castells, *The Rise of Network Society*, vol. 1 of *The Information Age: Economy, Society, and Culture*, 2nd ed. (Oxford: Blackwell, 2000). Michel de Certeau, *Culture in the Plural* (1974; Minneapolis: University of Minnesota Press, 1997), 145. Clifford, *Routes*. Alan Isaacs, ed., "Force," in *A Dictionary of Physics* (Oxford and New York: Oxford University Press, 2000), 176. For an attempt to defend the use of "system" as metaphor, and to apply "systems theory" to the humanities (although not to religion), see William Rasch and Cary Wolfe, eds., *Observing Complexity: Systems Theory and Postmodernity* (Minneapolis: University of Minnesota Press, 2000).

6. Gilles Deleuze and Félix Guattari, *A Thousand Plateaus: Capitalism and Schizophrenia* (Minneapolis: University of Minnesota Press, 1987), 361, 372. Bruno Latour, "On Recalling ANT," Keynote Address, "Actor Network and After" Workshop, Keele University, July 1997. Available online at: *http://www.comp.lancs.ac.uk/ fss/sociology/papers/Latour-Recalling-ANT.pdf*. In a very different use of aquatic images, Hans Blumenberg suggested that we imagine life as a sea voyage and draw on the metaphors of seafaring and shipwreck. Hans Blumenberg, *Shipwreck with Spectator: Paradigm of a Metaphor for Existence* (Cambridge: MIT Press, 1997). This is an intriguing suggestion, though I think it is less adequate as metaphor because it implies that movement begins only when humans leave land. To turn to another image, the religious do not, as the sociologist Peter Berger suggested, erect "sacred canopies." Religions are too complex and too dynamic for that. As Christian Smith suggested in a playful corrective, itinerant individuals and transient traditions open countless "sacred umbrellas," which have the advantage of being small, hand-held, and—most important—portable. Christian Smith, *American Evangelicalism: Embattled and Thriving* (Chicago: University of Chicago Press, 1998), 106.

7. F. Max Müller, *Introduction to the Science of Religion: Four Lectures* (1873; London: Longmans, Green, 1882). Hendrik Kraemer, *The Christian Message in a*

Non-Christian World (London: Edinburgh House, 1938). Rudolf Otto, *The Idea of the Holy* (London and Oxford: Oxford University Press, 1958). The passages from Müller, Kraemer, and Otto were quoted in an article that I have found useful for clarifying the issues, although I do not follow the author on all matters: Daniel L. Pals, "Is Religion a *Sui Generis* Phenomenon?," *Journal of the American Academy of Religion* 55.2 (Summer 1987): 259–282. A number of interpreters have held that religion is *sui generis*—not only Müller, Kraemer, and Otto, but also Nathan Söderblom, Gerardus Van der Leeuw, Joachim Wach, and Mircea Eliade. During the mid-1980s and early-1990s, there was a good deal of conversation about that question and the concomitant issue of whether "reductionistic" approaches are defensible. Pals, Donald Wiebe, and Robert Segal were the most energetic and articulate interlocutors in that conversation. For example, see Robert Segal, "In Defense of Reductionism," *Journal of the American Academy of Religion* 51.1 (March 1983): 97–124; Donald Wiebe, "Beyond the Sceptic and the Devotee: Reductionism in the Scientific Study of Religion," *Journal of the American Academy of Religion* 52.1 (March 1984): 156–165; Daniel L. Pals, "Reductionism and Belief," *Journal of Religion* 66.1 (January 1986): 18–36. Michael Mann has argued that "societies are constituted of multiple overlapping and intersecting sociospatial networks of power," and his model is helpful for reminding us that power as well as meaning is involved, though as I have made clear by now I think that *flow* is a better metaphor than *network* for cultural analysis. Michael Mann, *The Sources of Social Power,* vol. 1, *The History of Power from the Beginning to* A.D. *1760* (Cambridge: Cambridge University Press, 1986), 1.

8. I return to this "blind spot" about personal agency in the book's Conclusion.

9. Appadurai, *Modernity at Large,* 33. Immanuel Wallerstein, *The Modern World System,* 2 vols. (New York and London: Academic Press, 1974). Building on Appadurai's scheme, Elizabeth McAlister made a similar suggestion in a footnote: "It is possible here to think of 'religio-scapes' as the subjective maps (and attendant theologies) of diasporic communities who are also in global flow and flux." Elizabeth McAlister, "The Madonna of 115th Street Revisited: Vodou and Haitian Catholicism in the Age of Transnationalism," in R. Stephen Warner and Judith G. Wittner, eds., *Gatherings in Diaspora: Religious Communities and the New Immigration* (Philadelphia: Temple University Press, 1998), 156. Like Tsing's comment about the limits of *flow* as metaphor, Manuel A. Vásquez and Marie Friedmann Marquardt have helpfully noted the same possible limitation with the talk about *scapes:* "it may lead to an understanding of globalization as the product of impersonal, utterly dislocated flows." So we have to have the same corrective in mind:

there are always personal and transpersonal forces at work. Manuel A. Vásquez and Marie Friedmann Marquardt, *Globalizing the Sacred: Religion across the Americas* (New Brunswick, N.J.: Rutgers University Press, 2003), 37.

10. On the procession through Echternach, see Mary Lee Nolan and Sidney Nolan, *Christian Pilgrimage in Modern Western Europe* (Chapel Hill: University of North Carolina Press, 1989), 94. H. A. R. Gibb, trans. and ed., *The Travels of Ibn Battuta, A.D. 1325–1354*, 3 vols. (Cambridge: Cambridge University Press for the Hakluyt Society, 1958, 1961, 1971). Theda Perdue and Michael D. Green, eds., *The Cherokee Removal: A Brief History with Documents* (Boston and New York: St. Martin's Press, 1995). On the artist who painted the image of the Trail of Tears shown in Figure 5, Jerome Tiger, see the appreciative account by his wife: Peggy Tiger, *The Life and Art of Jerome Tiger: War to Peace, Death to Life* (Norman: University of Oklahoma Press, 1980). Here is another pragmatic advantage of this definition of religion. The emphasis on trails invites a consideration of religion's role in environmental destruction. For example, we might ask how the traditional Christian view that humans have "dominion" over the natural world has left traces on the landscape. We might consider different kinds of traces or trails. Imagine the markings left by a hiker on a mountain trail: the footprints, the charred logs, the candy wrappers, the snapped branches. Or, in more ominous signs, the smoke streaming from factories, toxins seeping into the soil, oceans rising from global warming.

11. M. M. Bakhtin, *The Dialogic Imagination*, ed. Michael Holquist (Austin: University of Texas Press, 1981). On the notion of *glocalities* and *glocalization*, see Roland Robertson, "Glocalization: Time-Space and Homogeneity-Heterogeneity," in Mike Featherstone, Scott Lash, and Roland Robertson, eds., *Global Modernities* (London: Sage, 1995).

12. Charles Taylor, *Varieties of Religion Today: William James Revisited* (Cambridge, Mass.: Harvard University Press, 2002), 5. Taylor also mentions three contemporary "phenomena" that a Jamesean perspective does not illumine (111–116). A. A. Goldenweiser, Review, "Émile Durkheim—Les Formes élémentaires de la vie religieuse. Le système totémique en Australie, 1912," *American Anthropologist* 17 (1915): 719–735. Reprinted in W. S. F. Pickering, ed., *Durkheim on Religion* (Atlanta: Scholars Press, 1994). The quoted passage is on page 212.

13. Dan Sperber, "Anthropology and Psychology: Towards an Epidemiology of Representations," *Man*, n.s., 20.1 (March 1985): 78–79. Harvey Whitehouse, *Inside the Cult: Religious Innovation and Transmission in Papua New Guinea* (Oxford: Clarendon Press, 1995), 220. Robert N. McCauley and E. Thomas Lawson, *Bringing Ritual to Mind: Psychological Foundations of Cultural Forms* (Cambridge: Cam-

bridge University Press, 2002), 104. McCauley and Lawson actually attributed the position to Whitehouse, rather than Sperber, though they certainly were aware that it originated with Sperber. Boyer, *Religion Explained*, 2. E. B. Tylor, *Primitive Culture*, vol. 1 (London: John Murray, 1920).

14. Clifford Geertz, "Culture, Mind, Brain/Brain, Mind, Culture," in Clifford Geertz, *Available Light: Anthropological Reflections on Philosophical Topics* (Princeton, N.J., and Oxford: Princeton University Press, 2000), 215, 203, 205–206. Scott Atran, *In Gods We Trust: The Evolutionary Landscape of Religion* (New York: Oxford University Press, 2002), 10–13. On emotion—and the interaction of emotion, perception, and cognition—see E. Eich, J. F. Kihlstrom, G. H. Bower, J. P. Forgas, and P. M. Niedenthal, *Cognition and Emotion* (Oxford: Oxford University Press, 2000); J. P. Forgas, *Feeling and Thinking: The Role of Affect in Social Cognition* (Cambridge: Cambridge University Press, 2000); R. D. Lane and L. Nadel, eds., *The Cognitive Neuroscience of Emotion* (Oxford: Oxford University Press, 2000); A. Damasio, *The Feeling of What Happens: Body and Emotion in the Making of Consciousness* (New York: Harcourt, 1999).

15. For an example of the use of tropes in art, literature, and science, see Gerald Holton's discussion of the symbol of the microcosm. As that historian of science points out, the symbol appeared in Rembrandt Harmenszoon van Rijn's 1652 etching "Faustus" and Johann Wolfgang von Goethe's 1808 dramatic poem *Faust,* and, through Goethe's work, it also influenced Albert Einstein's beliefs about unity in nature. Holton, "Einstein and the Cultural Roots of Modern Science," in Peter Galison, Stephen R. Graubard, and Everett Mendelsohn, eds., *Science in Culture* (New Brunswick, N.J.: Transaction, 2001), 1–44. See Chapter 2, and the accompanying notes, for my view of tropes. I also return to the issue in Chapter 4. Following philosophers Donald Davidson and Richard Rorty, here and elsewhere I suggest that it is helpful to emphasize metaphors' effects and uses. It is helpful to highlight the ways that metaphors direct and redirect speakers' attention and transport users back and forth between domains of language, experience, and practice. New metaphors can prompt, in my terminology, new sightings and crossings. In noting metaphors' role as an agent of change I am indebted to Rorty's analysis—and Frankenberry's insightful interpretation of Rorty's position—but I also am indebted to work in cognitive science. For example, Dedre Gentner and her colleagues have analyzed the "progressive abstraction" of conventional metaphors over time and the ways that novel metaphors introduce change, and Keith J. Holyoak and Paul Thagard have talked about the role of analogy in cultural change. Donald Davidson, "What Metaphors Mean," in Donald Davidson, *Inquiries into Truth and Interpretation,* 2nd ed. (Oxford: Clarendon Press, 2001),

245–264. Richard Rorty, "Unfamiliar Noises: Hesse and Davidson on Metaphor," in Rorty, *Philosophical Papers,* vol. 1 (Cambridge: Cambridge University Press, 1991), 162–172. Nancy K. Frankenberry, "Religion as a 'Mobile Army of Metaphors,'" in Frankenberry, ed., *Radical Interpretation in Religion* (Cambridge: Cambridge University Press, 2002), 171–187. Dedre Gentner, Brian F. Bowdle, Phillip Wolff, and Consuelo Boronat, "Metaphor Is Like Analogy," in Dedre Gentner, Keith J. Holyoak, and Boicho N. Kokinov, eds., *The Analogical Mind: Perspectives from Cognitive Science* (Cambridge and London: MIT Press, 2001), 199–253. Keith J. Holyoak and Paul Thagard, *Mental Leaps: Analogy in Creative Thought* (Cambridge: MIT Press, 1996). Latour, *Modern,* 104. On a very different issue, although I use different terms here and shift the focus slightly, I agree with Bruce Lincoln's claim that definitions of religion must be flexible enough to attend to four "domains": discourse, practice, community, and institution. His typology of "minimalist" and "maximalist" models of culture—as well as his distinction among religions of the status quo, religions of resistance, religions of revolution, and religions of counterrevolution—also provides a helpful way of talking about the relation between religion and culture. Those typologies, and his criteria for adequate definition, emerge from his concern to reflect on the meaning of religion in the contemporary political context, as the title of his volume signals. Lincoln, *Holy Terrors: Thinking about Religion after September 11* (Chicago and London: University of Chicago Press, 2003), 5–8, 41–61, 77–92.

16. Charles Darwin, *The Expression of the Emotions in Man and Animals* (New York: Oxford University Press, 1998). Paul Ekman, "Biological and Cultural Contributions to Body and Facial Movement in the Expression of Emotion," in Amelie Rorty, ed., *Explaining Emotions* (Berkeley: University of California Press, 1980), 73–101. Anna Wierzbicka, *Emotions across Languages and Cultures: Diversity and Universals* (Cambridge: Cambridge University Press, 1999), 34–35. Jean Briggs, *Never in Anger: Portrait of an Eskimo Family* (Cambridge, Mass.: Harvard University Press, 1970). Catherine Lutz, "Ethnopsychology Compared to What?: Explaining Behavior and Consciousness among the Ifaluk," in Geoffrey M. White and John Kirkpatrick, eds., *Person, Self, and Experience: Exploring Pacific Ethnopsychologies* (Berkeley: University of California Press, 1985), 35–80. Michelle Rosaldo, *Knowledge and Passion: Illongot Notions of Self and Social Life* (Cambridge: Cambridge University Press, 1980). For a collection that explores the question of universals, see Paul Ekman and Richard J. Davidson, eds., *The Nature of Emotion: Fundamental Questions* (New York: Oxford University Press, 1994). On the cultural production of emotions, see the somewhat dated but still useful overview in Catherine Lutz and Geoffrey M. White, "The Anthropology of Emotions,"

Annual Review of Anthropology 15 (1986): 405–436. I am indebted to John Corrigan for his help on the recent research about religion and emotion. His written work also is very useful, especially John Corrigan, ed., *Religion and Emotion: Approaches and Interpretations* (New York: Oxford University Press, 2004); and John Corrigan, Eric Crump, and John Kloos, *Emotion and Religion: A Critical Assessment and Annotated Bibliography* (Westport, Conn.: Greenwood, 2000). Corrigan lays out the continuum of positions I describe here in his introduction to *Religion and Emotion*, 7–13.

17. On filial sentiments in Kongzi (Confucius) see, for example, *The Analects* 1.6 and 2.7. There is a sense that the Confucian virtues, for example *ren* or humaneness, sprout from sentiments, as in this comment in *The Analects* 1.2: "The gentleman applies himself to the roots. Once the roots are firmly planted, the Way will grow therefrom. Might we thus say that filiality and brotherly respect represent the root of *ren*?" Philip J. Ivanhoe and Bryan W. Van Norden, eds., *Readings in Classical Chinese Philosophy* (New York and London: Seven Bridges Press, 2001), 3–6. For a translation of the key passage about the feeling of absolute dependence (*das Gefühl der schlechthinigen Abhängigkeit*), see Friedrich Schleiermacher, *The Christian Faith*, vol. 1 (New York: Harper and Row, 1963), 12–18. For an analysis of how the experience of displacement shapes the cultural productions of diasporic groups, see Matthew Frye Jacobson, *Special Sorrows: The Diasporic Imagination of Irish, Polish, and Jewish Immigrants in the United States* (Berkeley: University of California Press, 2002). For an interesting meditation on the Christian encoding of sadness, and the "gift of tears," see E. M. Cioran, *Tears and Saints*, trans. Ilinica Zarifopol-Johnston (Chicago and London: University of Chicago Press, 1995).

18. Even though Durkheim believed, as I do not, that exploring "primitive religions" provided special insight into the nature and function of religion, he did reject attempts to speculate on "absolute first beginnings," suggesting, as I have, that such questions must be "resolutely set aside." Durkheim, *Elementary Forms*, 7. In emphasizing joy, I am reaffirming a comment made by William James, who argued that "happiness" is the central concern of humans: "How to gain, how to keep, how to recover happiness, is in fact for most men at all times the secret motive of all they do, and of all they are willing to endure." I return to this issue in Chapter 5. William James, *The Varieties of Religious Experience* (New York: Penguin, 1982), 78.

19. David Hume, *Dialogues and Natural History of Religion* (New York: Oxford University Press, 1993), 139–140. Max Weber, *Sociology of Religion* (Boston: Beacon, 1964), 139. Peter Berger, *The Sacred Canopy* (Garden City, N.Y.: Anchor, 1969), 53.

20. Grace M. Jantzen, *Becoming Divine: Towards a Feminist Philosophy of Reli-*

gion (Bloomington: Indiana University Press, 1999), 2. Berger, *Sacred Canopy*, 51. Hume, *Dialogues and Natural History of Religion*, 143. As Van Harvey has pointed out, Ludwig Feuerbach's later work offered a multicausal account of religion that acknowledged the significance of nature as well as varied subjective factors. Among the subjective factors at work in religion, Feuerbach suggested in his *Lectures on the Essence of Religion* (1851), was not only a "feeling of dependency" that included anxiety about limitation and death but also *Glückseligkeitstrieb*, a drive-to-happiness. Although I would not affirm most of Feuerbach's conclusions—including the claim that religion is a mistaken interpretation of the natural environment—it is important to acknowledge that he and some others in the Western philosophical tradition did identify other emotions at work in religion. For the later Feuerbach, those sentiments include joy, love, awe, and gratitude. Ludwig Feuerbach, *Lectures on the Essence of Religion* (New York, Evanston, and London: Harper and Row, 1967). Harvey, *Feuerbach*, 161–180.

21. On anthropomorphism and religion, see, for example, Stewart Guthrie, *Faces in the Clouds: A New Theory of Religion* (New York: Oxford University Press, 1993). As specialists have pointed out, it is difficult to know how to interpret *dao* and *li*, but they are certainly better analogized as forces than as persons. On *dao*, I have in mind the classic Daoist philosophical texts. See Philip Ivanhoe, trans., *The Daodejing of Laozi* (New York: Seven Bridges Press, 2002). On *li*, I have in mind the writings of the Neo-Confucian Chinese philosopher Ju Xi (1130–1200), who used two basic metaphysical terms *li* (principle) and *qi* (material force or life energy). But, as Wing-Tsit Chan noted, *principle* is logically and ontologically prior, and it is identified with the *Great Ultimate*. Note that Chan translates a key passage in Ju Xi's writings this way: "The Great Ultimate is nothing other than principle." Wing-Tsit Chan, ed. and trans., *A Source Book in Chinese Philosophy* (Princeton, N.J.: Princeton University Press, 1963), 634, 638.

22. Thomas A. Tweed, *Our Lady of the Exile: Diasporic Religion at a Cuban Catholic Shrine in Miami* (New York: Oxford University Press, 1997), 93. Another volume published that same year also used *dwelling* in useful ways, as it championed *travel* as a root metaphor: Clifford, *Routes*, 1–13. Even if I came to the terms *dwelling* and *crossing* by other "routes"—reflection on my fieldwork in Miami—I am indebted to Clifford for enriching and complicating my understanding of the interpretive possibilities of these terms. I have learned a great deal from cultural geographers about *spatial practices*, but for that phrase, and much more, I am indebted to Michel de Certeau. Clifford acknowledges his debt to that French theorist too (53). See Michel de Certeau, *The Practice of Everyday Life* (Berkeley: University of California Press, 1984), 91–130.

23. Charles H. Long, *Significations: Signs, Symbols, and Images in the Interpretation of Religion* (1986; Aurora, Colo.: Davies Group, 1995), 7. Henri Bergson identified two sources or forms of religion, static and dynamic, but he used the terms in very different ways. See Henri Bergson, *The Two Sources of Morality and Religion* (New York: H. Holt, 1935).

24. The passage quoted is from the popular Tamil text *The Four Hundred Quatrains (Nāḷaḍinānnūrru)*: Ainslie T. Embree, ed., *Sources of Indian Tradition*, vol. 1, 2nd ed. (New York: Columbia University Press, 1988), 73. Other interpreters have pointed to the significance of "boundaries" and "limits" for religion. See, for example, Catherine L. Albanese, *America: Religions and Religion*, 3rd ed. (Belmont, Calif.: Wadsworth, 1999), 4–6.

25. In this paragraph and the next one I return to a question I addressed earlier in the chapter: is religion *sui generis*? I already have answered that—by suggesting that it is in a weak sense but not in a strong sense. By suggesting here that other cultural forms do not usually appeal to suprahuman forces, map cosmic space, or prescribe ways to cross the ultimate horizon, I am not saying that art, music, or literature do not sometimes include religious (or quasi-religious) themes. They do. To cite an obvious example, the Italian poet Dante Alighieri's *Commedia* appeals to supranatural forces and maps cosmic spaces as it recounts the poet's travels through hell, purgatory, and heaven. In my terms, however, that long vernacular poem is an example of the confluence of cultural flows. It emerges from the transfluence of religion and literature. As I see it, we can expect a definition of religion to mark religion's boundaries, but a useful definition also will be malleable enough to offer illuminating interpretations of cultural forms that do not fully overlap with the religious. Whether we talk about quasi-religious impulses—those that have some but not all the features of religion—or whether we talk about the transfluence of cultural flows—as I do more often—the account I offer here avoids some of the vagueness of Tillich's definition of religion as "ultimate concern" while still claiming the elasticity to have something to say about the complex ways that, for example, nationalism or poetry sometimes can emerge at the intersection of religious and secular cultural flows. Dante Alighieri, *The Divine Comedy*, trans. Charles H. Sisson (New York: Oxford University Press, 1993).

26. David L. Haberman, *Journey through the Twelve Forests: An Encounter with Krishna* (New York and Oxford: Oxford University Press, 1994), 25.

27. Wilfred Cantwell Smith, *The Meaning and End of Religion* (1962; San Francisco: Harper and Row, 1978), 195. Malory Nye, "Religion, Post-Religionism, and Religioning: Religious Studies and Contemporary Cultural Debates," *Method and Theory in the Study of Religion* 12.4 (2000): 447–476.

28. Gustavo Benavides, "The Tyranny of the Gerund in the Study of Religion," in Giulia Sfameni Gasparro, ed., *Themes and Problems of the History of Religions in Contemporary Europe / Temi e problemi della Storia delle Religioni nell'Europa contemporanea* [Hierá, Collana di studi storico-religiosi, 6] (Cosenza, Italy: Lionello Giordano, 2002), 53–66. Benavides himself argues for a combination of ethological, cognitive, and ecological approaches that also try to avoid thinking about religion in static terms, since they analyze religion as the "result of biological and social evolutionary processes" (7).

29. Michel Serres with Bruno Latour, *Conversations on Science, Culture, and Time* (Ann Arbor: University of Michigan Press, 1995), 101, 102, 127. Whitehead, *Process and Reality*, 22. Relationality also is emphasized in several ways in the writings of Deleuze and Guattari. Consider, for example, their notion of "reciprocal presupposition," which they use to trace the interaction between content and expression. Deleuze and Guattari, *A Thousand Plateaus*, 145–146. As I already have hinted by my neologisms *transtemporal* and *translocative*, prefixes can be as useful as prepositions. For example, the prefix *trans* is useful for gesturing toward a dynamic and relational theory, as the anthropologist Fernando Ortiz noted when he explained his reasons for preferring *transculturation* to *acculturation:* "I am of the opinion that the word transculturation better expresses the different phases of the *process of transition* from one culture to another because this does not consist merely in acquiring another culture, which is what the English word acculturation really implies, but the process also necessarily involves loss or uprooting of a previous culture." Fernando Ortiz, *Cuban Counterpoint: Tobacco and Sugar* (1947; Durham, N.C.: Duke University Press, 1995), 102. Emphasis mine.

4. Dwelling

Epigraphs: Charles H. Long, *Significations: Signs, Symbols, and Images in the Interpretation of Religion* (1986; Aurora, Colo.: Davies Group, 1995), 7. James Clifford, *Routes: Travel and Translation in the Late Twentieth Century* (Cambridge, Mass.: Harvard University Press, 1997), 36.

1. This account of the consecration of the shrine is taken from Thomas A. Tweed, *Our Lady of the Exile: Diasporic Religion at a Cuban Catholic Shrine in Miami* (New York: Oxford University Press, 1997), 99. See also Chuck Gomez and Miguel Perez, "Cubans Flock to Dedication of Shrine," *Miami Herald*, December 3, 1973, 1B, 2B. An estimate of the crowd, and other details about that ceremony are

included (with photographs) in Bob O'Steen, "Young and Old Showed Emotion: Flags Waved in 'Silent Applause,' " *The Voice*, December 7, 1973, 13; "Que la Virgen de la Caridad una al Exilio y lo conduzca a la liberación . . . ," and Gustavo Pena Monte, "Miles de Cubanos en la dedicación de la Ermita," *La Voz*, Suplemento en Español, December 7, 1973, 16. The dedication mass was concelebrated in front of the shrine by Cardinal John Krol of Philadelphia, president of the U.S. Conference of Bishops; Archbishop Coleman Carroll of Miami; Auxiliary Bishop René Gracida of Miami; Monsignor Eduardo Boza Masvidal; Father Orlando Fernández; and Monsignor Bryan Walsh, director of the Apostolate for Immigrants and Refugees. On *los taburetes*, the traditional Cuban chairs that are still built by farmers in the Cuban countryside, see the brief pamphlet published by the shrine: "La Virgen de la Caridad en Miami" (Miami: Ermita de la Caridad, n.d.). Agustín Román also mentions the chairs, and other features I describe here, in "La Virgen de la Caridad en Miami," in *Ermita de la Caridad* (Miami: Ermita de la Caridad, [1986]), 6–8. As I learned in an interview with the contractor, the tiled image of the Virgin over the central portal was done by a local subcontractor, Rivera Tile Company, from a painting by Teok Carrasco, who also executed the mural inside the shrine. Interview, Donald W. Myers (shrine contractor), 6 September 1994, Miami, Florida. I discuss the mural—as well as the busts, statue, and building—in chapter 5 of *Our Lady of the Exile.*

2. "Dwell," *Oxford English Dictionary Online* (2001). The philosopher Martin Heidegger used the term *dwelling (wohen)* to discuss humanity's situatedness in the world. For him, humans are in "the fourfold"—on the earth, under the sky, with the divinities, and with other mortals—by dwelling. Further, he linked the verb to dwell with the verb to build *(bauen)*. Martin Heidegger, "Bauen Wohen Denken," in *Vorträge und Aufsätze* (Pfullingen: Neske, 1954). For an English translation, see "Building Dwelling Thinking," in Heidegger, *Poetry, Language, and Thought* (London: Harper and Row, 1971), 145–161. A number of social theorists also have used the term *dwelling*, though I make it one of two central tropes for my theory. In a very different context, for example, Michel de Certeau talked about dwelling as an "everyday practice" akin to reading, talking, and cooking, and he suggested that his research "concentrated above all on the use of space, the ways of frequenting or dwelling in a place." Michel de Certeau, *The Practice of Everyday Life* (Berkeley: University of California Press, 1984), xxi–xxii. In a published response to James Clifford's suggestion that we use *travel* as the central metaphor for understanding culture, Stuart Hall encouraged Clifford to "conceptualize what 'dwelling' means" and answer the question "what stays the same even when you travel"? Clifford, in turn, did not really offer a full analysis of dwelling, but he did

take Hall's criticism to heart when he suggested that "comparative cultural studies" should focus on "everyday practices of dwelling and traveling: traveling-in-dwelling, dwelling-in-traveling." James Clifford, *Routes: Travel and Translation in the Late Twentieth Century* (Cambridge, Mass.: Harvard University Press, 1997), 44, 36. In a sense, what I do in this chapter is take up Hall's suggestion—to conceptualize dwelling—but I do so in a project—to define religion—that neither Hall nor Clifford have expressed much sustained interest in.

3. Satoshi Shioiri, Sadanori Ito, Kentaro Sakurai, and Hirohisa Yaguchi, "Detection of Relative and Uniform Motion," *Journal of the Optical Society of America* 19.11 (November 2002): 2169–79.

4. Ludwig Wittgenstein, "Lecture on Ethics," *Philosophical Review* 74.1 (January 1965): 8. Paul Tillich, *Systematic Theology*, vol. 1 (Chicago: University of Chicago Press, 1951), 163. Pascal Boyer, *Religion Explained: The Evolutionary Origins of Religious Thought* (New York: Basic Books, 2001), 13. In Chapter 5, I return to a related issue when I consider the differences between more and less abstract formulations of the problem of evil.

5. Tweed, *Our Lady of the Exile*, 107–110.

6. Ibid., 102–103.

7. On the Muslim pocket watch, see Carl Ernst, *Following Muhammad: Rethinking Islam in the Contemporary World* (Chapel Hill and London: University of North Carolina Press, 2003), 154. The inscription on the pocket watch identifies its original owner. For that and other information about the artifact, see also the account on the museum's Web site: Five Faiths Project, Ackland Art Museum, University of North Carolina at Chapel Hill, August 18, 2004, *www.ackland.org/fivefaiths*.

8. J. Gibbon, C. Malapani, C. Dale, and C. R. Gallistel, "Toward a Neurobiology of Temporal Cognition: Advances and Challenges," *Current Opinion in Neurobiology* 7.2 (April 1997): 170. D. Zakay and R. A. Block, "Temporal Cognition," *Current Directions in Psychological Science* 6.1 (February 1997): 12–16. J. H. Wearden, "Prescriptions for Models of Biopsychological Time," in M. Oaksford and G. Brown, eds., *Neurodynamics and Psychology* (London: Academic Press, 1994), 215–236. M. C. More-Ede, F. M. Sulzman, and C. A. Fuller, *The Clocks That Time Us: Physiology of the Circadian Timing System* (Cambridge, Mass.: Harvard University Press, 1982). G. J. Whitrow, *Time in History: Views of Time from Prehistory to the Present Day* (Oxford: Oxford University Press, 1988). Gisa Aschersleben, Talis Bachmann, and Jochen Müsseler, eds., *Cognitive Contributions to the Perception of Spatial and Temporal Events*, Advances in Psychology 121 (Amsterdam: Elsevier, 1999). For helpful overviews of the literature about temporal

perception, see John Gibbon and Chariklia Malapani, "Time Perception and Timing, Neural Basis of," in *Encyclopedia of Cognitive Science*, vol. 4 (New York and Tokyo: Nature Publishing Group, 2003), 401–406; and Lorraine G. Allan, "Time Perception," in Alan E. Kazdin, ed., *Encyclopedia of Psychology*, vol. 8 (New York and Oxford: Oxford University Press, 2000), 84–87. For another overview see Julio Artieda and María A. Pastor, "Neurophysiological Mechanisms of Temporal Perception," in María A. Pastor and Julio Artieda, eds., *Time, Internal Clocks, and Movement*, Advances in Psychology 15 (Amsterdam: Elsevier, 1996), 1–25.

9. On the distinction between "semantic" memory (for example, for Cubans in Miami, remembering how to act at the annual festival) and "episodic" or "flashbulb" memory (for example, for Americans, remembering 9/11 or the assassination of John F. Kennedy), see E. Tulving, *Elements of Episodic Memory* (Oxford: Clarendon Press, 1983) and Roger Brown and James Kulik, "Flashbulb Memories," in U. Neisser, ed., *Memory Observed* (San Francisco: W. H. Freeman, 1982), 23–40. For applications and revisions of that theory in the analysis of religious ritual, see Harvey Whitehouse, *Arguments and Icons: Divergent Modes of Religiosity* (Oxford: Oxford University Press, 2000), 50–53, 112–124; and Robert N. McCauley and E. Thomas Lawson, *Bringing Ritual to Mind: Psychological Foundations of Cultural Forms* (Cambridge: Cambridge University Press, 2002), 38–88. When I suggest here that artifacts "anchor" symbols, I am following the suggestion of the archeologist Steven Mithen. He has talked about artifacts as "anchors" of religious symbols that cross cognitive domains and argued that "religious ideas that are presented in material form gain survival value for the process of cultural transmission." Steven Mithen, "Symbolism and the Supernatural," in Robin Dunbar, Chris Knight, and Camilla Power, eds., *The Evolution of Culture: An Interdisciplinary View* (New Brunswick, N.J.: Rutgers University Press, 1999), 162, 164.

10. Burrow discussed "autocentric" and "allocentric" personality types: Trigant Burrow, *The Social Basis of Consciousness: A Study in Organic Psychology Based upon a Synthetic and Societal Concept of the Neuroses* (London: K. Paul, Trench, Trubner; New York: Harcourt, Brace, 1927). Much of the more recent scholarly literature refers to the first as "egocentric," but I think that term has some unhelpful moral implications—as in "he's so egocentric"—so I use Burrow's term, "autocentric." On spatial cognition, neurophysiological research, and the two models of representation, see N. Burgess, K. J. Jeffrey, and J. O'Keefe, eds., *The Hippocampal and Parietal Foundations of Spatial Cognition* (Oxford: Oxford University Press, 1999); R. G. Golledge, ed., *Wayfinding Behavior: Cognitive Mapping and Other Spatial Processes* (Baltimore: Johns Hopkins Press, 1999); and Babara Tversky, "Functional Significance of Visuospatial Representations," in Priti Shah

and Akira Miyake, eds., *Handbook of Higher-Level Visuospatial Representations* (Cambridge: Cambridge University Press, forthcoming). My discussion of the neurological and psychological processes involved in spatial representation is especially indebted to the work of Tversky and Burgess, including their useful overviews: Tom Hartley and Neil Burgess, "Spatial Cognition, Models of," in *Encyclopedia of Cognitive Science*, vol. 4, 111–119; Barbara Tversky, "Spatial Cognition, Psychology of," in *Encyclopedia of Cognitive Science*, vol. 4, 120–125. For an interesting analysis of the history of philosophical and psychological theories of spatial perception, see Gary Hatfield, *The Natural and the Normative: Theories of Spatial Perception from Kant to Helmholtz* (Cambridge: MIT Press, 1990). Some scholars have suggested that spatial perception and representation are gendered in some ways. For example, see I. Silverman and M. Eals, "Sex Differences in Spatial Abilities: Evolutionary Theory and Data," in J. Barkow et al., *The Adapted Mind: Evolutionary Psychology and the Generation of Culture* (New York: Oxford University Press, 1992). Steven Pinker also has pointed to a number of gendered differences in spatial abilities, including that men are better at manipulating three-dimensional objects while women have better depth perception. Steven Pinker, *The Blank Slate: The Modern Denial of Human Nature* (New York: Viking, 2002), 344–345. Among the influential interpreters of religion, William James offered the most substantial theory of spatial perception, though he did not apply that theory in any systematic way in his analysis of religion. See William James, *The Principles of Psychology*, vol. 2 (New York: Dover, 1950), 134–282.

11. My analysis of the role of language is taken from the work of Stephen C. Levinson, especially *Space in Language and Cognition: Explorations in Linguistic Diversity* (Cambridge: Cambridge University Press, 2002). A summary of some of that work can be found in his entry "Spatial Language," in *Encyclopedia of Cognitive Science*, vol. 4, 131–137. Levinson mentions Inuit spatial representation on page 134 of that entry.

12. F. Max Müller, *Lectures on the Science of Religion* . . . (New York: Scribner's Sons, 1881), 12, 119–123. Emile Durkheim, *The Elementary Forms of Religious Life*, trans. Karen Fields (New York: Free Press, 1995), 233. Stewart Guthrie, *Faces in the Clouds: A New Theory of Religion* (New York: Oxford University Press, 1993). For a report on experiments designed to identify the use of personification in narratives about the divine, and an assessment of Guthrie's theory, see Justin L. Barrett and Frank C. Keil, "Conceptualizing a Nonnatural Entity: Anthropomorphism in God Concepts," *Cognitive Psychology* 31.1 (December 1996): 219–247. Max Weber, *The Sociology of Religion* (Boston: Beacon, 1964), 9–10. Some twentieth-century phenomenologists, sociologists, and anthropologists (for example, Mircea Eliade,

Victor Turner, and Clifford Geertz) did attend to some tropes—especially symbol and myth—although metaphor, simile, and other forms of analogical language did not play a significant role in their analyses. Like Guthrie, other cognitive theorists of religion seem more concerned with personification, especially in their emphasis on "minimally counterintuitive supernatural agents," and they have not considered fully the ways that tropes mediate cognition and emotion.

13. Müller, *Lectures on the Science of Religion*, 118. Durkheim, *Elementary Forms*, 10–11. On the role of tropes in constructing collective identity, see Pablo Vila, *Crossing Borders, Reinforcing Borders: Social Categories, Metaphors, and Narrative Identities on the U.S.-Mexico Frontier* (Austin: University of Texas Press, 2000), 232–235. There is a vast literature on tropes, especially metaphor and symbol, in other fields, including cognitive anthropology, evolutionary biology, linguistics, computer science, and cognitive psychology. Some anthropologists have been exploring the intersection of cognition and culture for some time. Mary Douglas pondered "the social control of cognition" and focused on the role of "founding analogies": Mary Douglas, *How Institutions Think* (Syracuse: Syracuse University Press, 1986). In a similar way, building on the work of linguist George Lakoff and anthropologist W. H. Goodenough, among others, contributors to Dorothy Holland and Naomi Quinn's *Cultural Models in Language and Thought* (Cambridge: Cambridge University Press, 1987) offered a "cognitive view of cultural meaning" (3). Much of this literature refers, as I have, to metaphor's mapping of one cognitive domain onto another; see cognitive scientist Gilles Fauconnier's *Mappings in Thought and Language* (Cambridge: Cambridge University Press, 1997). Some psychologists and philosophers involved in cognitive science conversations have highlighted, as I have, the role of analogy in cultural innovation: Keith J. Holyoak and Paul Thagard, *Mental Leaps: Analogy in Creative Thought* (Cambridge: MIT Press, 1996). The archeologist Steven Mithen makes a compelling, if overstated, argument for the importance of "cognitive fluidity" and the capacity for cross-domain mapping in human culture, including art and religion: Steven Mithen, *The Prehistory of the Mind* (London: Phoenix, 1998). Although I would not go that far, some cognitive scientists, like Douglas R. Hofstadter, even have argued that analogical language is fundamental to *all* cognition: Douglas R. Hofstadter, "Epilogue: Analogy as the Core of Cognition," in Dedre Gentner, Keith J. Holyoak, and Boicho N. Kovinov, eds., *The Analogical Mind: Perspectives from Cognitive Science* (Cambridge: MIT Press, 2001), 499–538.

14. As I noted in Chapter 3, I borrow, and adapt, the term *chronotope* from the literary theorist Mikhail Bakhtin: M. M. Bakhtin, *The Dialogic Imagination*, ed. Michael Holquist (Austin: University of Texas Press, 1981), 84. Religions map, con-

struct, and inhabit many different sorts of spaces, or chronotopes. I should acknowledge that it is misleading to focus on just four: the body, the home, the homeland, and the cosmos. Religions also imagine and transform other spaces—including the street, the temple, the shrine, the neighborhood, the region, and the city—and by identifying these four I seem to be suggesting they are autonomous and static. They are not. These are only some of the myriad, shifting, and interpenetrating sites that religious women and men chart, make, and occupy. Yet I hope to show that analyzing these spaces in a very preliminary way—and I don't try to do more than that—can offer some hints about how dwelling practices function. On a different issue, I want to express my gratitude to William Paden, who discussed drafts of several chapters of this book and pointed to the term *habitat*. I had been talking about dwelling, inhabiting, and homes, but *habitat*, even though it is not a central term for me, does add some meanings that help me say what I want.

15. On unconscious circumspatial awareness, see James H. Austin, *Zen and the Brain* (Cambridge: MIT Press, 1999), 488, 496. Yi-Fu Tuan, *Space and Place: The Perspective of Experience* (Minneapolis: University of Minnesota Press, 1977), 34, 35. Alfred Schutz, *Collected Papers: The Problem of Reality*, vol. 1 (The Hague: Martinus Nijhoff, 1971), 262. I am grateful to my colleague Christian Smith for pointing me to the passage in Schutz: quoted in Christian Smith, *American Evangelicalism: Embattled and Thriving* (Chicago: University of Chicago Press, 1998), 106n7.

16. The passages from *The Questions of King Melinda* are included in Edward Conze, ed., *Buddhist Scriptures* (London and New York: Penguin, 1959), 147–149. The passages from the Hebrew Bible (Genesis 1:26–27; 5:1–3) are taken from Bruce M. Metzger and Roland E. Murphy, eds., *The New Oxford Annotated Bible*, New Revised Standard Version (New York: Oxford University Press, 1991), 3, 7–8. Alan Williams, "Zoroastrianism and the Body," in Sarah Coakley, ed., *Religion and the Body* (Cambridge: Cambridge University Press, 1997), 156, 158.

17. Ellen Gould Harmon White, *Counsels on Diet and Foods: A Compilation from the Writings of Ellen G. White* (Takoma Park, Md.: Review and Herald Pub. Association, 1976). For a study of Protestants and food, see Daniel Sack, *Whitebread Protestants: Food and Religion in American Culture* (New York: St. Martin's, 2000). Food practices, like other practices, are gendered; see R. Marie Griffith, *Born Again Bodies: Flesh and Spirit in American Christianity* (Berkeley: University of California Press, 2004).

18. William R. LaFleur, "Body," in Mark C. Taylor, ed., *Critical Terms in Religious Studies* (Chicago: University of Chicago Press, 1998), 38–40. Marcel Mauss

first published his analysis of "Les techniques du corps" in *Journal de Psychologie Normale et Pathologique* 35 (1935): 271–293. An English translation of that important essay can be found in Marcel Mauss, *Sociology and Psychology: Essays*, trans. Ben Brewster (London: Routledge & Kegan Paul, 1979), 97–123. Fredrik Barth, *Ritual and Knowledge among the Baktaman of New Guinea* (New Haven, Conn.: Yale University Press, 1975), 35, 74, 130.

19. Barbara Schreier, *Becoming American Women: Clothing and the Jewish Immigrant Experience, 1880–1920* (Chicago: Chicago Historical Society, 1994). Sandra Lee Evenson and David J. Trayte, "Dress and the Negotiation of Relationships between the Eastern Dakota and Euroamericans in Nineteenth-Century Minnesota," in Linda B. Arthur, ed., *Religion, Dress, and the Body* (Oxford and New York: Berg, 1999), 95–116. On the relation of the physical body to the social body see Mary Douglas, *Natural Symbols: Explorations in Cosmology* (New York: Pantheon, 1982), 65–81.

20. Mary Douglas also talks about trance, citing Raymond Firth's typology (spirit possession, spirit mediumship, and shamanism), and suggests a fourth type: Douglas, *Natural Symbols*, 75. Raymond Firth, *Tikopia Ritual and Belief* (London: Allen & Unwin, 1967). For an analysis of interpretations of trance, see Ann Taves, *Fits, Trances, and Visions: Experiencing Religion and Explaining Experience from Wesley to James* (Princeton, N.J.: Princeton University Press, 1999); and Mary Keller, *The Hammer and the Flute: Women, Power, and Spirit Possession* (Baltimore: Johns Hopkins University Press, 2002). See also Michel Foucault, *Abnormal: Lectures at the Collège de France, 1974–1975* (New York: Picador, 2003), 201–230. Janice Boddy, "Spirits and Selves in Northern Sudan: The Cultural Therapeutics of Possession and Trance," *American Ethnologist* 15.1 (1988): 4–27. R. Laurence Moore, *In Search of White Crows: Spiritualism, Parapsychology, and American Culture* (New York: Oxford University Press, 1977). Ann Braude, *Radical Spirits: Spiritualism and Women's Rights in Nineteenth-Century America* (Boston: Beacon, 1989). Gladys A. Nomland, "A Bear River Shaman's Curative Dance," *American Anthropologist*, n.s., 33.1 (January–March 1931): 38–41. Michael Saso, "The Taoist Body and Cosmic Prayer," in Coakley, *Religion and the Body*, 231–232. See also Kristofer Marinus Schipper, *Le corps taoïste: Corps physique, corps social* (Paris: Fayard, 1982).

21. Robert David Sack, *Homo Geographicus: A Framework for Action, Awareness, and Moral Concern* (Baltimore: Johns Hopkins University Press, 1997), 15. See also David Benjamin et al., eds., *The Home: Words, Interpretations, Meanings, and Environments* (Brookfield: Aldershot, 1995). Richard B. Lee, *The !Kung San: Men, Women, and Work in a Foraging Society* (Cambridge, Mass.: Harvard University Press, 1979).

22. Barth, *Ritual and Knowledge among the Baktaman,* 278–279 (Myth 3). See also Robert A. Orsi's compelling analysis of the *domus* in *The Madonna of 115th Street: Faith and Community in Italian Harlem,* 1880–1950 (New Haven, Conn.: Yale University Press, 1985), 75–149.

23. Shampa Mazumdar and Sanjoy Mazumdar, "Creating the Sacred: Altars in the Hindu American Home," in Jane Naomi Iwamura and Paul Spickard, eds., *Revealing the Sacred in Asian and Pacific America* (New York and London: Routledge, 2003), 143–157. Raymond Brady Williams, *Religions of Immigrants from India and Pakistan: New Threads in the American Tapestry* (Cambridge: Cambridge University Press, 1988), 42–47. Juan E. Campo, *The Other Sides of Paradise: Explorations into the Religious Meanings of Domestic Space in Islam* (Columbia: University of South Carolina Press, 1991). Aminah Beverly McCloud, "'This Is a Muslim Home': Signs of Difference in the African-American Row House," in Barbara Daly Metcalff, ed., *Making Muslim Space in North America and Europe* (Berkeley: University of California Press, 1996), 65–73. Tweed, *Our Lady of the Exile,* 32. Dana Salvo, *Home Altars of Mexico* (Albuquerque: University of New Mexico Press, 1997), 29. Methodist Church (U.S.), "The Dedication of a Home," *Doctrines and Discipline of the Methodist Church: 1940* (Nashville: Methodist Publishing House, 1940), 709–711. On religious artifacts and Protestant domestic space, see also Colleen McDannell, *The Christian Home in Victorian America, 1840–1900* (Bloomington: Indiana University Press, 1986); A. Gregory Schneider, *The Way of the Cross Leads Home: The Domestication of American Methodism* (Bloomington: Indiana University Press, 1993); David Morgan, ed., *Icons of American Protestantism: The Art of Warner Sallman* (New Haven, Conn.: Yale University Press, 1996). See also David Morgan, *Protestants and Pictures: Religion, Visual Culture, and the Age of American Mass Production* (New York: Oxford University Press, 1999). Observant Jewish homes might include Sabbath candlesticks, a menorah, and a bookshelf with devotional texts of various kinds; and *kashruth,* or Jewish dietary laws, shape the nature and functions of the kitchen in Orthodox homes; see Jenna Weismann Joselit, *The Wonders of America: Reinventing Jewish Culture, 1880–1950* (New York: Hill and Wang, 1994), 151. Muslim kitchens also are organized around the storage and preparation of Halal meat, which is slaughtered according to Islamic law. Many Muslims also subdivide intimate space further, by following the prescriptions not to linger in the bathroom since it is inhabited by *jinn,* or spirits; see McCloud, "'This Is a Muslim Home,'" 72. Not only did one article in a Catholic periodical in 1953, on the eve of the papally declared Marian year, exhort American devotees to build domestic altars so family members would maintain their devotion, "lukewarm Catholics will become fervent—and non-Catholic friends will remark about it," but the article also offered blueprints and

directions: "measure approximately 4'6" and 6'6" up from the floor and mark with a pencil," the printed instructions began. Charles B. Broschart, "A Shrine to Our Lady in Every Home," *Ave Maria*, December 5, 1953, 12–13.

24. Tweed, *Our Lady of the Exile*, 54. On Cuban American yard shrines, see also James R. Curtis, "Miami's Little Havana: Yard Shrines, Cult Religion, and Landscape," *Journal of Cultural Geography* 1.1 (Fall–Winter 1980): 1–15. Howard Finster, as told to Tom Patterson, *Stranger from Another World: Man of Visions Now on This Earth* (New York: Abbeville, 1989), 106. Another millennialist Protestant, James Hampton, rented a nearby garage space when it became clear that his room in a Washington, D.C., boardinghouse would be too small to contain the elaborate altar that the African American custodian was building from found objects and tin foil. That 250-piece structure, *The Throne of the Third Heaven of the Nations Millennium General Assembly*, not only sacralized space but narrated religious history: the pieces to the right of the throne represent Moses and the teaching of the Old Testament, while pieces to the left relate to Jesus and the New Testament. Throughout are references to the place and time of the world's consummation, the coming of the Kingdom of God. On Hampton, see Elinor Lander Horwitz, *Contemporary American Folk Artists* (Philadelphia and New York: J. B. Lippincott, 1975), 127–132. Etan Diamond, *And I Will Dwell in Their Midst: Orthodox Jews in Suburbia* (Chapel Hill: University of North Carolina Press, 2000), 51–52. See also Yosef Gavriel Bechhofer, *The Contemporary Eruv: Eruvin in Modern Metropolitan Areas* (Jerusalem and New York: Feldheim, 1998). For the Talmudic reflections on the *eruv* see Jacob Neusner, trans., *The Talmud of the Land of Israel: A Preliminary Translation and Explanation,* vol. 12, *Erubin* (Chicago: University of Chicago Press, 1991).

25. There is a vast social scientific literature on forms of social organization in multiple cultural contexts—including studies of nomads, clans, tribes, chiefdoms, nations, and empires—as well as analyses of a variety of other social spaces—including streets, barrios, cities, provinces, and regions. As anthropologist Hugo G. Nutini points out, ethnographic research on Mesoamerican communities has contributed a good deal to that scholarly discussion, including refinements of the concepts of "folk societies," "barrios," and "ritual kinship." See Nutini, "Mesoamerican Community Organization: Preliminary Remarks," *Ethnology* 35.2 (Spring 1996): 81–92. Sociologist James V. Spickard proposes an alternative Islamic model, which emphasizes the distinction between *tribes* and *cities*, as he persuasively argues that the standard categories of social organization—and those I use here—are not universal. They emerged from particular Western intellectual traditions and attention to European and American history. See Spickard, "Tribes and

Cities: Towards an Islamic Sociology of Religion," *Social Compass* 48.1 (March 2001): 103–116. On the Iroquois confederacy of six nations, see William N. Fenton, *The Great Law and the Longhouse: A Political History of the Iroquois Confederacy* (Norman: University of Oklahoma Press, 1998). I take the phrase "imagined communities" from Benedict Anderson, *Imagined Communities: Reflections on the Origin and Spread of Nationalism,* rev. ed. (London and New York: Verso, 1991). Expanding and revising Ernest Gellner's term "diasporic nationalism," I defined and analyzed it in Tweed, *Our Lady of the Exile,* 83–90. Ernest Gellner, *Nations and Nationalism* (Ithaca, N.Y.: Cornell University Press, 1983), 101–109. See also Akhil Gupta and James Ferguson, eds., *Culture, Power, Place: Explorations in Critical Anthropology* (Durham, N.C.: Duke University Press, 1997).

26. There is an enormous literature on social stratification and taxonomies. One of the most helpful studies is Thomas Hylland Eriksen, *Ethnicity and Nationalism: Anthropological Perspectives* (London and Boulder: Pluto Press, 1993). See also Gustavo Benavides, "Stratification," in Willi Braun and Russell T. McCutcheon, eds., *Guide to the Study of Religion* (London and New York: Cassell, 2000), 297–313. On the class and caste systems, see Brian K. Smith, *Classifying the Universe: The Ancient Indian Varna System and the Origins of Caste* (New York: Oxford University Press, 1994).

27. Zdzislaw Mach, *Symbols, Conflict, and Identity: Essays in Political Anthropology* (Albany: State University of New York Press, 1993). Tweed, *Our Lady of the Exile,* 110–112. On Martí, see John Kirk, *José Martí: Mentor of the Cuban Nation* (Tampa: University Presses of Florida, 1983). On Varela, see Carlos Manuel de Céspedes, *Pasión por Cuba y por la iglesia: Aproximación biográfica al Padre Félix Varela* (Madrid: Biblioteca de Autores Cristianos, 1998).

28. Diana Eck, *Banaras: City of Light* (Princeton, N.J.: Princeton University Press, 1982), 34–42. *The New Oxford Annotated Bible,* Genesis 12:1–7; 17:1–8. On the Sumerian understanding of the city-state, see Milton Covensky, *The Ancient Near Eastern Tradition* (New York: Harper and Row, 1966), 28. *Deep Significance of the Spring and Autumn Annals* is by the scholar Dung Jung-shu, and it is one of the most important philosophical works of the early Han. That passage (section 19, 6:7a–8a) is included in William Theodore de Bary, Wing-tsit Chan, and Burton Watson, eds., *Sources of Chinese Tradition,* vol. 1 (New York: Columbia University Press, 1960), 162–163.

29. On Ayodhyā, see Mark Jurgensmeyer, *The New Cold War?: Religious Nationalism Confronts the Secular State* (Berkeley: University of California Press, 1993), 81–90.

30. Barbara E. Mundy, *The Mapping of New Spain: Indigenous Cartography*

and the Maps of the Relaciones Geográficas (Chicago: University of Chicago Press, 1996). On the Purāṇic cosmograph of the *Vishṇu Purāṇa*, and on cosmology in other traditions, see "Cosmology," in Jonathan Z. Smith, ed., *The Harper Collins Dictionary of Religion* (San Francisco: HarperSanFrancisco, 1995), 291–294. On Rüst, and early European cartography, see Tony Campbell, *The Earliest Printed Maps, 1472–1500* (London: British Library, 1987), 79–84. On the ways that medieval European maps inscribed religious symbols and served spiritual purposes, see David Woodward, "Reality, Symbolism, Time, and Space in Medieval World Maps," *Annals of the Association of American Geographers* 75 (1985): 510–521.

31. Zhang Heng's account is included in de Bary, Chan, and Watson, *Sources of Chinese Tradition,* vol. 1, 193–194. The Roman Catholic Church's teaching on purgatory, a place or condition for souls who need purification before entering heaven, was clarified at the church councils of Florence (1439) and Trent (1563). See Joseph A. Dinoia, "Purgatory," in Richard P. McBrien, ed., *The Harper Collins Encyclopedia of Catholicism* (San Francisco: HarperSanFrancisco, 1995), 1070. The passage from the Qur'án is from "Divorce" (65:12): N. J. Dawood, trans., *The Koran* (Middlesex, U.K.: Penguin, 1974), 386. Descriptions of the six realms are numerous in texts from almost every Buddhist tradition. For a relevant selection from the *Tibetan Book of the Dead,* see Conze, *Buddhist Scriptures,* 230–231. Some Buddhists also have complicated this picture by suggesting that there are multiple world systems, many Buddha fields: Vasubandhu speculated there were a billion such systems. On Buddhist cosmology, see Rupert Gethin, *The Foundations of Buddhism* (New York: Oxford University Press, 1998), 112–132. Armin W. Geertz, *Hopi Indian Altar Iconography* (Leiden: E. J. Brill, 1987), 19, 29. The photograph of the ceremonial altar I describe is plate XXI. On the Hopi, see also John D. Loftin, *Religion and Hopi Life,* 2nd ed. (Bloomington: Indiana University Press, 2003). On indigenous traditions of the Southwest, including the Hopi, see the still useful overview by Peter M. Whiteley, "The Southwest," in Lawrence E. Sullivan, ed., *Native American Religions: America,* Selections from the *Encyclopedia of Religion* edited by Mircea Eliade (New York: Macmillan; London: Collier Macmillan, 1989), 45–63.

32. Geertz, *Hopi Indian Altar Iconography,* 8. The Hopi myth is included in Barbara C. Sproul, ed., *Primal Myths: Creation Myths around the World* (San Francisco: HarperSanFrancisco, 1991), 269–284.

33. My typology, and my analysis below, is indebted to a number of works on cosmogony. First, I am indebted to Charles H. Long's *Alpha: The Myths of Creation* (New York: G. Braziller, 1963). I also profited from the collections of creation myths, not only Sproul's *Primal Myths,* but other anthologies such as Ulli Beier, *The Origin of Life and Death: African Creation Myths* (London, Ibadan [etc.]:

Heinemann, 1966); and Charles Doria and Harris Lenowitz, eds., *Origins: Creation Texts from the Ancient Mediterranean* (New York: Anchor Books, 1976). Sproul organizes the myths geographically, but Doria and Lenowitz use a thematic arrangement that offers an interesting typology of myths from the ancient Mediterranean world, dividing them into two basic types (creation through the word and elemental creation) and then subdividing the latter into three types (rising, falling, dividing). James C. Livingston offered a typology of creation stories that helped shape my views too: *Anatomy of the Sacred: An Introduction to Religion* (New York: Macmillan, 1989), 198–221. See also David Adams, *Encyclopedia of Creation Myths* (Santa Barbara, Calif.: ABC-CLIO, 1994).

34. According to one text in the Theravada Buddhist canon, the *Dīgha Nikāya* (3.28ff.), the Buddha directly challenged the Hindu account of Brahmā's role as creator: Ainslie T. Embree, ed., *Sources of Indian Tradition*, vol. 1, 2nd ed. (New York: Columbia University Press, 1988), 127–128. The parable of the arrow is quoted, and analyzed, in Gethin, *Foundations of Buddhism*, 66–68. In that passage, Gethin also persuasively interprets the Buddha's reluctance to answer metaphysical questions about origins: it is because they are unanswerable, at least as they are usually formulated, since the cosmogonic question incorrectly presumes a substantial, enduring "world" that is populated by substantial, enduring "selves." On the other hand, Pali texts suggest that the Buddha taught that all things—including worlds and selves—are empty of substantial, enduring reality.

35. E. W. Nelson, *The Eskimo about Bering Strait: 18th Annual Report of the Bureau of American Ethnology* (Washington, D.C.: Government Printing Office, 1899), 452–462.

36. Sproul, *Primal Myths*, 192–194.

37. The excerpt from the *Enuma Elish* is included in Sproul, *Primal Myths*, 92. See also Alexander Heidel, *The Babylonian Genesis*, 2nd ed. (Chicago: University of Chicago Press, 1963). Julius Eggeling, trans., *Śatapatha-brāhmaṇa*, Sacred Books of the East, vol. 44, ed. F. Max Müller (Oxford: Clarendon, 1900), 12–15.

38. The anthropologist Alfred Gell wrote an insightful essay about the Tahitian creation myth that emphasized the importance of differentiation in the creative process: Alfred Gell, "Closure and Multiplication: An Essay on Polynesian Cosmology and Ritual," in Daniel de Coppet and André Iteanu, eds., *Cosmos and Society in Oceania* (Oxford: Berg, 1995), 21–56. He also cited the often-quoted Tahitian cosmogony from Teuria Henry, *Ancient Tahiti*, Bishop Museum Bulletin, 48 (Honolulu: Bishop Museum Press, 1928), 339–340. Mircea Eliade discussed that myth too: *Patterns of Comparative Religion* (New York: Meridian, 1974), 413. Sproul includes that myth, reprinting Henry's narrative, in *Primal Myths*, 350–351.

Sproul's *Primal Myths* also anthologized the other two myths I cite here, from the Pelasgians (156–157) and the Jivaros (308–313). On the Jivaran Indians, see Phillipe Descola, *La nature domestique: Symbolisme et praxis dans l'écologie des Achuar* (Paris: Editions de la Maison des sciences de l'homme, 1986). The Jewish and Christian traditions have emphasized monotheism, of course, but some translations of the Priestly creation account in the Hebrew Bible render the supernatural as plural—"the gods said Light." See Doria and Lenowitz, trans. and eds., *Origins*, 37–40.

5. Crossing

Epigraphs: Richard Kearney, *Strangers, Gods, and Monsters: Interpreting Otherness* (London and New York: Routledge, 2003), 230. Katherine K. Young, "Tīrtha and the Metaphor of Crossing Over," *Studies in Religion* 9 (1980): 61.

1. Edwin S. Gaustad, *Historical Atlas of Religion in America* (New York: Harper and Row, 1962), 159. On genetic migrations, see Luca Cavalli-Sforza, Paolo Menozzi, and Alberto Piazza, *The History and Geography of Human Genes* (Princeton, N.J.: Princeton University Press, 1994). Somewhat more accessible treatments of the topic can be found in Luca Cavalli-Sforza, *Genes, Peoples, and Languages* (London: Penguin, 2000) and Spencer Wells, *The Journey of Man: A Genetic Odyssey* (Princeton, N.J.: Princeton University Press, 2002). Peter N. Stearns, *Cultures in Motion: Mapping Key Contacts and Their Imprints in World History* (New Haven, Conn.: Yale University Press, 2001). James Clifford, *Routes: Travel and Translation in the Late Twentieth Century* (Cambridge: Harvard University Press, 1997), 2. Many other observers have commented on the significance of migrations in earlier periods, of course. In a volume that appeared in 7 B.C.E., Strabo, the Greek geographer who traveled in southern Europe, northern Africa, and western Asia, discussed "the changes resulting from the migrations of peoples": he pointed to the transregional movements of Egyptians, Iberians, and Persians. Strabo, *Geography*, vol. 1, Loeb Classical Library (Cambridge, Mass.: Harvard University Press, 1917), 227–229.

2. "Transport Revolution," in *Encyclopedia of World History* (New York: Oxford University Press, 1998), 674–675. My account of Chinese shipbuilding is from Manuel Castells, who also offers insights about the implications of the changes in communication technology: Manuel Castells, *The Rise of the Network Society*, vol. 1 of *The Information Age: Economy, Society, and Culture,* 2nd ed. (Oxford: Blackwell,

2000), 8. There is much less research on the relation between travel technology and religious practice than on communication media and religions, but there is a voluminous literature on early modern European voyages of "discovery" and evangelization, including works on the Portuguese. On their presence in Japan during this period, for example, see Peter Milward, ed., *Portuguese Voyages to Asia and Japan in the Renaissance Period,* Renaissance Monographs 20 (Tokyo: Sophia University's Renaissance Institute, 1994). For a volume that collects the interpretations of the early missionaries to Japan, including many Portuguese, see Michael Cooper, ed., *They Came to Japan: An Anthology of European Reports on Japan, 1543–1640* (Berkeley: University of California Press, 1965). There are a number of good studies of transcultural contact and exchange in Meiji Japan: see, for example, Judith Snodgrass, *Presenting Japanese Buddhism to the West: Orientalism, Occidentalism, and the Columbian Exposition* (Chapel Hill: University of North Carolina Press, 2003). On the significance of the railroad for African Americans, see John M. Giggie, "'When Jesus Handed Me a Ticket': Images of Railroad Travel and Spiritual Transformations among African Americans, 1865–1917," in David Morgan and Sally M. Promey, eds., *The Visual Culture of American Religions* (Berkeley: University of California Press, 2001), 249–266. On American Hindus' practice of traveling to the homeland, see Raymond Brady Williams, *Religions of Immigrants from India and Pakistan: New Threads in the American Tapestry* (Cambridge: Cambridge University Press, 1988), 289. On the Unchained Gang, see Rich Remsberg, *Riders for God: The Story of a Christian Motorcycle Gang* (Urbana: University of Illinois Press, 2000). I am indebted to Timothy Barrett of the School of Oriental and African Studies at the University of London for making a casual aside about "quadruped Buddhism" in the question-and-answer period at a conference at Duke University on February 21, 2004, "Global Flows and the Restructuring of Asian Buddhism in an Age of Empire." While everyone else in the room went on with the discussion about Chinese Buddhism, I began to sketch out the typology I offer here about the relation between transport technology and religion.

3. "Communications Revolution," in *Encyclopedia of World History* (New York: Oxford University Press, 1998), 155–156. Castells, *Rise of Network Society,* 8. Mark U. Edwards, *Printing, Propaganda, and Martin Luther* (Berkeley: University of California Press, 1994), 1. On print, see also Elisabeth Eisenstein, *The Printing Press as an Agent of Change: Communications and Cultural Transformations in Early Modern Europe,* 2 vols. (New York: Cambridge University Press, 1979). Philip Goff, "'We Have Heard the Joyful Sound': Charles E. Fuller's Radio Broadcast and the Rise of Modern Evangelicalism," *Religion and American Culture* 9.1 (Winter 1999):

67–95. B. Meyer, "Popular Ghanaian Cinema and 'African Heritage,'" *Africa Today*, 46.2 (Winter 1999): 95–113. B. Meyer, *Translating the Devil: Religion and Modernity among the Ewe in Ghana* (Edinburgh: Edinburgh University Press, 1999). M. Gillespie, "The Mahābhārata: From Sanskrit to Sacred Soap," in D. Buckingham, ed., *Reading Audiences: Young People and the Media* (Manchester: Manchester University Press, 1993), 48–73. On religion and computers, see Stephen D. O'Leary, "Cyberspace as Sacred Space: Communicating Religion on Computer Networks," *Journal of the American Academy of Religion* 64.4 (Winter 1996): 781–808; Brenda Brasher, *Give Me That Online Religion* (San Francisco: Jossey-Bass, 2001); Bruce B. Lawrence, *The Complete Idiot's Guide to Religion Online* (Indianapolis: Alpha Books, 2000); and Lorne L. Dawson and Douglas E. Cowan, eds., *Religion Online: Finding Faith on the Internet* (New York: Routledge, 2004). For a helpful overview of research trends and theoretical frameworks in the study of religion and communication since the mid-twentieth century, see Stewart M. Hoover, "The Culturalist Turn in Scholarship on Media and Religion," *Journal of Media and Religion* 1.1 (2002): 25–36. See also Hent de Vries and Samuel Weber, *Religion and Media* (Stanford, Calif.: Stanford University Press, 2001); Stewart M. Hoover and Lynn Schofield Clark, eds., *Practicing Religion in the Age of the Media: Explorations in Media, Religion, and Culture* (New York: Columbia University Press, 2002); and Jolyon Mitchell and Sophia Marriage, *Mediating Religion: Conversations in Media, Religion, and Culture* (London and New York: T & T Clark, 2003).

4. For an account of Mohan Singh's rolling journey toward Pakistan, see Paul Watson, "Saint, Peace Seeker, Hero by Turns," *Los Angeles Times*, June 1, 2004, A1. As far as I can tell from an online search of the English-language news reports from India, Pakistan, Britain, and the United States, Ludkan Baba apparently did not achieve his goal of entering Pakistan. Confirming reports from periodicals in Pakistan and India, a story in the *Los Angeles Times* suggested that he had to turn back after the Pakistani government refused him entry: "After more than 1,500 miles, Ludkan Baba, the Hindu ascetic who is rolling across India for peace, suspended his quest after being rebuffed at the Pakistani border. The holy roller decided Friday to return to his hometown of Ratlam with his 11-member, hymn-singing entourage." Shankhadeep Choudhury, "Indian Holy Man's Roll of a Lifetime Stopped at Border," *Los Angeles Times*, September 25, 2004, A.3.

5. On holy wells, see Michael P. Carroll, *Irish Pilgrimage: Holy Wells and Popular Catholic Devotion* (Baltimore: Johns Hopkins University Press, 1999). On Shikoku, see Oliver Statler, *Japanese Pilgrimage* (New York: William Morrow, 1983) and Ian Reader, *Making Pilgrimages: Meaning and Practice in Shikoku* (Honolulu: University of Hawaii Press, 2005). On Lourdes, and other European Catholic

shrines, see Mary Lee Nolan and Sidney Nolan, *Christian Pilgrimage in Modern Western Europe* (Chapel Hill: University of North Carolina Press, 1989). See also Ruth Harris, *Lourdes: Body and Spirit in the Secular Age* (New York: Viking, 1999). For the Muslim journey to Mecca, see F. E. Peters, *The Hajj: The Muslim Pilgrimage to Mecca and the Holy Places* (Princeton, N.J.: Princeton University Press, 1994), and Michael Wolfe, ed., *One Thousand Roads to Mecca: Ten Centuries of Travelers Writing about the Muslim Pilgrimage* (New York: Grove, 1997). The typology of pilgrimages I mention is from Alan Morinis, "Introduction: The Territory of the Anthropology of Pilgrimage," in Morinis, *Sacred Journeys: The Anthropology of Pilgrimage* (Westport, Conn.: Greenwood Press, 1992), 10. I also offer a typology of shrines and an overview of the approaches to the study of pilgrimage in two encyclopedia entries: Thomas A. Tweed, "Pilgrimage" and "Shrine" in Wade Clark Roof, ed., *Contemporary American Religion,* vol. 2 (New York: Macmillan, 2000), 534–536, 674–676. For a helpful review of some recent works on pilgrimage, see J. E. Llewellyn, "Pilgrimage as Bounded Entity: A Review Essay," *Religious Studies Review* 27.1 (January 2001): 38–46. Llewellyn notes that—as my work at the Cuban shrine also confirms—pilgrims visit shrines for many reasons, including what some observers might label as nonreligious motives: "Rather, pilgrimage centers are places people go to make money, to score points against their political adversaries, to gain social status, and even to have fun" (44). So pilgrims often are driven by multiple, overlapping motives. Among anthropologists, John Eade and Michael J. Sallnow have challenged Victor Turner's consensus model of pilgrimage, with its emphasis on "communitas," and so have the authors of a number of other recent studies, including Jill Dubisch. Victor Turner and Edith Turner, *Image and Pilgrimage in Christian Culture: Anthropological Perspectives* (New York: Columbia University Press, 1978). John Eade and Michael J. Sallnow, eds., *Contesting the Sacred: The Anthropology of Christian Pilgrimage* (London: Routledge, 1991). Jill Dubisch, *In a Different Place: Pilgrimage, Gender, and Politics at a Greek Island Shrine* (Princeton, N.J.: Princeton University Press, 1995). A good deal of the conversation has focused on Christian pilgrimage, but there are many works on pilgrimage in other cultures as well. For an overview, see Simon Coleman and John Elsner, *Pilgrimage: Past and Present in the World Religions* (Cambridge, Mass.: Harvard University Press, 1995). A number of fine studies of pilgrimage in India and Japan also have appeared, too many to cite here. On India, see Anne Feldhaus, *Connected Places: Region, Pilgrimage, and Geographical Imagination in India* (New York: Palgrave Macmillan, 2003) and David L. Haberman, *Journey through the Twelve Forests: An Encounter with Krishna* (New York: Oxford University Press, 1994). On Japan, see not only the works on Shikoku by Statler and Reader cited above but also the brief but helpful work by Ian Reader: *Sendatsu and the Development of Contemporary Japanese Pilgrimage* (Oxford: Nissan Institute of Japanese Studies, 1993).

6. Matthew 28:19. Acts 28:31. Stephen Neill, *A History of Christian Missions,* 2nd ed. (Middlesex, U.K.: Penguin, 1986). There is some evidence that Lull's own thought was influenced by the encounter with Muslims he sought to convert. See Charles Lohr, "The Arabic Background to Ramón Lull's *Liber Chaos* (ca. 1285)," *Traditio* 55 (2000): 159–170. However, as John Bossy points out, Lull was much more hostile toward Jews: John Bossy, *Christianity in the West, 1400–1700* (New York and Oxford: Oxford University Press, 1985), 84. On Charlemagne, see Matthias Becher, *Charlemagne,* trans. David S. Bachrach (New Haven: Yale University Press, 2003). For a translation of the *Capitulatio de partibus Saxoniae,* see the passages in Dana Carleton Munro, ed., *Selections from the Laws of Charles the Great* (Philadelphia: Department of History of the University of Pennsylvania; London: P. S. King, 1900). On the Fāṭimid caliphate, see Farhad Daftary, *A Short History of the Ismailis: Traditions of a Muslim Community* (Princeton, N.J.: Markus Wiener, 1998), 63–119. It is Daftary who translates *dāʿīs* as "religio-political missionaries" (64). On Aśoka, see John S. Strong, *The Legend of King Aśoka* (Princeton, N.J.: Princeton University Press, 1983). Of course, Buddhist emissaries also have transmitted practices, artifacts, and beliefs in other times and places, for example as monks from the Paekche kingdom (18 B.C.E–660 C.E.) brought Buddhism from Korea to Japan. On the role of Korean Buddhists in East Asia, see Robert E. Buswell, Jr., ed., *Currents and Countercurrents: Korean Influences on the Buddhist Traditions of East Asia* (Honolulu: University of Hawaii Press, 2005). On Buddhists as active agents in the propagation of their faith since the nineteenth century, see Linda Learman, ed., *Buddhist Missionaries in the Era of Globalization* (Honolulu: University of Hawaii Press, 2004).

7. On Cuban *balseros,* including their devotion to Our Lady of Charity, see Alfredo Antonio Fernández, *Adrift: The Cuban Raft People* (Houston: Arte Publico Press, 2000). See also the analysis of that book by Dora Amador Morales, "La fe de los balseros y la Virgen," *La Voz Católica* 49 (September 2001). This can be found online at: *http://www.vozcatolica.org/44/febalsa.htm.* Miguel Leon-Portilla, ed., *The Broken Spears: The Aztec Account of the Conquest of Mexico* (Boston: Beacon, 1992), 51. See also Davíd Carrasco and Eduardo Matos Moctezuma, eds., *Moctezuma's Mexico: Visions of the Aztec World,* rev. ed. (Boulder: University Press of Colorado, 2003). For a Spanish eyewitness account, which varies from the Nahuatl narratives, see Bernal Díaz, *The Conquest of New Spain* (London: Penguin, 1963). There is a voluminous literature on New Spain. For helpful overviews of the origins of

colonization in the Americas and the history of New Spain, see Daniel Vickers, ed., *A Companion to Colonial America* (Malden, Mass., and Oxford: Blackwell, 2003), 25–43, 451–468.

8. There also has been a great deal of scholarly interest in the Silk Road. A useful distillation of that scholarship, and the source of the information I mention in this paragraph, is Richard C. Foltz, *Religions of the Silk Road: Overland Trade and Cultural Exchange from Antiquity to the Fifteenth Century* (New York: St. Martin's, 1999), 71, 11, 8–9. I refer here to Faxian (ca. 337–ca. 418), who was the first Chinese monk to travel to India, as far as we know, and his account of that fifteen-year journey, *Faxian Zhuan* (416), has appeared in two English translations. For the more recent one, see Herbert A. Giles, trans., *The Travels of Fa-hsien (399–414 A.D.), or, Record of the Buddhistic Kingdoms* (1923; London: Routledge and Kegan Paul, 1956). See also Michel Strickmann, "India in the Chinese Looking-Glass," in Deborah E. Klimburg-Salter, ed., *The Silk Route and the Diamond Path: Esoteric Buddhist Art on the Trans-Himalayan Trade Routes* (Los Angeles: UCLA Art Council, 1982), 52–63.

9. Of the many works on the class and caste systems in India, see Brian K. Smith, *Classifying the Universe: The Ancient Indian Varna System and the Origins of Caste* (New York: Oxford University Press, 1994), 26–85. Gāndhi's challenges to the caste system in India are well known, and in his autobiography he recounted how some attempted to block his own journey to England on caste grounds: Mohandās K. Gāndhi, *An Autobiography: The Story of My Experiments with Truth* (1927; Boston: Beacon Press, 1957), 40–41, 90–91. On Ambedkar, see Christopher S. Queen, "Dr. Ambedkar and the Hermenutics of Buddhist Liberation," in Christopher S. Queen and Sallie B. King, eds., *Engaged Buddhism: Buddhist Liberation Movements in Asia* (Albany: State University of New York Press, 1996), 45–72. Jo Ann Kay McNamara, *Sisters in Arms: Catholic Nuns through Two Millennia* (Cambridge, Mass.: Harvard University Press, 1996), 237, 245. Malcolm X, with the assistance of Alex Haley, *The Autobiography of Malcolm X* (1964; New York: Grove, 1966), 339. Russell H. Conwell, *Acres of Diamonds* (New York: Harper and Brothers, 1915), 17–20.

10. The statistics I cite above about the number of times Conwell gave his famous lecture and the information about his ordination are from his authorized biography: Agnes Rush Burr, *Russell H. Conwell and His Work: One Man's Interpretation of Life* (Philadelphia: John C. Winston, 1926), 307, 184. Davíd Carrasco, *Religions of Mesoamerica* (San Francisco: HarperSanFrancisco, 1990), 110. On the Maya, see also Claude F. Baudez, *Une histoire de la religion des Mayas* (Paris: A. Michel, 2002) and Meredith Paxton, *The Cosmos of the Yucatec Maya: Cycles and*

Steps from the Madrid Codex (Albuquerque: University of New Mexico Press, 2001). E. Thomas Lawson, *Religions of Africa* (San Francisco: HarperSanFrancisco, 1985), 51–56. See also Andrew Apter, *Black Critics and Kings: The Hermeneutics of Power in Yoruba Society* (Chicago: University of Chicago Press, 1992) and Margaret Thompson Drewal, *Yoruba Ritual: Performers, Play, Agency* (Bloomington: Indiana University Press, 1992). As Lawson also noted, Yorùbá traditions have not remained static over time, and for a study of contact and exchange with Christianity, see John David Yeadon, *Religious Encounter and the Making of the Yoruba* (Bloomington: Indiana University Press, 2000). There are other well-known examples of rulers who have religious as well as political significance, as in the traditional Japanese understanding of the emperor.

11. Samuel B. How, *Slaveholding Not Sinful: Slavery, the Punishment of Man's Sin; Its Remedy, the Gospel of Christ: An Argument before the General Synod of the Reformed Protestant Dutch Church, October 1855* (New Brunswick, N.J.: J. Terhune's Press, 1856). Frederick Douglass, *Narrative of the Life of Frederick Douglass, an American Slave . . .* (1845; New York: Signet, 1968), 68. For two analyses of gendered seating in synagogues in very different settings, see Sharon Lea Mattila, "Where Women Sat in Ancient Synagogues: The Archeological Evidence in Context," in John S. Kloppenborg and Stephen G. Wilson, eds., *Voluntary Associations in the Graeco-Roman World* (London: Routledge, 1996), 266–286, and Jonathan D. Sarna, "Seating and the American Synagogue," in Philip R. Vandermeer and Robert P. Swierenga, eds., *Belief and Behavior: Essays in the New Religious History* (New Brunswick, N.J.: Rutgers University Press, 1991), 189–206. On gender and religious sites in Okinawa, see William P. Lebra, *Okinawa Religion: Belief, Ritual, and Social Structure* (Honolulu: University of Hawaii Press, 1966) and Susan Starr Sered, *Women of the Sacred Groves: Divine Priestesses of Okinawa* (New York: Oxford University Press, 1999). The practice of systematic gender exclusion seems to have changed somewhat in recent years. My colleague Christopher T. Nelson, an anthropologist who works on this region, told me that he found no evidence that men were regularly excluded from sacred sites or groves on the main island of Okinawa as of the mid-1990s. Pers. comm., Christopher T. Nelson to the author, February 8, 2005. As with religion and racism in other times and places, Christianity both supported and challenged apartheid in South Africa. On Dutch Calvinism in South Africa, see Piet Strauss, "Church and State and Apartheid in South Africa: A Perspective on the Dutch Reformed Church (1962–1998)," *European Journal for Church and State Research* 8 (2001): 327–346. On religion in South Africa, see J. S. Kruger, *Along the Edges: Religion in South Africa: Bushman, Christian, Buddhist* (Pretoria: University of South Africa Press, 1995) and David Chidester,

Religions of South Africa (London and New York: Routledge, 1992). On Hindu marriage, see Lindsey Harlan and Paul B. Courtright, eds., *From the Margins of Hindu Marriage: Essays on Gender, Religion, and Culture* (New York: Oxford University Press, 1995). See also Bhaiyārām Śarmā, *The Vivāha: The Hindu Marriage Saṃskāras* (Delhi: Motilal Banarsidass, 1993).

12. For an overview of Hindu rites of passage or *saṃskāras*, including marriage, see Gavin Flood, "Hinduism," in Jean Holm with John Bowker, eds., *Rites of Passage* (London and New York: Pinter, 1994), 66–89. See also Vasumathi K. Duvvury, *Play, Symbolism, and Ritual: A Study of Tamil Brahmin Women's Rites of Passage* (New York: Peter Lang, 1991).

13. Max Weber, *Sociology of Religion* (Boston: Beacon, 1964), 139. Before and after Weber, other interpreters have highlighted religion's function as an explanation of disorder or evil. See Peter Berger, who followed Weber's interpretation, in *The Sacred Canopy: Elements of a Sociological Theory of Religion* (Garden City, N.Y.: Anchor, 1969), 53–80. Grace E. Jantzen has argued persuasively that theorists of religion have been preoccupied with "violence, sacrifice, and death." She proposes instead a philosophy of religion that "begins with birth, and with hope and possibility and wonder implicit in it": Grace E. Jantzen, *Becoming Divine: Towards a Feminist Philosophy of Religion* (Bloomington: Indiana University Press, 1999), 2. Even though my own thinking heads in another direction, I am very much in sympathy with Jantzen's basic critique—and with the suggestion that we might profit from thinking about natality as much as mortality. In a similar way, I emphasize the significance of wonder—and wonders—for religion.

14. It is important to note that the religious sometimes have suggested that the crossing of embodied limits involves pain. As Ariel Glucklich has suggested, pain is sometimes the proposed solution to pain, or at least to suffering, if we make a distinction between pain (as a sensation associated with tissue damage) and suffering (as a cognitive and affective reaction to a wide range of sources, including pain). A variety of painful practices have been held up as spiritually efficacious, including self-flagellation, initiatory ordeals, fasting, pilgrimage journeys, and even martyrdom. Ariel Glucklich, *Sacred Pain: Hurting the Body for the Sake of the Soul* (New York: Oxford University Press, 2001), 11–13.

15. Weber, *Sociology of Religion*, 138–150. The translation of the passage from Job (Job 38:4) is taken from Bruce M. Metzger and Roland E. Murphy, eds., *The New Oxford Annotated Bible*, New Revised Standard Version (New York: Oxford University Press, 1991). For a comparative analysis of responses in Judaism, Christianity, Islam, Hinduism, Buddhism, Zoroastrianism, Manichaeism, and Jainism, see John Bowker, *Problems of Suffering in Religions of the World* (Cambridge: Cam-

bridge University Press, 1970). As Bowker's title makes clear, there is no single way that evil presents itself in all religious traditions, and there are many tradition-specific studies, especially of Christianity and Judaism. In the history of Christianity, several approaches have predominated—Irenaen, Augustinian, and Process theodicies. For an anthology of Christian theological responses, including examples of each of those three types, see Michael L. Peterson, ed., *The Problem of Evil: Selected Readings* (Notre Dame: Notre Dame University, 1992). As Clifford Geertz suggested in an essay on Bali, Max Weber's typology of "traditional" religions and "rationalized" religions provides a lens for interpreting the differing formulations of the problem of suffering. Traditional religions tend to frame the issue in more personal and "piecemeal" terms—why did my daughter die?—and rationalized religions tend to frame the issue in more abstract and systematic terms—why do humans die? Geertz argued that a transformation was occurring in Bali from one mode of religion and one framing of evil to another during the process of religious rationalization. Clifford Geertz, "'Internal Conversion' in Contemporary Bali," in *The Interpretation of Culture* (New York: Basic Books, 1973), 172. As Geertz notes, E. E. Evans-Pritchard makes a similar point in *Witchcraft, Oracles, and Magic among the Azande* (Oxford: Clarendon, 1937). Max Weber discusses religious rationalization in several works. See, for example, his comparison of two forms of religious rationalism, Confucianism and Puritanism, in *The Religion of China* (New York: Free Press, 1964), 226–249.

16. Job 42:1–6; 3:11, taken from Metzger and Murphy, eds., *The New Oxford Annotated Bible*. Lawson, *Religions of Africa*, 56. On healing in Yorùbá traditions, see also Mary Olufunmilayo, *The Yorùbá Traditional Healers of Nigeria* (New York: Routledge, 2003). On the "atonement-healing idea" in Pentecostalism, see Grant Wacker, *Heaven Below: Early Pentecostals and American Culture* (Cambridge, Mass.: Harvard University Press, 2001), 3.

17. The relevant passages in Mengzi are 6A1, 6A6, 2A6, 2A2, 6A7–8. On Mengzi's use of horticultural metaphors—*sprouts* and *cultivation*—see Philip J. Ivanhoe and Bryan Van Norden, eds., *Readings in Classical Chinese Philosophy* (New York and London: Seven Bridges Press, 2001), 112. On pages 121–146, Van Norden provides a translation of the passages I cite. See also the translation by D. C. Lau: *Mencius* (Middlesex, U.K.: Penguin, 1970). For interpretations of Mengzi, see Alan K. L. Chan, ed., *Mencius: Context and Interpretations* (Honolulu: University of Hawaii Press, 2002) and Xiusheng Liu and Philip J. Ivanhoe, eds., *Essays on the Moral Philosophy of Mengzi* (Indianapolis: Hackett, 2002). For the passage from Book VIII of the *Confessions*, see Saint Augustine, *Confessions* (Middlesex, U.K.: Penguin, 1961), 164–165.

18. A great deal has been written about the religious significance of the Holocaust for Jews—too much to cite here. But it is important to note that Jewish responses also included those who spent little time trying to work out a new theological defense (or condemnation) of God. For example, anthropologist Samuel Heilman points out that post-Holocaust *haredim*, or so-called ultra-Orthodox, had a "sense of mission": they felt they had an obligation to triumph over the Holocaust by resurrecting the pre-Holocaust world they remembered. Samuel Heilman, *Defenders of the Faith: Inside Ultra-Orthodox Jewry* (New York: Schocken, 1992), 31–32, 58–59. By noting that the more challenging public responses began only in the late 1960s, I am recognizing that in some ways the public Jewish theological response to the Holocaust was delayed for a generation. It was only in the late 1960s and the 1970s that Jewish thinkers began to emphasize the significance of the Holocaust for theology. I am indebted to my colleague Yaakov Ariel for this insight. Richard Rubenstein's *After Auschwitz: History, Theology, and Contemporary Judaism* (Indianapolis: Bobbs-Merrill, 1966). Arthur Hertzberg, *Jews: The Essence and Character of a People* (San Francisco: HarperSanFrancisco, 1998), 268. John Wesley, "Serious Thoughts Occasioned by the Late Earthquake at Lisbon," in Thomas Jackson, ed., *The Works of John Wesley*, vol. 11 (London: Wesleyan Methodist Book Room, 1872; reprint edition, Grand Rapids, Mich.: Zondervan, 1958–59), 6–7. See also J. W. Haas, Jr., "John Wesley's Vision of Science in the Service of Christ," *Perspectives on Science and Christian Faith* 47.4 (December 1995): 234–243. Joseph McCabe, trans., *Toleration and Other Essays by Voltaire* (New York and London: G. P. Putnam's Sons, 1912), 255–256. The philosopher Jean Jacques Rousseau criticized Voltaire's poem, and his interpretation of the earthquake, in a letter dated August 18, 1756. See J. A. Leigh, ed., *Correspondence complète de Jean Jacques Rousseau*, vol. 4 (Geneva: Institut et musée Voltaire, 1967), 37–50. For a geological explanation of the Lisbon earthquake, see Marc-André Gutscher, "What Caused the Great Lisbon Earthquake?" *Science* 305.5688 (August 27, 2004): 1247–48. Of course there have been many other powerful earthquakes, including the one in Japan's Kanto region that killed approximately 105,000 people and left millions homeless in 1923. For an account of the 1923 earthquake, see Bureau of Social Affairs, Home Office, Japan, compiled by Morihiko Fujisawa, *The Great Earthquake of 1923 in Japan* (Tokyo: Bureau of Social Affairs, Home Office, 1926). There are some studies of religious responses to particular earthquakes, hurricanes, and other natural disasters from ancient to contemporary times, but as far as I know no overview of religion and natural disasters has appeared.

19. The two O'Connor short stories, "A Good Man Is Hard to Find" and "A

Temple of the Holy Ghost," can be found in Flannery O'Connor, *The Complete Stories* (New York: Noonday, 1971), 117–133, 236–248. Lucien Stryk, trans., *On Love and Barley: Haiku of Bashō* (Middlesex, U.K.: Penguin, 1985), 54. I use Stryk's translation of Bashō's 1690 poem because it best suits my purposes here, but I should note the poem is complex and several other translations have appeared. The American Zen teacher Robert Aiken, for example, rendered it this way: "Come / to the true flower viewing / of the life of pilgrimage." Robert Aiken, *A Zen Wave: Bashō's Haiku and Zen* (New York: Weatherhill, 1978), 142. Reginald Horace Blyth translated it as "come, come / to the real flower viewing / of this life of poverty." Reginald Horace Blyth, *A History of Haiku*, vol. 1 (Tokyo: Hokuseido Press, 1963), 128. The grass pillow *(kusa makura)* referred to in the first line of the original is a standard reference for being on a journey, so in broad terms the poem is about viewing flowers during a journey. In that sense, Stryk's translation is not that distinct, even if it renders the implied hardships of the journey as "painful world" and emphasizes the reality of the flowers rather than the authenticity of the viewing. I am grateful to David Barnhill for discussing the nuances of the Japanese original and the English translations with me. To mirror common English usage, I use the term "haiku" to describe Bashō's poetry. However, the issue is complicated, since in the narrowest sense that term refers to an independent poetic form that was popularized by Masaoka Shiki (1867–1902). Bashō was a master of *haikai no renga,* a form of linked verse that was popular in the seventeenth century, and that linked verse opened with a first stanza *(hokku)* that introduced the poem. So some interpreters refer to his verse as *hokku.* For a discussion of the terminological issues, see David Barnhill, *Bashō's Haiku: Selected Poems of Matsuo Bashō* (Albany: State University of New York Press, 2004), 3–5. On linked verse, and its religious significance, see Gary Ebersole, "The Buddhist Ritual Use of Linked Poetry in Medieval Japan," *Eastern Buddhist* 16 (1983): 50–71.

20. Giambattista della Porta, *Natural Magick . . . Wherein Are Set Forth All the Riches and Delights of the Natural Sciences* (London: Thomas Young and Samuel Speed, 1658). The quote from Faraday, as well as mention of della Porta, is in a volume by a prominent physicist who took his title from Faraday's comment: Philip Morrison, *Nothing Is Too Wonderful to Be True* (Woodbury, N.Y.: American Institute of Physics, 1995), 52. On Chinese landscape painting, see Michael Sullivan, *The Birth of Landscape Painting in China* (Berkeley: University of California Press, 1962) and Michael Sullivan, *Symbols of Eternity: The Art of Chinese Landscape Painting in China* (Stanford, Calif.: Stanford University Press, 1979). Samuel Taylor Coleridge, *The Complete Poems* (London and New York: Penguin Books, 1997). For Coleridge's religious views, see Samuel Taylor Coleridge, *Aids to Reflection*

(Princeton, N.J.: Princeton University Press, 1993). See also Douglas Hedley, *Coleridge, Philosophy, and Religion: Aids to Reflection and the Mirror of the Spirit* (Cambridge: Cambridge University Press, 2000). Ralph Waldo Emerson, *Selected Essays* (London and New York: Penguin, 1982), 58, 37. On the rice *kami*, see "Mountains, Sacred" in Jonthan Z. Smtih, ed., *Harper Collins Dictionary of Religion* (San Francisco: HarperSanFrancisco, 1995), 737.

21. On the Green Corn Ceremony, see Charles Hudson, *The Southeastern Indians* (Knoxville: University of Tennessee Press, 1976), 365–375. On the Inuit Bladder Feast, see Inge Kleivan, "Inuit," in Lawrence E. Sullivan, ed., *Native American Religions: North America*, Selections from *The Encyclopedia of Religion*, edited by Mircea Eliade (New York: Macmillan; London: Collier Macmillan, 1989), 114.

22. Arnold van Gennep, *The Rites of Passage* (1909; Chicago: University of Chicago Press, 1960). Douglas Davies, "Introduction," in Jean Holm with John Bowker, eds., *Rites of Passage* (London: Pinter, 1994), 3. Kleivan, "Inuit," 113. As one historical anthropologist notes, "not all birthing is blessed in its outcome. Mothers and babies can die during pregnancy and birthing. And in many regions of the world mothers and babies still do die in large numbers." She goes on to note that the Southwest Pacific is one such region, including Fiji, Papua New Guinea, and Tonga: Margaret Jolly, "Introduction," *Birthing in the Pacific: Beyond Tradition and Modernity?* (Honolulu: University of Hawaii Press, 2002), 3.

23. On the Wana's gendered views of pregnancy, see Masao Ishii, "Childbirth and Gender in Central Sulawesi," in Katsuhiko Yamaji, ed., *Kinship, Gender, and the Cosmic World: Ethnographies of Birth Customs in Taiwan, the Philippines, and Indonesia*, 2nd ed. (Taipei: SMC, 1991), 197. On the Bukidnon cosmology and childbirth practices, see Toshimitsu Kawai, "The Navel of the Cosmos: A Study of Folk Psychology of Childbirth and Child Development among the Bukidnon," in Yamaji, *Kinship, Gender, and the Cosmic World*, 106–114. Other peoples, in Asia and elsewhere, also affirm that spirits are involved in the childbirth process and perform rituals to interact with those spirits. For example, the Laujé of Central Sulawesi, Indonesia, believe that birth spirits inhabit the mother's placenta and nurture the fetus in the womb and the child after birth. See Jennifer W. Nourse, *Conceiving Spirits: Birth Rituals and Contested Identities among Laujé of Indonesia* (Washington, D.C., and London: Smithsonian Institution Press, 1999).

24. On childbirth practices in Islam, see Clinton Bennett, "Islam," in Holm, *Rites of Passage*, 93–98.

25. Michael D. McNally, "An Apache Girl's Initiation Feast," in Colleen McDannell, ed., *Religions of the United States in Practice*, vol. 2 (Princeton, N.J.: Princeton University Press, 2001), 194–204. See also the "further readings" suggested by

McNally, including the works by Inéz Talamantez. Franz Boas, *Chinook Texts,* Bulletin no. 20, Bureau of American Ethnology (Washington, D.C.: Government Printing Office, 1894), 246–247. Debra Reed Blank, "Jewish Rites of Adolescence," in Paul F. Bradshaw and Lawrence A. Hoffman, eds., *Life Cycles in Jewish and Christian Worship* (Notre Dame, Ind.: University of Notre Dame Press, 1996), 81–110.

26. The translation of the Shintō wedding ceremony is from Cherish Pratt, "The Shintō Wedding Ceremony: A Modern Norito," in George Tanabe, ed., *Religions of Japan in Practice* (Princeton, N.J.: Princeton University Press, 1999), 135–138. See also Donald L. Phillipi, *Norito: A Translation of the Ancient Japanese Ritual Prayers* (Princeton, N.J.: Princeton University Press, 1990). James T. Duke, "Eternal Marriage," in Daniel H. Ludlow, ed., *Encyclopedia of Mormonism*, vol. 2 (New York: Macmillan, 1992), 857–859. Among the relevant passages from LDS sacred texts are the following: *The Doctrines and Covenants of the Church of Jesus Christ of Latter Day Saints* (Salt Lake City: Church of Jesus Christ of Latter Day Saints, 1981), 124:93; 131:1–4; 132:19. There were 61 Mormon temples (of 120 total) outside the United States as of July 2005. On the Tokyo Temple and the other LDS temples see the official LDS Web site: *www.lds.org.*

27. The passage about LDS funerals is from a published exhortation by Elder Boyd K. Packer of the Quorum of the Twelve Apostles: Boyd K. Packer, "Funerals?: A Time for Reverence," *Ensign* (November 1988): 18. Louis-Vincent Thomas, "Funeral Rites," in Lawrence E. Sullivan, ed., *Death, Afterlife, and the Soul,* Selections from the *Encyclopedia of Religion* (New York: Macmillan, 1989), 31.

28. The tenth-century account of the Viking funeral is by Ibn-Fadlan, a representative of the Caliph of Baghdad to the people of middle Volga, where he encountered Scandinavians. See the summary in Mike Parker Pearson, *The Archeology of Death and Burial* (College Station: Texas A&M Press, 2000), 1–3. For a translation of the text by Ibn-Fadlan see G. Jones, *A History of the Vikings* (Oxford: Oxford University Press, 1968), 425–430. The German text (and English translation by Katherine E. Carté) of Susanna Zeisberger's memoir (Bethlehem Diary, vol. XLV, 107–110) is included in the Bethlehem Digital History Project, which has collected and posted archival sources from the Moravian Archives in Bethlehem, Pennsylvania, and the Moravian Historical Society in Nazareth, Pennsylvania: *http://bdhp.moravian.edu.* On Moravian women and their memoirs, see Katherine Faull, *Moravian Women's Memoirs: Their Related Lives, 1750–1820* (Syracuse: Syracuse University Press, 1997) and Beverly Smaby, "Female Piety among Eighteenth Century Moravians," *Pennsylvania History* 64 (1997): 151–167. For an overview, see Elisabeth W. Sommer, *Serving Two Masters: Moravian Brethren in Germany and North Carolina, 1727–1801* (Lexington: University Press of Kentucky, 2000). On the

trombone choir, which dates from 1731 in Herrnhut, Germany, see the Glenwood Moravian Trombone Choir's useful Web page: *http://webpages.charter.net/gmtc/GMTCmain.html*, July 20, 2004.

29. Sewa Singh Kalsi, "Sikhism," in Holm and Bowker, *Rites of Passage*, 149–153. On Sikhism, see W. H. McLeod, *Sikhs and Sikhism* (New York and New Delhi: Oxford University Press, 1999) and Gurinder Singh Mann, *Sikhism* (Upper Saddle River, N.J.: Prentice Hall, 2004).

30. There has been a great deal of conversation and controversy about *satī*. Among the several helpful scholarly volumes are John Stratton Hawley, ed., *Sati, the Blessing and the Curse* (New York: Oxford University Press, 1994) and Lata Mani, *Contentious Traditions: The Debate on Sati in Colonial India* (Berkeley: University of California Press, 1998). Pearson, *The Archeology of Death and Burial*, 1. Kalsi, "Sikhism," 143, 151. Many interpreters would suggest that another compelled corporeal passage is female "circumcision," or clitorectomy. On that practice in Africa, see Bettina Shell-Duncan and Ylva Hernlund, eds., *Female "Circumcision" in Africa: Culture, Controversy, and Change* (Boulder, Colo.: Lynne Rienner, 2000).

31. "Telos," in *Oxford English Dictionary Online* (Oxford: Oxford University Press, 2003). Drawing on selections from a number of Indian texts, as well analysis of them, Embree offers a helpful overview of these four ends of humans: Ainslie T. Embree, ed., *Sources of Indian Tradition*, vol. 1, 2nd ed. (New York: Columbia University Press, 1988), 213–341.

32. Peter M. Whitely, "The Southwest," in Lawrence E. Sullivan, ed., *Native American Religions: North America* (New York: Macmillan, 1989), 49–50. Carrasco, *Religions of Mesoamerica*, 67. See also Michael E. Smith, *The Aztecs* (Malden, Mass.: Blackwell, 2003). Fredrik Barth, *Ritual and Knowledge among the Baktaman of New Guinea* (New Haven, Conn.: Yale University Press; Oslo: Universitetsforlaget, 1975), 123–130. Julien Ries, "Immortality," in Sullivan, *Death, Afterlife, and the Soul*, 274–275. The prominence of the metaphor of crossing in Indian religions has been noted by many scholars. Rupert Gethin, for example, suggested that "one of the ancient and recurring images of Indian religious discourse is of 'crossing the ocean of existence,' that is, crossing over from the near shore, which is fraught with dangers, to the further shore, which is safe and free from danger. This is equivalent to escaping or transcending the endless round of rebirth that is *saṃsāra* and the condition of *duḥkha*." Rupert Gethin, *The Foundations of Buddhism* (New York: Oxford University Press, 1998), 64.

33. I am indebted to Max Weber's typology of paths to salvation, although I depart from that scheme in a number of ways. For that typology, and his analysis of "this-worldly" and "other-worldly" piety, see Weber, *Sociology of Religion*, 166–

206. For a helpful overview of Chan Buddhism, and its lineages elsewhere in Asia, see John Jorgensen, "Chan School," in Robert E. Buswell, Jr., ed., *Encyclopedia of Buddhism*, vol. 1 (New York: Macmillan, 2004), 130–137. On its history in Japan, including the Sōtō school, see Heinrich Dumoulin, *Zen Buddhism: A History*, vol. 2, Japan (New York: Macmillan, 1990). Transforming insight has been important in Vedānta Hinduism, including the Advaita (or nondualistic) school founded by Śaṅkara who wrote about 800 C.E. For an analysis of his thought, see Roger Marcaurelle, *Freedom through Inner Renunciation: Śaṅkara's Philosophy in a New Light* (Albany: State University of New York Press, 2000). For a collection of primary sources, see Eliot Deutsch and A. B. van Buitenen, eds., *A Source Book of Advaita Vedānta* (Honolulu: University Press of Hawaii, 1971). On Manichaeism, see Julien Ries, "Immortality," in Sullivan, *Death, Afterlife, and the Soul*, 274–275, and Jason BeDuhn, *The Manichaean Body: In Discipline and Ritual* (Baltimore: Johns Hopkins University Press, 2000). On Daoism, health, and longevity, see Michel Strickmann, *Chinese Magical Medicine* (Stanford, Calif.: Stanford University Press, 2002) and Kenneth Dean, *Taoist Ritual and Popular Cults of Southeast China* (Princeton, N.J.: Princeton University Press, 1993). See also Peter Nickerson's translation and interpretation of "The Great Petition for Sepulchral Plaints," which shows the role of Daoist priests in healing illness caused by the unhappy spirits of deceased family members, in Stephen R. Bokenkamp, *Early Daoist Scriptures* (Berkeley: University of California Press, 1999), 230–274. Some religious movements in Melanesia, as well as Africa and the Americas, came to be called "cargo cults" because participants awaited not only a social utopia but the goods carried by missionaries, traders, and colonial administrators. For two interesting accounts of cargo cults, see Harvey Whitehouse, *Inside the Cult: Religious Innovation and Transmission in Papua New Guinea* (New York: Oxford University Press, 1995) and Andrew Lattas, *Cultures of Secrecy: Reinventing Race in Bush Kaliai Cargo Cults* (Madison: University of Wisconsin Press, 1998). Many works about the Social Gospel have appeared. See, for example, Susan Curtis, *A Consuming Faith: The Social Gospel and Modern American Culture* (Columbia: University of Missouri Press, 2001). On the role of women in the movement, see Wendy J. Deichman Edwards and Carolyn De Swarte Gifford, eds., *Gender and the Social Gospel* (Urbana: University of Illinois Press, 2003). On environmental activism as quasi-religion, I am indebted to an unpublished paper by Laurel Zwissler, "Pilgrimage and Protest: Travel by Religiously Motivated Activists to Anti-Globalization Protests," Anthropology of Religion Consultation, American Academy of Religion Annual Meeting, Atlanta, Georgia, November 23, 2003.

34. Kenneth Surin, "Liberation," in Mark Taylor, ed., *Critical Terms for Religious Studies* (Chicago: University of Chicago Press, 1998), 180. Philip B.

Yampolsky, trans., *The Platform Sutra of the Sixth Patriarch* (New York: Columbia University Press, 1967), 142–153. Walter Rauschenbusch, *A Theology for the Social Gospel* (1917; New York and Nashville: Abington, 1945), 7, 95. One of the classic texts of Latin American liberation theology, which has Catholic and Protestant analogues in Asia, Africa, Europe, and North America, is Gustavo Gutiérrez's *Teología de la liberación: Perspectivas* (Lima, Peru: CEP, 1971). The first English translation appeared in 1973: Gustavo Gutiérrez, *A Theology of Liberation: History, Politics, and Salvation* (1973; Maryknoll, N.Y.: Orbis Books, 1988). For an introduction to the movement, consult Christopher Rowland, ed., *The Cambridge Companion to Liberation Theology* (Cambridge and New York: Cambridge University Press, 1999).

35. Klievan, "The Inuit," 113. Inuit views of the afterlife include a notion of rebirth. See Antonia Mills and Richard Slobodin, eds., *Amerindian Rebirth: Reincarnation Beliefs among North American Indians and Inuit* (Toronto: University of Toronto Press, 1994). Shigematsu Akihisa, "An Overview of Japanese Pure Land," trans. Michael Solomon, in James Foard, Michael Solomon, and Richard K. Payne, eds., *The Pure Land Tradition: History and Development*, Berkeley Buddhist Studies Series, no. 3 (Berkeley: Regents of the University of California, 1996), 267–312. Lawson, *Religions of Africa*, 76. The Qur'ánic passages are translated and interpreted in Michael Sells, trans., *Approaching the Qur'án: The Early Revelations* (Ashland, Ore.: White Cloud Press, 1999), 42–43, 56–59. Zeisberger memoir (Bethlehem Diary, vol. XLV, 107–110), Bethlehem Digital History Project. For a translation of Bonaventure's *Itinerarium Mentis ad Deum*, see Saint Bonaventura, *The Mind's Road to God*, trans. George Boas (New York: Liberal Arts Press, 1953). For an online version, with the parallel Latin text, see The Franciscan Archive, Historical Documents, *http://www.franciscanarchive.org/bonaventura/opera/itinerl.html*, June 15, 2004. John Bunyan, *The Pilgrim's Progress* (1678, 1684; New York: Oxford University Press, 2003).

36. Katherine K. Young, "Tīrtha and the Metaphor of Crossing Over," *Studies in Religion* 9 (1980): 61–68. Feldhaus, *Connected Places*, 39. Diana Eck, *Banaras: City of Light* (Princeton, N.J.: Princeton University Press, 1982), 34–42. Gregory Schopen, "Stūpa and Tīrtha: Tibetan Mortuary Practices and an Unrecognized Form of Burial Ad Sanctos at Buddhist Sites in India," *Buddhist Forum* 3 (1994): 273–293. For a translation of an important sixteenth-century Sanskrit text on *tīrthas* and pilgrimage see Richard Salomon, trans., *The Bridge to the Three Holy Cities: The Sāmānya-praghaṭṭaka of Nārāyaṇa Bhaṭṭa's Tristhalīsetu* (Delhi: Motilal Banarsidass, 1985). Śāntideva, *The Way of the Bodhisattva*, trans. Padmakara Translation Group (Boston and London: Shambhala, 1997), 100, 51. Śāntideva also appeals to transforming teleographies in that same text, for example in the chapter

on "Meditation" (110–136), where he talks about the goal of personal and collective enlightenment. That is another illustration of how both types are advocated within the same tradition, and even within the same text and by the same person. John E. Cort, *Jains in the World: Religious Values and Ideology in India* (New York and Oxford: Oxford University Press, 2001), 22–23. On Jain images, see Jyotindra Jain and Eberhard Fischer, *Jaina Iconography: Part One: The Tīrthaṅkara in Jaina Scriptures, Art, and Rituals* (Leiden: E. J. Brill, 1978).

37. Bruno Latour, "Another Take on the Science and Religion Debate," paper delivered in Santa Barbara, Calif., for the Templeton Series on Science, Religion, and Human Experience, May 2002, second version, English uncorrected, *http://www.ensmp.fr/~latour/articles/article/086.html*, 7, 16.

38. Ibid., 12. Fra Angelico's apprentice was Benozzo Gozzoli, who painted the three women on the right. On Fra Angelico's work at the Convento di San Marco, see William Hood, *Fra Angelico at San Marco* (New Haven, Conn.: Yale University Press, 1993). The scriptural passage is from Mark 16:5–7. The note on verse 5 in *The New Oxford Annotated Bible* suggests that "the young man's clothes indicate him to be a heavenly messenger." Metzger and Murphy, *The New Oxford Annotated Bible*, NT 74.

39. Latour, "Another Take on the Science and Religion Debate," 12.

40. Zenkei Shibayama, *Zen Comments on the Mumonkan* (San Francisco: Harper and Row, 1974), 67. As Morten Schlütter notes in his brief but helpful overview, the Japanese pronunciation of the term *kōan*, which is an administrative and legal term meaning "public case," has become standard in English usage, and I follow that practice here, as I do in using the Japanese title for the Chinese collection and Chan master. Morten Schlütter, "Kōan," in Robert E. Buswell, Jr., ed., *Encyclopedia of Buddhism*, vol. 1 (New York: Macmillan, 2004), 426–429. On the *Mumonkan* and its editor, see Heinrich Dumoulin, *Zen Buddhism: A History*, vol. 1, *India and China* (New York: Macmillan, 1990), 250–252. For a helpful collection of essays, see Steven Heine and Dale S. Wright, eds., *The Kōan: Texts and Contexts in Zen Buddhism* (New York and Oxford: Oxford University Press, 2000).

41. Shibayama, *Mumonkan*, 69.

42. Burton Watson, trans., *The Zen Teachings of Master Lin-chi* (Boston and London: Shambhala, 1993), 23.

Conclusion

1. Another way to put the point I am trying to make in this paragraph and the next is to suggest, as Hilary Putnam does, that both epistemic values and ethical values are at work in the assessment and selection of theories. Citing the

classical pragmatists (Charles Sanders Pierce, William James, and John Dewey), Putnam notes that epistemic values—for example, coherence, simplicity, and so on—are introduced as we assess theories of all sorts. He has theory in the natural and social sciences in mind, but the same holds for theories of religion. For example, I appeal directly or indirectly to internal coherence, methodological self-consciousness, epistemological humility, theoretical generativity, definitional adequacy, professional utility, analytical complexity, historical relevance, social justice, and gender inclusiveness. As I do so, I am identifying and enacting epistemic values, moral values, and—to the extent that coherence and complexity are about beauty as well—even aesthetic values. Hilary Putnam, *The Collapse of the Fact/Value Dichotomy and Other Essays* (Cambridge, Mass.: Harvard University Press, 2002), 30–32.

2. A visual record of the flight by the nuns to Miami can be found in a photograph in the Archives, *La Voz Católica,* Archdiocese of Miami, Pastoral Center, Miami Springs, Florida. The inscription indicates that it is the Apostolate of the Sacred Heart of Jesus arriving on a flight from Havana to Miami in 1961.

3. Marshall Sahlins, "Two or Three Things That I Know about Culture," *Journal of the Royal Anthropological Institute* 5.3 (September 1999): 399–421.

4. David Ruelle, *Chance and Chaos* (Princeton, N.J.: Princeton University Press, 1991), 90. It was John D. Eigenauer who worried about the "morass of causes." John D. Eigenauer, "The Humanities and Chaos Theory: A Response to Steenburg's 'Chaos at the Marriage of Heaven and Hell,'" *Harvard Theological Review* 86.4 (October 1993): 455–469. The article Eigenauer was responding to was David Steenburg, "Chaos at the Marriage of Heaven and Hell," *Harvard Theological Review* 84.4 (October 1991): 447–466. The social scientists who argued that for chaotic systems, including social systems, the only attainable goal is understanding, not prediction or control, are Hal Gregersen and Lee Sailer. They made this point, and outlined five other implications for social science research, in "Chaos Theory and Its Implications for Social Science Research," *Human Relations* 46.7 (1993): 777–802. Among the earliest and most influential works to emphasize that nonlinear systems are "sensitive to initial conditions" is the famous article by meteorologist Edward Lorenz: "Deterministic Nonperiodic Flow," *Journal of the Atmospheric Sciences* 20 (March 1963): 130–141. Since the 1960s, there has been an enormous scientific literature on chaos theory, and a few attempts at popularization, including James Gleick's *Chaos: Making of a New Science* (New York: Penguin, 1987). Some reference books are helpful, including Willi-Hans Steeb, *A Handbook of Terms Used in Chaos and Quantam Chaos* (Mannheim: B. I. Wissenschaftsverlag, 1991). As my citations above suggest, there also has been some conversation about the implications of chaos theory for the humanities,

behavioral sciences, and social sciences. For a sampling of that literature, see George A. Reisch, "Chaos, History, and Narrative," *History and Theory* 30.1 (February 1991): 1–20; Harriet Hawkins, *Strange Attractors: Literature, Culture, and Chaos Theory* (New York: Prentice Hall/Harvester Wheatsheaf, 1995); Rae Fortunato Blackerby, *Application of Chaos Theory to Psychological Models* (Austin, Tex.: Performance Strategies Publications, 1998); N. Pradhan, P. E. Rapp, and R. Sreenivasan, eds., *Nonlinear Dynamics and Brain Functioning* (Commack, N.Y.: Nova Science, 1999); and L. Douglas Kiel and Euel Elliott, ed., *Chaos Theory in the Social Sciences* (Ann Arbor: University of Michigan Press, 1996). Some cultural theorists I have cited in this book explicitly mention chaos theory, not only Gilles Deleuze and Félix Guattari, but also Arjun Appadurai and Brian Massumi. Arjun Appadurai, *Modernity at Large: Cultural Dimensions of Globalization* (Minneapolis and London: University of Minnesota Press, 1996), 46–47. Brian Massumi, *Parables for the Virtual: Movement, Affect, Sensation* (Durham, N.C.: Duke University Press, 2002), 8, 19, 32, 37, 109–110, 147, 223–227, 229, 237, 244–245, 261. Massumi also mentions complexity theory, which is not the same thing, as Mark C. Taylor notes in his compelling exploration of the implications of complexity theory for a philosophy of culture. Mark C. Taylor, *The Moment of Complexity: Emerging Network Culture* (Chicago: University of Chicago Press, 2001). Some Christian theologians also have considered the topic. See Robert John Russell, Nancey Murphy, and Arthur R. Peacocke, eds., *Chaos and Complexity: Scientific Perspectives on Divine Action* (Vatican City State: Vatican Observatory; Berkeley, Calif.: Center for Theology and the Natural Sciences, 1995). However, as far as I know, there has been no systematic attempt to lay out the implications of chaos theory or complexity theory for the study of religion. This effort has not gone further than gesturing toward metaphors, as I have done here.

5. For a biography of Fidel Castro, see Sebastian Balfour, *Castro,* 2nd ed. (London and New York: Longman, 1995). See also Manuel Fernández Carcassés, *Tivolí: La casa donde vivió Fidel* (La Habana, Cuba: Artex: Pablo de la Torriente, 1997). For his own account of his childhood, see Fidel Castro, *My Early Years,* ed. Deborah Shnookal and Pedro Álvarez Tabío (Melbourne, Australia, and New York: Ocean Press, 1998). There is a substantial literature in English and Spanish on the Cuban wars for independence. On the war of 1898, and U.S.-Cuban ties, see Louis A. Pérez, *The War of 1898: The United States and Cuba in History and Historiography* (Chapel Hill: University of North Carolina Press, 1998). On the royal slaves and devotion to Our Lady of Charity, see María Elena Díaz, *The Virgin, the King, and Royal Slaves of El Cobre: Negotiating Freedom in Colonial Cuba, 1670–1780* (Stanford, Calif.: Stanford University Press, 2000).

6. Clifford Geertz, "Culture, Mind, Brain/Brain, Mind, Culture," in Clifford

Geertz, *Available Light: Anthropological Reflections on Philosophical Topics* (Princeton, N.J., and Oxford: Princeton University Press, 2000), 215, 203, 205–206.

7. On Bishop Román's role in the history of devotion at the Miami shrine, see Thomas A. Tweed, *Our Lady of the Exile: Diasporic Religion at a Cuban Catholic Shrine in Miami* (New York and Oxford: Oxford University Press, 1997), 6, 8, 36, 38–39, 44, 46–48, 54–55, 59, 67, 96, 112, 124–125, 127.

8. On John Winthrop, see Edmund Sears Morgan, *The Puritan Dilemma: The Story of John Winthrop* (Boston: Little, Brown, 1958) and Francis J. Bremer, *America's Forgotten Founding Father* (New York: Oxford University Press, 2003). There are many works on King. For example, see Vincent Harding, *Martin Luther King, the Inconvenient Hero* (Maryknoll, N.Y.: Orbis, 1996). On Eddy, see Gillian Gill, *Mary Baker Eddy*, Radcliffe Biography Series (Reading, Mass.: Perseus Books, 1998). By analyzing King as a *tīrthaṅkara* I am employing a comparative strategy used by Max Weber and refined by William A. Clebsch. Clebsch called this method of comparing each in terms of the other a "dialogical" approach. He suggested that it went beyond homological comparisons yielding genotypes to "xenological" comparisons yielding allotypes. While this strategy by itself is not sufficient, in my view, it is a useful first step in transcultural comparison. William A. Clebsch, "Apples, Oranges, and Manna: Comparative Religion Revisited," *Journal of the American Academy of Religion* 49.1 (March 1981): 10–12. For other attempts to rethink comparative analysis, see Kimberly C. Patton and Benjamin C. Ray, eds., *A Magic Still Dwells: Comparative Religion in the Postmodern Age* (Berkeley: University of California Press, 2000). There are a number of theoretical resources for emphasizing, as I do here, the "interplay" of human and nonhuman agency in religion. Borrowing from science studies, for example, we might adapt Andrew Pickering's notion of "the mangle of practice." He used that notion to interpret the practice of science, but it also might prove useful for talking about the ways that human and nonhuman agency are "reciprocally and emergently intertwined" in religions. Andrew Pickering, *The Mangle of Practice: Time, Agency, and Science* (Chicago and London: University of Chicago Press, 1995), 21.

9. Max Müller, *Lectures on the Science of Religion* (New York: Scribner's Sons, 1881), 11. Still useful for thinking about the introductory course is Mark Jurgensmeyer, ed., *Teaching the Introductory Course in Religious Studies: A Sourcebook* (Atlanta: Scholars Press, 1991). Around the same time as that volume appeared, the American Academy of Religion released a report that considered the place of religious studies in the liberal arts: Stephen Crites, scribe, AAR Task Force on the Religion Major, "Liberal Learning and the Religion Major," American Academy of Religion, 1990. That report had been sponsored by the Association of American Colleges, and the report on the religion major was included in the sub-

sequent volumes: Association of American Colleges, *Liberal Learning and the Arts and Sciences Major: Project on Liberal Learning, Study-in-Depth, and the Arts and Sciences Major,* 2 vols. (Washington, D.C.: Association of American Colleges, 1990, 1991). As I am framing it, religious studies is interdisciplinary, and the scholarly literature on that theme in higher education is also relevant, especially in its call for clarity about disciplinary identity and difference. See Rick Szostak, "'Comprehensive' Curricular Reform: Providing Students with a Map of the Scholarly Enterprise," *Journal of General Education* 52.1 (2003): 27–49. For background on those issues, see also Julie Thompson Klein, *Crossing Boundaries: Knowledge, Disciplinarities, and Interdisciplinarities* (Charlottesville: University Press of Virginia, 1996) and L. Salter and A. Hearn, *Outside the Lines: Issues in Interdisciplinary Research* (Montreal: McGill-Queen's University Press, 1996).

10. Although I use the term "bracketing" here, I do not mean to signal an uncritical or unconditional acceptance of the phenomenological approach advocated by, among others, Van der Leeuw. He describes the phenomenological approach to the study of religion and its "intellectual suspense" *(epoché)* in G. Van der Leeuw, *Religion in Essence and Manifestation,* vol. 2 (1933; New York: Harper and Row, 1963), 683–689. I use the term in a more restricted sense. To talk about pedagogical positioning also raises many vexing legal, moral, religious, and educational issues about the relation between religion and institutions of higher education. That situation varies across cultures, of course, and across regions in North America. On the situation in Canada, see the Study of Religion in Canada series sponsored by the Canadian Corporation for Studies in Religion. For example, Harold Remus, *Religious Studies in Ontario: A State-of-the-Art Review* (Waterloo, Ont.: Published for the Canadian Corporation for Studies in Religion/Corporation canadienne des sciences religieuses by Wilfred Laurier University Press, 1992). On the United States, see Victor H. Kazanjian Jr. and Peter L. Laurence, eds., *Education as Transformation: Religious Pluralism, Spirituality, and a New Vision for Higher Education in America* (New York: Peter Lang, 2000) and Warren A. Nord, *Religion and American Education: Rethinking a National Dilemma* (Chapel Hill: University of North Carolina Press, 1995). Like Nord's volume, much recent writing on the subject has been critical about the place of religion in higher education. See *Religion and the American University: A Report by the Faith and Reason Institute* (Washington, D.C.: Faith and Reason Institute, 2001). See also George Marsden, *The Soul of the American University: From Protestant Establishment to Established Unbelief* (New York: Oxford University Press, 1994) and Darryl G. Hart, *The University Gets Religion: Religious Studies in American Higher Education* (Baltimore: Johns Hopkins University Press, 1999). For an attempt to describe the place of religion on U.S. cam-

puses, see Conrad Cherry, Betty A. DeBerg, and Amanda Porterfield, *Religion on Campus* (Chapel Hill: University of North Carolina Press, 2001). For a review of that book, and nine others on religious studies and higher education, see Susan Henking, "Religion, Religious Studies, and Higher Education into the 21st Century," *Religious Studies Review* 30 (April/July 2004): 129–136.

11. Novalis was the pseudonym for Georg Friedrich Philipp von Hardenburg (1772–1801). The aphorism can be found in Arthur Versluis, trans., *Pollen and Fragments: Selected Poetry and Prose of Novalis* (Grand Rapids, Mich.: Phanes, 1989), 84. Novalis put it slightly differently: "The learned know how to appropriate the alien, and how to make the familiar strange." He made a similar point in an aphorism about how to "romanticize" the world: "I give the common sense a higher sense, the quotidian a longing, homesick aspect, the familiar the majesty of the unfamiliar" (56). Among the many texts that encourage "active learning" and "inquiry-based learning" in the university—ideas that go back at least to John Dewey—is the influential report by the Boyer Commission: Boyer Commission on Educating Undergraduates in the Research University, *Reinventing Undergraduate Education: A Blueprint for America's Research Universities* (Stony Brook, N.Y.: State University of New York at Stony Brook for the Carnegie Foundation for the Advancement of Teaching, 1998). Its first and second recommendations dealt with inquiry-based learning. See also Association of American Colleges, *Strong Foundations: Twelve Principles for Effective General Education Programs* (Washington, D.C.: Association of American Colleges, 1994). On "active learning," see for example David W. Johnson, Roger T. Johnson, and Karl A. Smith, *Active Learning: Cooperation in the College Classroom* (Edina, Minn.: Interaction Book Co., 1991) and Melvin L. Silberman, *Active Learning: 101 Strategies to Teach Any Subject* (Boston: Allyn and Bacon, 1996).

12. Of these different interpretive tasks, in some ways it is translation that seems to have received the least theoretical attention in the study of religion, as Steven Engler and the other contributors to a helpful roundtable discussion on the process of translation point out. Steven Engler, Susan Bassnett, Robert Bringhurst, and Susan M. DiGiacomo, "Consider Translation: A Roundtable Discussion," *Religious Studies Review* 30 (April/July 2004): 107–120.

13. I analyzed my spontaneous prayer, and considered the interpreter's position, in Thomas A. Tweed, "On Moving Across: Translocative Religion and the Interpreter's Position," *Journal of the American Academy of Religion* 70.2 (2002): 253–277. I draw on that analysis here. Scholars also move from isolation to community, as they congregate to present the results of their research in professional meetings, and from specialization to generalization, as they speak to the media or

give public lectures. As David Damrosch argues, both isolation and specialization are particular problems in the contemporary university: David Damrosch, *We Scholars: Changing the Culture of the University* (Cambridge, Mass.: Harvard University Press, 1995).

14. To suggest that scholars are moving back and forth between fact and value reaffirms that scholarship, like teaching, is not "value free," as I suggested in Chapter 1, though it still can be in accord with the United States Constitution's First Amendment requirement to neither "establish" religion nor prohibit its "free exercise." For an interesting exploration of these moral issues, see Robert A. Orsi, "Snakes Alive: Resituating the Moral in the Study of Religion," in Richard Wightman Fox and Robert B. Wesbrook, eds., *In Face of the Facts: Moral Inquiry in American Scholarship* (Cambridge: Cambridge University Press; and Washington, D.C.: Woodrow Wilson Center Press, 1998), 201–226. In suggesting that scholars move back and forth between inside and outside, I am proposing that they are not permanently or fully inside *or* outside when they study religion. For a helpful collection of essays that address the insider-outsider problem, see Russell T. McCutcheon, ed., *The Insider-Outsider Problem in the Study of Religion: A Reader* (London and New York: Cassell, 1999).

ILLUSTRATION CREDITS

Figure 1. Photograph by Aracelli Cantero. Courtesy *La Voz Católica.*

Figure 2. The Ruth and Sherman Lee Institute for Japanese Art, Hanford, California. Gift of Dr. and Mrs. Robert Feinberg.

Figure 3. Freud Museum, London.

Figure 4. From *Buddha: The Living Way* by deForest Trimingham (Paget, Bermuda). Photographs copyright © 1998 by deForest Trimingham. Essay copyright © by Peter Iyer. Used by permission of Random House, Inc.

Figure 5. Copyright Margaret Lois (Peggy) Tiger. Reprinted courtesy Peggy Tiger.

Figure 6. Diagram designed by the author.

Figure 7. Courtesy *La Voz Católica.* Reprinted by permission of Oxford University Press from Thomas A. Tweed, *Our Lady of the Exile: Diasporic Religion at a Cuban Catholic Shrine in Miami* (New York and Oxford: Oxford University Press, 1997), 38.

Figure 8. Photograph by Ada Orlando. Courtesy Ada Orlando.

Figure 9. Ackland Fund, selected by the Ackland Associates, 96.3.2. Ackland Museum, The University of North Carolina at Chapel Hill.

Figure 10. Photograph by William Henry Ilingworth. By permission of the Minnesota Historical Society. LOC #E91p13. Neg #22837.

Figure 11. Courtesy Shambhala Publications.

Figure 12. Photograph by Dana Salvo. By permission of Dana Salvo.

Figure 13. Photograph by Victor Faccinto. By permission of Victor Faccinto and V. F. Productions.

Figure 14. The Pierpont Morgan Library, New York. PML 19921.

Figure 15. The Voth Collection, Mennonite Library and Archives. Bethel College, North Newton, Kansas. Voth photograph 1535.

Figure 16. Photograph by Rich Remsberg. By permission of Rich Remsberg.

Figure 17. *Los Angeles Times* photograph by Paul Watson.

Figure 18. © Ali Kazuyoshi Nomachi / Pacific Press Service.

Figure 19. © Walt Michot / The Miami Herald.

Figure 20. Photograph by Graham Harrison. By permission of Graham Harrison.

Figure 21. Réunion des Musées Nationaux / Art Resource, N.Y.

Figure 22. Photograph by permission of *www.sacredsites.com* and Martin Gray.

Figure 23. Erich Lessing / Art Resource, N.Y.

Figure 24. Photograph by Ana Rodríguez-Soto. Courtesy *La Voz Católica*.

ACKNOWLEDGMENTS

To acknowledge is "to recognize or confess." In this book, I have tried to recognize my position as interpreter, and some readers may think I have done more than enough confessing. Those who start to squirm at the first hint of autobiographical disclosure can relax. I won't do much more of that here. However, there are more things to recognize: my debts and my gratitude. If scholarship is crossing and theory is itinerancy, as I have argued, this journey has been an especially long and demanding one. I spent five years working on the book, and, as I noted in Chapter 1, it really began earlier, in 1993, when I first reflected on the annual feast-day celebration for Our Lady of Charity in Miami. As with all long journeys, the debts have accumulated.

I am indebted, first, to the Cuban American pilgrims at the shrine of Our Lady of Charity in Miami. I remain grateful for their kindness to me over the years. I have thanked them before in print, and I returned to the annual festival after *Our Lady of the Exile* appeared to acknowledge their help and offer my thanks. Yet I am continually reminded of how profoundly my experiences at the shrine transformed me and my work. This book, which began with reflections on those experiences, only accrues more debts.

Because I wander across all sorts of boundaries in this book—both across disciplinary boundaries and across those that mark subfields in religious studies—I have turned to many scholars for help along the way, too many to mention them all here. I was interested in thinking about movement, a central theme in my theory, so I took a brief course on dynamical systems offered by several colleagues in mathematics— what was I thinking?—and those classroom conversations, especially on fluid dynamics and chaos theory, were helpful, even if very little of that found its way into the text in explicit ways. One of those instructors, Sue Goodman, also gave me citations and helped me to ponder the implications of chaos theory for the humanities. So did the physicist Laurie McNeil. As a testimony to their collegiality, both Sue and Laurie also read passages from this book, which, needless to say, is far from their areas of specialization. Colleagues from other fields, whether they remember it or not—or want to admit it—also helped by discussing ideas or providing citations, including Stephen Birdsall (geography), Mark Evan Bonds (music), Donald Garrett (philosophy), John McGowan (English), James Peacock (anthropology), William Race (classics), and Christian Smith (sociology).

Chris Smith also read the whole manuscript, and his comments prompted several exchanges that helped me clarify what I was doing— and not doing—in this book, and other colleagues in the study of religion at Carolina and Duke helped in many ways as well. I tested ideas in a departmental colloquium, where Laurie Maffly-Kipp asked a good question about the static in religion. At a crucial juncture, this query reconfirmed my sense that I had to talk about dwelling as well as crossing. Others also helped in various ways, including Yaakov Ariel, Carl Ernst, Zlatko Plese, Barry Saunders, Randall Styers, and Ruel Tyson.

Carl talked with me about some of the Islamic examples I have used. Several colleagues from Duke have been wonderful conversation partners: Julie Bryne, Stanley Hauerwas, Richard Jaffe, Bruce Lawrence, and Grant Wacker. Co-teaching a course with Richard on religion and transnationalism helped to clarify my thinking about what I have called terrestrial crossings. As always, Grant was a kind and helpful colleague. Even though this book is not at all the sort Stanley would write, early in the process he provided encouragement and read chapters, and Bruce, Julie, and Richard offered penetrating comments all along the way. Bruce gave an exceptionally careful reading of the completed manuscript. Graduate students at Carolina and Duke read portions of the book: Maryellen Davis, Shannon Hickey, Katie Lofton, Mary Ellen O'Donnell, Chad Seales, Isaac Weiner, Jeff Wilson, and Ben Zeller. Katie discussed ideas and checked endnotes. Jeff served as my research assistant during the final phase of the book, and I am grateful for his help.

Before the book reached the final phase, I published some work-in-progress. Portions of the first chapter and the conclusion, in revised form, are taken from my article "On Moving Across: Translocative Religion and the Interpreter's Position," which appeared in the *Journal of the American Academy of Religion* 70 (June 2002): 253–277; I use that material here by permission of Oxford University Press. An earlier version of Chapter 2 appeared in *History of Religions* in February 2005 (© by the University of Chicago Press). Writing the latter, which at the time I imagined as a portion of a longer chapter, helped me to reorganize the book. Oxford University Press also granted me permission to use two paragraphs and one photograph from my book *Our Lady of the Exile: Diasporic Religion at a Cuban Catholic Shrine in Miami* (New York and Oxford: Oxford University Press, 1997). I am grateful to these publishers for allowing me to reprint revised versions of this work here.

And I am grateful for other support. Margaretta Fulton and Elizabeth Gilbert, editors at Harvard University Press, helped in many ways. So did my family. My wife, Margaret McNamee, was the first reader of each newly drafted chapter, and my children, Kevin and Bryn, gracefully put up with my tendency to cloister myself in the study when I am trying to finish a book. Actually finishing the book was made easier by other kinds of support. A summer stipend from the National Endowment for the Humanities helped me to put down on paper my first thoughts about the project, and a semester-long research leave funded by the College of Arts and Sciences at Carolina allowed me time to draft the first two chapters. Granting me that time to write was especially generous since I was in the middle of a five-year term as associate dean for undergraduate curricula, and deans don't usually get research leaves. The College also generously awarded me a distinguished professorship, which comes with research support that aided the project in countless ways. So did the cross-disciplinary conversations that I enjoyed as a Hettleman Fellow at UNC's Institute for Arts and Humanities.

Although that semester at the Institute I tossed around some ideas with the other fellows, especially Mark C. Taylor, who later commented on a chapter, my first public exploration of the ideas that became this book was in the Robert C. Lester Lecture at the University of Colorado. I am grateful to the faculty and students there for all the good questions they asked. At a later stage, I got helpful feedback from faculty and students at Syracuse University's Department of Religion, especially Gail Hamner and the late Charles Winquist. The Department of Religion at Boston University invited me to give their annual lecture, and several faculty members—including Nancy Ammerman, John Berthrong, Ray Hart, and Stephen Prothero—nudged me to rethink the implications of my theory. Scholars at Harvard and Stanford, where I attended graduate school, might recognize their influence. Even if they don't—or aren't sure they like what I have done with what they taught me—I am grateful to Carl Bielefeldt, the late William Clebsch, Diana Eck, William Graham, Van Harvey, William Hutchison, Gordon Kaufman, Richard Niebuhr, and Lee Yearley. Gordon also sent along encouraging comments on some early writing, and Van asked incisive questions about the book proposal. My enduring gratitude to Van, who taught me much of what I know about modern Western religious thought, is so great that I have dedicated this book to him. Other scholars discussed ideas or provided citations, including Catherine Brekus, John Corrigan, Rosalind Hackett, Michael McNally, Gordon Newby, and James Treat. I also am grateful to those who read some or all of the writing that became this book, including David Barnhill, Gustavo Benavides, Jason Bivins, Ann Burlein, David Chidester, Nancy Frankenberry, Russell McCutcheon, Robert Orsi, William Paden, Daniel Pals, Kenneth Surin, Ann Taves, and Harvey Whitehouse. Ann Burlein, Nancy, Dan, Ken, and Jason read the first draft of the manuscript and gently pressed me to rethink some important issues. Ann Taves read it all too, and—with her usual flurry of probing questions and imaginative suggestions—she let me try out ideas before they had fully formed. All these scholars have saved me from some mistaken assertions and unclear formulations, though surely some remain. As with all the other debts I have accumulated along the way, just because I thank these interlocutors does not mean that they agree with all that I have said here. They don't. It means only that I recognize how much they have helped me during this demanding but rewarding intellectual journey.

INDEX

Abraham, 112, 140

Africa: Christian missions to, 129; and cinema, 127; and clitorectomies, 100; emergence of civilizations in, 124; first humanoid species in, 124; Islam in, 103, 131; northern, 139; and slaves to Cuba, 173; South, 136; Tonga in, 31; and trance, 103; Yorùbá in, 6, 135, 139, 153, 155

African Americans, 96, 100, 125, 134, 170, 176, 178, 182, 226n24

afterlife, 147–156. *See also* salvation; soteriology; teleographies

agency, 210n9; human and nonhuman, 249n8; of individuals, 174–176; institutions and, 68; and the metaphor of flow, 60–61, 174–176; and moral evil, 139–140; and personal and transpersonal forces, 211n9; supernatural, 120, 174

allegories, 68, 155. *See also* tropes

altar: "astrosphere," 116–117; domestic, 106–108; Marian, 225n23; Mexican home, 107; at the Miami shrine, 87–88, 175–176

anātman (no-self), 55

ancestors, 39, 105–106, 147, 152, 155, 177

Angelico, Fra, 158–161, 163

animals, 74, 95, 101, 116, 124, 143, 145

animism, 95

anthropology, 23–24; constitutive term of, 30; and the interpretation of transnationalism, 57; and the "reflexive turn," 20; and spatial representation,

gion, 67; scholarly focus on, 166; as social space, 105; "techniques," 100

Bosteels, Bruno, 9–10

boundaries: between this world and the other world, 152–153, 155–156; crossing, 54, 74, 98, 123, 152; economic, 134; and embodied limits, 136–150; encountering, 86; of the home and homeland, 110–111; marking, 123, 165. *See also* ultimate horizon

Boyer, Pascal, 65, 86

Buddha, 55, 73, 118, 155, 162, 228n31; Amida, 77, 155; -nature: 73, 154, 162

Buddhism, 23, 26, 39, 40, 55–56, 70, 73, 76–77, 99, 101, 106, 115, 118, 125, 127, 128, 132, 137, 141, 152, 154, 155, 155, 156, 161–163, 208n3, 231n2

Bukidnon, 145

Burke, Kenneth, 45

Calvinists, 136

Canada, 108–109, 250n10

Caroline Islands, 69

Carter, Paul, 58

caste, 75, 111, 134, 150

Catholicism. *See* Roman Catholicism

Chambers, Iain, 10, 58

chaos, 57, 121, 172–173, 247n4

Cherokee, 62, 63, 72

Chidester, David, 42

children, 43–44, 46, 53, 105, 145, 147, 167

China: and Buddhism, 11, 154, 161; and cartographies, 112; and Confucianism, 139–140; and cosmographies, 115; and landscape painting, 142; and Silk Road, 132, 134; and travel and communications technology, 124–125, 126

Chinook, 146, 150

Christianity, 23, 39, 70, 71, 73, 76, 96, 100, 101, 106–107, 108, 113, 114–115, 125, 127, 129, 132, 136, 139–140, 141, 145, 148, 152, 154, 155, 157–160, 176

Christian Science, 176

chronotopes, 64, 97, 97–122, 123, 166, 222n14. *See also* body; cosmos; home; homeland

circumcision, 100, 145; and female clitorectomies, 100

cities: Ayodhyā, 113; Banaras, 112, 127; as chronotopes, 223n14; Jerusalem, 113, 115; Mecca, 89, 94, 106, 129, 134, 178, 182; Mesoamerican, 110; and Puritan "city on a hill," 176; sacred, 75, 112, 113; and social organization, 226n25; Sumerian, 112

clans, 75, 95, 101, 105, 110, 124, 153

class, 111, 134

Clifford, James, 8, 58, 59, 80, 124, 215n22, 218n2

codes: and boundary marking, 123; Buddhist, 26; and the present, 162; racial, 178; spatial, 75

cognition: analogical, 68, 95–97; micromechanisms of, 65; and religion, 67–68, 70; spatial, 93–98; temporal, 91–93. *See also* mind

cognitive science, 65–66, 91–98, 204n30, 205n33, 212n15

colonialism, 11, 37, 38, 42, 111, 124, 131, 132

communication: micromechanisms of, 65; technology, 125–127; and types of religion, 127

comparison: of religions, 249n8; and this theory, 84–85

confluences, 54, 59–69, 167, 171–178

Confucianism: and *li*, 73, 215n21; and moral evil, 139–140; on sentiments and virtues, 70, 214n17 constitutive terms, 29–33; changing over time, 198n3; and disciplinary horizons, 53, 165; and educators, 178; limited elasticity of, 39–41

corporeal crossings, 136–150. *See also* body

cosmic crossings, 75–76, 150–163. *See also* cosmos

cosmogonies, 116, 118–122, 229n34; types of, 118, 229n33. *See also* myths

cosmographies, 115–116, 154, 170

cosmos: the body as, 98, 101, 103–104; as chronotope, 74, 97; and religion, 113–122

creation, 120–122. *See also* cosmogonies

crossing: boundaries, 123; compelled, 27, 135–136, 150, 166, 181–182, 243n30; concealed, 157–163; constrained, 22, 27, 135–136, 150, 166, 170; corporeal, 136–150, 243n30; cosmic, 150–163; and Cuban American piety, 169–171; and Indian traditions, 123, 243n32; linguistic, 47–48; metaphoric domain, 96; research and teaching as, 178–183; and religion, 54, 75–77; social space, 134–135; terrestrial, 124–136, 169–170; terrestrial, corporeal, and cosmic, 75, 76, 123, 169; translocative and transtemporal, 158, 163; usefulness of the trope of, 158–160

Cuba: and Fidel Castro, 1, 172; flag of, 2, 3, 112, 169; national anthem of, 3, 5, 169; and wars for independence, 2, 7, 87, 169, 172

Cuban Americans: and this theory of religion, 1–7, 20, 54, 167–171, 174–179. *See also balseros;* diaspora; diasporic religion; exile; hybridity; liberation; Our Lady of Charity; Santería; Shrine of Our Lady of Charity

cults: ancestor, 105, 152; cargo, 153; healing, 153

cultural mediations: and religion, 65–69; and spatial and temporal perception, 89, 91–98

cultural studies: comparative, 80; on power and position, 24; religious studies as, 37–38

culture: as anthropology's constitutive term, 30, 33; as constitutive term for religious studies, 37; challenges to the concept of, 201n15; classic conception of, 58; definitions of, 35–37; and mind, 65–66; "minimalist" and "maximalist" models of, 213n15; in motion, 124; and nature, 64–69, 173–174; network, 58; as "placeholder," 36; as trajectory, 58; translocal, 58

dancing, 31, 62, 99, 121

Daoism: and the body, 103–104; and *dao*, 73, 215n21; and health and longevity, 153

darśan: and *theōria*, 14; three kinds of, 191n15

Darwin, Charles, 56, 69

Davidson, Donald, 45, 46, 204n31, 212n15

death, 72, 98, 136–137, 147–150. *See also* mortality

de Certeau, Michel, 20, 58, 215n22, 218n2

definitions: and "exegetical fussiness," 32–33; as implying theories and employing tropes, 42–48; objections to, 36–42; suspicion of, 29–30; tropes in, 42–44, 48–52; types of, 33–36, 54, 199n9

Deleuze, Gilles, 54, 57, 59, 171, 189n8, 217n29

Dewey, John, 16, 191n17

dharma, 151, 155

diaspora, 67, 70, 81, 125, 153

diasporic religion, 168, 174, 181

divination, 135, 153

dress: and collective identity, 101; Cuban American, 2, 5, 101, 169; Eastern Dakota, 101–102; Jewish, 101; and religion, 68, 98–100; Sikh, 149

Dubuisson, Daniel, 198n1, 201n14

Durkheim, Emil, 50, 51, 52, 64, 73, 95–96, 214n18

dwelling: 54, 80–122; and Cuban American piety, 169; definition of, 81–83; -intravel, 80; as mapping, building, and inhabiting, 82; as movement, 83; philosophers and theorists on, 218n2; and religion, 74–75; research and teaching as, 178–183

dynamics. See flows; kinetics; movement

dynography, 11

Eastern Dakota, 101

economics: and the study of religion, 178. See also economy

economy: and capitalism, 6, 168; and economic boundaries, 134; and hardships of migration, 182; and poverty, 22; and prosperity as a religious goal, 134, 153; and religion, 18, 60–61, 168, 172; and trade, 131–132, 134

education: and active and inquiry-based learning, 180, 251n11; general, 178; goals of, 251n11; and isolation and specialization, 251n13; liberal arts, 178; and religion, 250n10; and universities' morally ambivalent past, 20. See also teaching

Eliade, Mircea, 50, 52, 61

emotions: common and variant, 69; among Cuban Americans, 5–6, 70, 93, 97, 101, 168, 177; Feuerbach on, 215n29; importance of, 66; and limits, 136; religion and, 67–72; and space, 96

environment: and activism, 153; built, 24, 27, 61–62, 181; joyful encounter with,

71; the destruction of, 211n10; transformation of, 66, 82

epistemologies, locative and supralocative, 16

epoché (bracketing), 20, 250n10

eruv, 108–109

ethnicity: and ethnoscapes, 61; and homeland, 110–113; religion and, 75, 110. See also race

ethnography, 2, 21, 23, 181. See also anthropology

Eucharist, 101, 157, 168

Europeans: and colonialism, 38, 111; and early maps, 115; and the Holy Roman Empire, 129, 131; and printing, 26; and scientific societies, 142; and ships, 125

evil: Cuban Americans on, 168; and the Holocaust, 140, 239n18; religious responses to, 71, 137–141, 237n15. See also suffering

evolution: and human history, 65; as metaphor in definitions, 46, 51, 52; and models of nature and culture, 56; religion and, 217n28

"exegetical fussiness," 32–33, 53, 77

exile: and disruption of time and place, 86–87; as metaphor, 67, 96–97, 131, 168, 169; as moral evil, 168; and the new land, 110; sadness of, 70

experience: channeling, 66; of the holy, 3, 46, 50; as inaccessible, 17, 192n17; of *mysterium tremendum*, 49; of the numinous, 60; Schleiermacher on, 49–50, 205n34

faith: as category for the study of religion, 201n14; faculty of, 60

family: exiles and separation from, 168, 182; and the father, 43; and the home, 103, 105, 107, 108; as institution, 68,

family *(continued)*
97; and intergenerational bonds, 6–7, 112, 167; and kinship networks, 101, 146; and memory, 97; as metaphor, 96
feelings. *See* emotions; experience
feminism, 20, 24, 188n4. *See also* gender
Fernandez, James W., 45, 48
Feuerbach, Ludwig, 51, 215n20
Finke, Roger, 34
Fitzgerald, Timothy, 29, 37–41, 42
flows: and "ambulant sciences," 54; chronotopic, 64; and the contemporary age, 22, 166; and the environment, 211n10; global cultural, 57, 61; Heraclitus on, 56; horizontal, vertical, and transversal, 62; and hydrodynamics, 59, 171–173, 176; limits of as metaphor, 60–61; as metaphor, 59, 210n7; nonreligious, 60; organic-cultural, 54, 62, 171–178; religion as, 59–69, 167–168; spaces of, 57; translocative and transtemporal, 64; transnational, 166
food: Cuban, 47; and fasting, 68, 98; and the home, 105; Muslim and Jewish, 101, 225n23; prohibitions on, 75; religious language and practices about, 99; Seventh Day Adventists and, 100–101; and Zen kōan, 161
forces: benevolent and malevolent, 99; economic, 178; human and suprahuman, 73, 168–169; impersonal, 61, 139; personal and transpersonal, 211n9; in physics, 59; psychological, 72; supernatural, 74–75; suprahuman, 54, 68, 76
Foucault, Michel, 9, 20
Frankenberry, Nancy, 45, 212n15
Freud, Sigmund, 19, 42–48, 50, 51, 52, 71, 96
funerals, functions of, 147–149. *See also* death; mortality

Gāndhi, Mohandās K., 134, 235n9
garden: of Eden, 108, 115, 147; Paradise, 108–109
Geertz, Armin: on the Hopi, 116; on "religion," 207n38
Geertz, Clifford: on evil, 238n15; on mind and culture, 65, 173; on "religion," 3, 51
gender: and assessment of theories, 166; and Baktaman domestic space, 105; and bodies, 98; and clitorectomies, 100; and constrained movement, 22; exclusion, 236n11; inversion, 150; and nuns, 134, 169, 182, 247n1; and ordination, 170; and rites of passage, 150; and spatial perception, 221n10; and the study of religion, 178
geographies: as cognitive maps, 113–115; as contested, 112–113
geography: as approach to the study of religion, 178; attempts to define, 32; constitutive term of, 30, 198n3; discipline of, 9, 24, 198n3; as distinct from "chorography" and "topography," 10; Ptolemy on, 10; and "spaces of flows," 57; and spatial practices, 215n22; Strabo on, 10, 230n1
geology, 57, 172
Giddens, Anthony, 9, 196n26
Gill, Sam, 10
globalization 22, 210n9. *See also* transnationalism
God, 46, 49, 73, 76, 79, 93, 99, 112, 139, 140, 141, 145, 149, 168. *See also* theism
goddesses: Apache, 146; Hindu, 106; Hopi, 118, Near Eastern, 121; Yorùbá, 6
Godlove, Terry, 204n31
gods: and Buddhist cosmography, 116; creator, 99, 120; and descent to earth, 158; exchanges with, 34; as father or mother, 96; Hindu, 14, 56, 62, 76, 106,

113, 119, 144; Inuit, 119; and Japanese *kami*, 142–143, 146; mountain, 75; as narrow category, 73; Sumerian, 112; Yorùbá, 135; Zoroastrian, 99

Goodman, Nelson, 48, 204n31

Greece, 13, 14, 19, 38, 56, 121

Guattari, Félix, 54, 57, 59, 171, 189n8, 217n29

gurus, 155

Guthrie, Stewart, 49, 51, 96

Haitians, 46–48

hajj, 129. *See also* pilgrimage

Hall, Stuart, 218n2

Harraway, Donna, 15–16, 18

Harvey, Van A., 51, 207n38, 215n20

healing: among the Bear River, 103; and the home, 105; among Pentecostals, 139; and pilgrimage sites, 129; as religious aim, 153, 154, 174; religious language and practices about, 99; and religion, 98; among the Yorùbá, 135, 139

heaven, 56, 76, 93, 115, 116, 145, 149, 154, 155, 170

Hegel, G. W. F., 46, 51

Heidegger, Martin, 218n2

hell, 116

Heraclitus, 56, 57, 208n

Hinduism, 14, 23, 40, 56, 62, 76, 106, 113–114, 115, 119, 120, 125, 127, 134, 136, 144, 150, 151, 152, 153, 155

history: as approach to study of religion, 178, 181; and chaos theory, 172–173

home: artifacts and shrines in, 225n23; and bodily needs, 105; as chronotope, 74, 97; definition of, 103, 105; and domestic furnishings, 68, 225n23; and the *eruv*, 108–109; and garages, 226n24; and gardens, 108–109; prescriptions

about, 106; religion and, 103–109; scholarly focus on, 166; shrines, 106–108; varied forms of, 103

homeland: conceptions of, 98; as contested territory, 112–113; and Cuban Americans, 81, 97, 169, 175; as imagined territory, 110; and religion, 74–75, 109–113; scholarly focus on, 166; and tropes, 110; as ultimate horizon, 153

homemaking: as chronotope, 74, 97; and collective identity, 111; as negotiating power and meaning, 112–113; as religious process, 75, 82–84

Hopi, 26, 116–118, 152

Huayan, 56

humanities, 7, 10, 20, 44–45, 178, 209n5, 247n4

Hume, David, 49, 50, 51, 71–72

hybridity: in Cuban Catholic piety, 6, 167; condemned as "syncretism," 6; and definitions, 48; and interreligious exchanges, 177; scholarly attention to, 166

ideal types, 8, 40, 202n19

identity: collective, 75, 79, 97, 101, 110–112, 119, 166, 177; disciplinary, 32; dress and, 101–102; ethnic, 75, 110; imagined communities and, 226n25; and myths, 119; national, 75, 110–112; religious, 60, 168, 171

Ifaluk, 69

illness, 98, 136, 139, 174

Incas, 110

India, 23, 38, 40, 76, 89, 94, 113, 119, 120, 123, 125, 127, 131, 134, 136, 144, 149, 150, 152–152, 155–156, 177

indigenous peoples: as heathens, 62; missions to, 148. *See also* Native traditions in the Americas

metaphor, 65–66; moral history of, 26, 27; as motherland or chosen land, 110, 153; natural, 74, 81, 98, 211n10; as Promised Land, 170; as sacred, 112–113, 142–143

Larson, Gerald, 51

Latin America, 10–11, 121, 132, 135, 154

Latour, Bruno, 58, 59, 78, 157–158, 160

Lawson, E. Thomas, 65

Leuba, James, 30, 36, 41, 49, 56

liberation: Cuban Americans and political, 2–3, 6, 168, 170, 181; in Hinduism, 151; in Jainism, 156; in Christian theology, 154. *See also* teleographies

life cycle, 72, 136. *See also* rites of passage

Lincoln, Bruce, 213n15

linguistics: constitutive term of, 30, 33; psycho-, 95; and spatial representation, 94–95

literary studies: as approach to study of religion, 178, 181; constitutive term of, 30

literature, 76, 141, 216n25. *See also* poetry

Long, Charles, 52, 74, 80, 81

Lopez, Donald, 42

lynching, 25, 100, 125, 196n27

magic, 96, 200n9

Mahāvīra, 156

Malcolm X, 134, 178, 182

Manichaeism, 121, 132, 142, 152, 153

Maoism, as quasi-religion, 77

mapping: cognitive, 74, 84–95, 113; as contested, 113; and ethnicity, 110; natal place and social space, 110–113; and nationalism, 110–111; religious dwelling as, 82; of symbolic landscape, 74; of terrestrial, subterranean, and celestial realms, 115–116; and tropes, 111–112. *See also* dwelling; homemaking; orientation

maps: Amerindian, 10–11, 113; early European, 114–115; as metaphor in theory, 10

marriage, 146–147; as crossing, 163; Hindu, 136; Mormon, 147; Shintō, 146–147

Marx, Karl, 18–19, 43, 51, 195n21; and Marxist utopianism, 153

Mary, Virgin, 67; apparitions of, 129; carrying, 167; home altars for, 225n23; medals of, 101; medieval devotion to, 173; as symbol, 111. *See also* Our Lady of Charity

Massumi, Brian, 57

mathematics, 57, 172

Mauss, Marcel, 100

Maya, 110, 135

McCauley, Robert, 65

McCutcheon, Russell, 78, 194n19

meaning: homemaking and, 113; interpreters and, 177; as negotiated by the religious, 6, 74, 113, 165; and power, 38, 74, 113, 177; scholars' construction of, 18; and terrestrial crossings, 131; and theory, 27

media, and religion, 125–127. *See also* communication

memory: and artifacts at the shrine, 87–89; episodic, 92, 173; familial, 97; long-term spatial, 93; personal and collective, 110; and religion, 67, 92; sense, 47; types of, 220n9

Mengzi (Mencius), 139–140

menstruation: and the Baktaman, 105–106; and rites of passage, 146, 150

Mesoamerica, 110, 113, 132, 135

Mesopotamia, 124

metaphors: approaches to the study of, 45, 204n30, 212n15; aquatic, 54, 59–61, 66, 73 168, 171–178; cartographic,

metaphors *(continued)*
10; definition of, 46–48, 212n15; direct
and indirect, 45–46, 207n38; exilic, 67,
96–97, 111, 131; horticultural, 139–140,
238n17; journey, 155–156; as orienting
trope, 68; and religion, 68; and religious representation of space, 96–97,
111–112; seafaring, 209n6; spatial, 52, 54,
59, 73–79; visual, 15–16. *See also* flows;
space; tropes
Methodists, 108, 140
Mexico, 113, 132
Miami. *See* Cuban Americans; Our Lady
of Charity; Shrine of Our Lady of
Charity
migrancy, as metaphor for theory, 58
migration: and assessing theories, 166;
forced, 62; of genes, 124; Hindu, 125;
within and across the homeland, 124;
and the interpreter's position, 181–183;
Latino and Asian, 22, 24; Puritan, 176;
religiously-inspired, 131
millennialism: and Adventists, 101; and
cargo cults, 153; and Howard Finster's
art, 108; and James Hampton's art,
226n24
mind: and body, 64; and culture, 65–66,
173; and "mental faculty," 95; and neural pathways and memory processes,
67, 173; and temporal and spatial perception, 91–98
missions, 129–131; and assessing theories,
166; Buddhist, 131; Catholic, 125, 129;
and local and global crossing, 62;
Moravian, 148; Muslim, 130–131; Protestant, 101, 125, 148; and "religion," 37
Mithen, Steven, 220n9
mokṣa, 76, 151, 153
Mongolia, 132
monotheism, 121, 152

Moravians, 148–149
Mormons: and marriage and funerals,
147–148; and temples, 147, 242n26
mortality, 75–76; as theme in theories of
religion, 71–72
motion, accelerated and unaccelerated,
83. *See also* movement
mountains, 75, 112, 142. *See also* nature
movement: between fact and value,
252n14; between immanence and transcendence, 158, 163; between inside and
outside, 182, 252n14; and "freeze-fram-
ing," 157–158; and the interpreter's position, 181–183; as metaphor for
transnationalism, 57; and religious
speech-acts, 157–158; social, 57, 60; as a
theme in this theory of religion, 5–7,
55, 77, 167, 181–183; theoretical resources for emphasizing, 55, 158, 208n3
Muhammad, 145
Müller, Friedrich Max, 18, 23, 46, 50, 60,
72, 95–96
music: at deaths, 148; definition of, 31–32;
at feast-day mass, 2, 5, 169; and marking boundaries, 76; as musicology's
constitutive term, 30; and the Tonga,
31
Muslims. *See* Islam
myths, 68; about the body, 99; Baktaman
ancestor, 106; cosmogonic, 116, 118–122;
Kwaio, 86; as orienting trope, 68; and
religious mapping, 111; solar, 95

narratives: biblical, 170; Cuban Catholic,
93; *kōan* as, 161–162; Moravian biographical, 148; and religion, 67–68; traditions of, 74. *See also* myths; texts
natality: as theme, 72; as
underemphasized, 237n13. *See also*
birth

nation, 110, 111. *See also* Iroquois

nationalism: Cuban American, 3; diasporic, 111, 169; and dress, 101; and imagined communities, 111; and landscape, 110; as quasi-religion, 77; and religious travel, 131–132; and symbols, 97. *See also* homeland

Native traditions in the Americas: and chiefdoms, 110; and maps, 10–11, 113; and shamanism, 103; and southeastern woodland tribes, 143. *See also* Apache; Aztecs; Cherokee; Chinook; Eastern Dakota; Hopi; Incas; indigenous peoples; Inuit; Iroquois; Jivarans; Maya; Sioux; Zuni

natural sciences, 8, 57, 68, 142, 157, 158, 178, 203n25, 212n15, 247n1

nature: as "ally" of religion, 142; changing "laws" of, 188n6; and culture, 64–69, 173–174; and god of rain and thunder, 56; mystics, 137; and natural disasters, 71, 136, 138, 140–141, 239n18; and "naturism," 95; and the seasons, 143; and sky, earth, and water gods, 119; and solar phenomena, 95, 121; and stars, 142; and water gods and moon goddesses, 112

network: institutional, 69; kinship, 101; as metaphor, 58, 210n7; social, 181

neuroscience, 69, 93–94, 178

New Guinea, 39, 100, 105, 152, 177

Nietzsche, Friedrich, 15, 56, 191n17

nirvāṇa, 39, 77, 141

nomads, 101, 110, 124

Novalis, 180, 251n11

Nye, Malory, 78

organic constraints: on emotions, 69; and religions, 65–69, 173–174; and spatial and temporal perception, 89, 91–98

orientation: and autocentric and allocentric representations, 84, 93–97; and "metaphysical shock," 86; philosophical, 16; religion as, 52, 74–75, 80–81, 166, 169; spatial and temporal, 66, 67, 74, 85–98, 100, 173; and tropes, 95–98. *See also* reference frames; space

orthodoxy, 60, 168, 171. *See also* hybridity

Ortiz, Fernando, 217n29

Otto, Rudolf, 3, 46, 49, 50, 60

Our Lady of Charity: confraternity of, 2, 3, 5, 67, 173; consecration of Miami shrine of, 80–83; devotees appeal to, 168, 170; discovery of, 5; as an exile, 5; feast-day celebration for, 1–7, 77, 108, 167–171, 175 181–182; as nationalist symbol, 97, 131, 169; as *Ọ̀ṣun*, 6, 108, 167, 170; and race relations in Miami, 46–47; as *tīrthaṅkara*, 170

pain, as distinguished from suffering, 237n14. *See also* suffering; evil

Pakistan, 127–128, 232n4

Palestine, 113, 132

parts of speech: adjectives and theories, 77–78; gerunds and theories, 78; prepositions and theories, 54, 77–79, 181–183; verbs and theories, 78

Pelasgians, 121

Pentecostalism, 71, 125–126, 139

personification, 45, 68, 73, 96. *See also* tropes

phenomenology, 20

Philippines, 145

philosophy: and "conceptual schemes," 204n31; and pragmatism, 191n17, 195n23; of prepositions, 54; process, 57; of religion, 71–72; tropes and concepts in, 189n8

physics, 59, 83, 142, 166, 188n6, 203n25, 240n20; geo-, 172; psycho-, 91 pilgrimage: by plane, 124; consensus and contestation models of, 233n5; as crossing, 163; in France, 129; in India, 134, 155, 156, 177; in Ireland, 128; in Japan, 128; as journey to the religious end, 155; life and death as, 149, 150; to Mecca, 128–129; as metaphor for the religious path and goal, 155; to Miami shrine, 2; and nonreligious motives, 233n5; and tourism, 131; types of, 128

place, as orienting metaphor for religion, 74. *See also* space

poetry: Bashō's, 13, 141–142, 191n15, 216n25, 240n19; Samuel Taylor Coleridge's, 142; Dante's, 216n25; T. S. Eliot's, 45–46; Ralph Waldo Emerson's, 142; John Hollander's, 31; Mộng-Lan's, 22; tropes in, 68; Voltaire's, 140–141

politics: as alternate constitutive term, 37–38; ancient Greek, 38; and Chinese rulers, 112; and civil religion, 153; and definitions of "culture" and "religion," 213n15; and democracy, 6, 168; and the Fāṭimid Dynasty, 130; and the Holy Roman Empire, 129, 135; and the Japanese emperor, 236n10; and the Mauryan Empire of Aśoka, 131; and Mayan kings, 135; and religion, 6, 60, 168, 172; and Yorùbá chiefs, 135

positionality: and anthropology, 188n4; and feminism, 20, 188n4; and locating this theory, 20–27, 181–183; and moral problems, 21; and other theories of religion, 183, 194n20; and pretenses to divine perspective, 15–16; and religion, 5–7; and research and teaching, 178–183; as a theme in this theory of religion, 5, 7, 13–20, 165–166, 167–171, 178; and theories, 28

possession, 98, 103, 152. *See also* trance

postmodernism: and positionality, 20–21; and pragmatism, 192n17; working definition of, 196n26

power: and controversies in religious studies, 197n29; definition of, 196n26; and mapping, 112–113; and meaning, 74; networks of, 210n7; and "politics," 38; and position, 24; and theories, 27, 166

practices: ascetic, 127; in definitions of religion, 51; of dwelling and crossing, 80; and figurative language, 45; gendered and racialized, 100; the mangle of, 249n8; and religion, 68; religious, 43, 70; retrospective and prospective, 169; spatial, 7, 79, 215n22; totemic, 95; transtemporal and translocative, 169. *See also* ritual

pragmatism, 20–21, 191n17, 195n23, 247n1

procession: at the Cuban shrine, 175; dancing, 62; Hindu, 14

projection, religion as, 51, 207n35

Protestants: and alleged iconophobia, 108; and communication media, 126–127; evangelical, 100, 127; and the home, 107–109; and missions, 101, 126; and the Reformation, 126; and the Social Gospel, 153, 154

psychology: as approach to the study of religion, 178, 181; in the early twentieth century, 56–57; and Freud, 43–44, 52; and Jung, 52; and Leuba, 30, 36, 41, 49, 56; and spatial perception, 93–95

puberty, rites of passage at, 145–146, 150

pūjā, 62, 106

Pure Land, Amida Buddha's, 77, 155

purgatory, 115, 228n31

Puritans, 127, 176

purity: and bodies, 98, 100, 149, 154; and spiritual or material pollution, 153

Putnam, Hilary: on epistemic and moral values, 26, 246n1; on the fact–value binary, 197n29; on interpretation, 193n18; on positionality, 21; and pragmatism, 21, 191n17, 195n23, 247n1; on "realism with a small r," 8, 16–17

quasi-religion: 77, 153, 216n25

race: and approaches to the study of religion, 178; and bodies, 98; and constrained movement, 22; and the Ku Klux Klan, 24–26, 196n27; and metaphor at the shrine, 46–47; and pilgrimage to Mecca, 134. *See also* ethnicity; identity
Rappaport, Roy, 39, 49
rebirth: in Buddhism, 77, 155; in Hinduism, 76; in Indian religions, 153; among the Inuit, 155, 245n35; in Jainism, 156
reference frames: autocentric and allocentric, 84, 93–97, 113, 169, 220n10; and geographies, cosmographies, cosmogonies, and teleographies, 113–122; and religions, 67, 173
reflexivity, 20–22, 24, 26, 33, 178. *See also* positionality
relation: and dependent co-origination (*pratītya-samutpāda*), 55; and intergenerational bonds, 6–7, 112, 167; and Jewel Net of Indra, 55–56; kinship, 101, 146, 109; Michel Serres on, 54; as theme for this theory of religion, 5–7, 55, 77–79, 166; theoretical resources for emphasizing, 55, 208n3, 217n29
relativism, cognitive, 27
religion: ancient, 96; as biological and cultural, 64; civil, 153; as concern, 50; as constitutive term for religious studies, 30–31, 60; and culture, 213n15,

216n25; definitions of, 3–4, 31, 41, 48–52; diasporic, 168, 181; as dwelling and crossing, 73–79; ethnic and universal, 53; as experience or feeling, 49–50; as form of life, 51; four "domains" of, 213n16; function of, 71–72; and hierophanies, 61; hydrodynamics of, 59–60, 171–172, 176; as illness, 42–44, 51; as individualistic and collective, 64; -in-general, 55; as institution, 3, 52, 207n38; intellectualist, affective, and volitional definitions of, 49; Bruce Lincoln's typology of, 213n15; as mediated by technology, 124–127; mutual intercausality with economy, society, and politics, 50; as narcotic, 51; and nonreligious cultural forms, 76; as not "universal," 36–37, 40–41, 55, 78; objections to defining, 36–42; as organic-cultural flows, 62–69; as orientation, 52, 74–75, 80–98; and orienting tropes, 68; orienting tropes in definitions of, 49–53; origin of, 70–71, 165, 214n18; as pictorial thought, 51, 53, 206n38; prepositional and verbal theory of, 77–79; primitive and civilized, 53; as projection, 51, 207n38; proposed definition of, 54, 167; as psychic capacity, 49, 50; and "religioning," 78; and the sacred, 50, 52, 61; as "second order concept," 33; as society, 51; as space, 52; as spatial practice, 73, 78; static and dynamic, 216n23; as *sui generis*, 60, 210n7; as system, 51; taxonomies of, 52–53, 62; themes for a theory of, 5, 182; and themes of close and distant, 157–158; theories of, 3–4; this-worldly and other-worldly, 153; as translocative and transtemporal flows, 64, 163; "traditional" vs. "rationalized," 238n15;

religion *(continued)*
  tribal, 95; and tropes for spatial representation, 95–98; as watch and compass, 85–98, 169; as Western category, 36–41; as worldview, 51
religious studies: and comparison, 249n8; controversies in, 197n29; "culture" as constitutive term for, 37; and the liberal arts, 249n9; "religion" as constitutive term of, 30–31, 60; research and teaching in, 178–183
representations: analogical, 95; as bodily and culturally mediated processes, 16; positioned, 13–20, 164; situated, 16; spatial, 93–98; temporal, 91–93; of the ultimate horizon, 151–156; verbal and nonverbal, 67, 173. *See also* space; time
research: as dwelling and crossing, 180–183; translation in, 251n12. *See also* interpretation; scholars
resurrection, 158–161, 169
revelation, special, 60
revolution, 1, 217n29
rites of passage, 143–150, 170
ritual: as action, 189n9; as alternate constitutive term, 37, 39; bath, 149; and the Bladder Feast, 143; and boundary marking, 123; calendar, 169; Cuban American feast-day, 1–7, 77, 93, 108, 167–171, 175, 181–182; Eucharistic, 101; funereal, 147–150; the Green Corn, 143; and the life cycle, 143–150; objects, 68, 89–90; observing, 181; performance, 74; postpartum, 145; and the present, 162; and religion, 67–68; and religious speech-acts, 157; and sensory pageantry and performance frequency, 92; Jonathan Z. Smith's theory of, 189n9; specialists, 103, 135, 145; temple, 77; translocative and transtemporal, 5, 81;

transmission of, 62. *See also* pilgrimage; practices; *pūjā;* rites of passage
Román, Agustín, 46–47, 174–176
Roman Catholicism: and Archdiocese of Miami, 167–168; and baptism, 100; and burial, 148; and Eucharist, 101; and liberation theology, 154; and literature, 141; in Luxembourg, 62; and medieval Marian devotion, 173; Mexican, 107, 132; and nuns, 134, 169–170, 182, 247n1; and ordination, 170; Portuguese, 125; and purgatory, 115; and shrines, 128–129; Spanish, 132, 167; and transubstantiation, 157; and virtual mass, 127. *See also* Cuban Americans; Our Lady of Charity; saints; Shrine of Our Lady of Charity
Rorty, Richard, 15, 45, 192n17, 212n15
Rose, Gillian, 21

sacroscapes, 61–62, 69, 210n9
Sahlins, Marshall, 171
saints, Roman Catholic: Barbara, 108; as metaphoric kinship system, 107; Lazarus, 93, 108; Theresa, 107; Willibrord, 62
salvation: as alternate category, 39; as social regeneration, 154–155; and the "desire for the new," 154; as transport and transformation, 170; types of, 243n33. *See also* soteriology; teleographies
saṃsāra, 141, 153
Santería, 6, 108, 167, 171
satī, 150
Schleiermacher, Friedrich: on definitions of religion, 49; on feeling of absolute dependence, 49, 70; and feelings, 3; on religion as feeling, intuition, and experience, 49–50, 205n34
scholars: and exchange networks and

geographical location, 181; and research and teaching, 178–183; role-specific obligations of, 17, 27, 30–33, 53, 54, 165; as situated, 16–20; and specialization and generalization, 251n13

Schutz, Alfred, 98

science. *See* natural sciences; social sciences

self: Christian ideas of, 70, 73, 140; Confucian ideas of, 73, 139, 215n21; Buddhist ideas of, 55, 73, 99; and limit situations, 137; Manichean ideas of, 153. *See also* body; mind

Serres, Michel, 29, 54, 57, 78–79

Seventh Day Adventists, 100–101

sex: and aroused bodies, 98; and the home, 105; and homosexuality, 100, 150; and intimacy, 136; prescriptions about, 101, 136, 150; as proximate human aim, 77; religious language and practices about, 99

shamanism: among the Bear River, 103; and the ultimate horizon, 152

Sharf, Robert H., 192n17

Shingon, 128

Shintō, 40, 125, 142–143, 146–147

Shrine of Our Lady of Charity (Miami): and busts of José Martí and Félix Varela, 111; consecration of, 80–83; cornerstone of, 87–89; Cuban flag at, 112; devotee kneeling at 88, 93; founding of 174; mural at, 87–89

shrines: domestic, 106–108; and pilgrimage, 128–129; yard, 108

Sikhism, 106, 149–150

Silk Road, 132, 134, 182

similes, 45, 68, 96, 111. *See also* tropes

sin, 70

Sioux, 101–102

slavery, 75, 110, 125, 148, 173, 197n27; as

compelled crossing, 27, 135–136, 150; religious justification of, 135–136

Smart, Ninia, 51

Smith, Christian: on "religion," 49; on "sacred umbrellas," 209n6

Smith, Jonathan Z., 33, 41, 49, 50, 78, 189n9

Smith, William Cantwell, 42, 77, 198n1, 201n14

social sciences, 7, 20, 44–45, 178, 247nn1,4

society: as networks of power, 210n7; regeneration of, 154–155; as religion, 51; and religion, 60; and rites of passage, 143–150; and "social construction," 188n6; and social hierarchies, 106, 112, 134–135; and social justice, 153; and social organization, 110, 226n25; and social roles, 135, 143–144; and social stratification, 111–112; and symbolism, 96

sociology: as approach to study of religion, 71, 178, 181; process, 209n4

Soja, Edward W., 9

Solomon Islands, 86

soteriology, 37–39. *See also* crossing; salvation; teleographies; ultimate horizon

space: as constitutive term for geography, 30; cultic, 106; and cultural theory, 9–10; and definitions of religion, 52, 54, 59; domestic, 100–101, 103, 105–109; domestic and public, 75, 108–109; as local and global, 62; moving through, 74; and Muslim watch and compass, 89–90, 92; perception and representation of, 93–98, 173; sacred, 52, 75, 105, 132, 236n11; social, 27, 74, 81, 100, 110–113, 134–135, 158; terrestrial, 113, 115; and time, 64; and unconscious circumspatial awareness, 98

Spain: and the Inquisition, 62; and New Spain, 113, 132, 167

Tonga, 31
totem, 95
Trail of Tears, 62–63
trajectory: culture as, 58, 65; in physics, 59
trance, 99, 152; forms of, 103; typology of, 224n20
transculturation, 217n29
transmission: and institutions, 68, 95; of religions, 69; of religious gestures, 62; of religious representations, 67; of tropes, artifacts, and rituals, 95; and the usefulness of artifacts for, 220n9
transnationalism, 22, 57–58, 61, 110–111, 124–125, 129–134, 166. See also globalization
transportation: technology, 124–126; and types of religion, 125
travel, 124–127; account by Abū 'Abdallah Ibn Battuta, 62; in-dwelling, 80; embodied, 9–13; as mediated by technology, 124–127; as metaphor for the religious end, 155–156; as metaphor for theory, 8, 58, 59; by motorcycle, 125–126; and other itinerant practices, 131–134; by raft, 22, 131–133, 182; religious, 124–131, 169–170; by rolling, 127–128; round-trip, 127–131; and "walking rhetorics," 188n7. See also colonialism; crossing; migration; pilgrimage
tricksters, 119
tropes: in art, literature, and science, 68, 212n15; aquatic and spatial, 54, 59, 66, 73, 155–156, 158, 168; and boundary marking, 123; definition of, 45, 204n30; in definitions of religion, 42–44, 48–52; as figurative tools, 68; and the five "macrotropes," 45; in humanities and social sciences, 44–45; and interactivity with definition and theory, 42–48; me-

teorological, 154; moral implications of, 42, 52–53; and the natural sciences, 57, 58, 203n25, 212n15; orienting, 29, 49–52, 68; and religion, 67–68, 177; and the religiously formed body, 99–100; and religious representation of space, 95–98; scholarship on, 204n30, 222n13. See also metaphors; myths; personification; similes; symbols
truth: awakening to, 162; coherence and pragmatic theories of, 16–17; correspondence theories of, 16, 17, 158; and Latour's "conditions of felicity," 157; Nietzsche's "perspectivist" analysis of, 191n17; and nonrepresentational or pragmatic realism, 8; and "warranted assertability," 16, 191n17
Tsing, Anna, 57–58, 60
Tuan, Yi-Fu, 98
Turner, Victor, 48
twelve-step programs: as quasi-religion, 77, 153; ultimate horizon of, 153
Tylor, E. B., 3, 49, 50, 52, 65, 95

ultimate horizon, 68, 76–77, 98, 122, 151–156, 163, 166, 168, 170, 174
United States: and exchanges with Japan, 125; and forced removal, 62; and its national map, 113; slavery and, 135; and the study of religion, 250n10

values: as entangled with "facts," 197n29; epistemic and moral, 26–27, 246n1; and normative judgments, 26–27; and religion, 68, 124; and scholars' role-specific obligations, 17, 27, 30–33, 53. See also codes
Van der Leeuw, Gerardus, 52
Van Gennep, Arnold, 143–144
Vedānta, 153

verstehen (understanding), rejected as a goal for interpretation, 17
Vikings, 148, 150
violence, 62, 72, 100, 113, 129, 131
visual culture, 37, 200n14. *See also* architecture; art; artifacts
Voltaire, 140

Wallerstein, Immanuel, 61
Wana, 144
war: for independence in Cuba, 2, 7, 87, 169, 172; and Mayan warriors, 135. *See also* colonialism; violence
Weber, Max, 40, 71–72, 96, 136, 138, 153, 238n15, 243n33
West, Cornell, 192n17
West, the: and communication technology, 126; and "geography," 10; modern, 124; and "music," 32; and preoccupation with death, 71–72; and "religion," 3, 36, 37, 42; and "soteriology," 39; and the theme of movement, 56

Whitehead, Alfred North, 52, 57, 79
Whitehouse, Harvey, 65
Wilson, E. O., 50
Wilson, John, 5
Wittgenstein, Ludwig, 21, 51, 85, 193n18, 195n23, 206n38
wonders, 72, 137, 142–143

Yorùbá, 134, 139, 153, 155
Young, Katherine Y., 123

Zen: and Bashō 141; and cosmic crossing, 154; Rinzai, 161–163; Sōtō, 70, 153
Zoroastrianism, 99–100, 103, 132
Zuni, 121